T0311874

The Mentor's Guide

A definitive resource that pulls together evidence from psychology, education, and organizational studies, this fully updated second edition translates research into practice and serves as a practical handbook on how to set up, run, and evaluate any mentoring program.

Despite ever-growing interest, there are few helpful resources for program managers and mentoring coordinators. This book sheds needed light on mentoring behaviors, the stages of mentoring, elements of high-quality relationships, and how to recognize and avoid dysfunctional ones. Step-by-step guidance will enable readers to:

- Understand what mentoring is (and is not)
- Assess their mentoring program using a clear framework
- Work through steps to design or redesign an effective mentoring program
- Draw on real-world examples to assess and improve programs
- Benefit from all-new material for this second edition, including a chapter on e-mentoring and in-depth case studies, as well as updated information on culturally intelligent mentoring and more

If you manage or support a mentoring program, then this handbook is for you. Human resource professionals across industries will gain ideas on how to improve the efficiency and effectiveness of mentoring, while administrators in higher education will value the content on formal mentorship programs for faculty members, graduate students, and undergraduates.

Laura Gail Lunsford is an expert in mentoring and leadership. She has written numerous articles, chapters, and books on mentoring and leadership, including co-editing the *Sage Handbook of Mentoring*. She is Assistant Dean and Full Professor of Psychology at Campbell University.

The Mentor's Guide

Five Steps to Build a Successful Mentoring Program

2nd Edition

Laura Gail Lunsford

Routledge
Taylor & Francis Group
NEW YORK AND LONDON

Second edition published 2022
by Routledge
605 Third Avenue, New York, NY 10158

and by Routledge
2 Park Square, Milton Park, Abingdon, Oxon, OX14 4RN

Routledge is an imprint of the Taylor & Francis Group, an informa business

First edition published by Routledge 2016

Library of Congress Cataloging-in-Publication Data
Names: Lunsford, Laura Gail, author.
Title: The mentor's guide : five steps to build a successful mentoring program / Laura Gail Lunsford.
Other titles: Handbook for managing mentoring programs
Description: 2nd edition. | New York, NY : Routledge, 2022. | Earlier edition published in 2016 as: A handbook for managing mentoring programs: starting, supporting and sustaining effective mentoring. | Includes bibliographical references and index.
Identifiers: LCCN 2021028830 (print) | LCCN 2021028831 (ebook) | ISBN 9780367757557 (hardback) | ISBN 9780367757519 (paperback) | ISBN 9781003163862 (ebook)
Subjects: LCSH: Mentoring.
Classification: LCC BF637.M45 .L86 2022 (print) | LCC BF637.M45 (ebook) | DDC 158.3--dc23
LC record available at https://lccn.loc.gov/2021028830
LC ebook record available at https://lccn.loc.gov/2021028831

ISBN: 978-0-367-75755-7 (hbk)
ISBN: 978-0-367-75751-9 (pbk)
ISBN: 978-1-003-16386-2 (ebk)

DOI: 10.4324/9781003163862

Typeset in Sabon
by MPS Limited, Dehradun

Thanks mom, for the work ethic and in loving memory of dad.

Contents

Figures

Tables

Case Studies

About the author

Laura Gail Lunsford, PhD, is a mentoring and leadership development expert. A US Fulbright Scholar, she has published over 40 articles and chapters on mentorship dysfunction, optimizing mentoring relationships, mentor benefits, evaluating mentoring, and leadership. She co-edited the *Sage Handbook of Mentoring* and *Mentoring Undergraduate Student*s and co-authored *Faculty Development in Liberal Arts Colleges*. Lunsford regularly consults with organizations on effective mentoring and coaching. Lunsford is Assistant Dean and Professor of Psychology at Campbell University, a beautiful liberal arts university in rural NC. In 2009, the International Mentoring Association (IMA) recognized her with the Dr. Hope Richardson Dissertation Award. She serves on the IMA Board of Directors, volunteers with the American Red Cross and is a Rotarian.

Preface

Great mentors make you feel good, motivated, and empowered. Terrific protégés give you a sense of satisfaction and well-being when you feel you have contributed to their success – but what about great mentoring programs, or even great mentoring program managers? I have found few resources to help program managers when they are responsible for starting, supporting, or sustaining formal mentoring efforts.

This new edition answers questions I received from program managers from the first edition. The design of a mentoring program is simplified into five steps. Information is added about ethics, diversity, and inclusion. Several chapters were added to focus in-depth on popular types of mentoring programs and updated resources were added throughout the book.

The information in this volume will assist you to make evidence-based decisions on how best to operate your mentoring program. This book may advance efforts to professionalize roles with duties related to formal mentoring programs or with titles such as "mentoring program manager," director, or coordinator. The broad, research-based coverage in the book also may be useful to those with an emerging scholarly interest in mentoring programs and to mentors and protégés.

A multidisciplinary approach frames the book. My scholarly interest in mentoring came from a conversation years ago with an expert in gifted education, Rena Subotnik, who is now Director of the Center for Psychology in Schools and Education, American Psychological Association. I have since worked with and studied mentoring programs in business, education, and community organizations. The book draws on research from business, education, psychology, and youth development. Positive psychology emphasizes flourishing and aligns well with the aim of sustaining effective mentoring programs.

May this handbook help you to facilitate successful mentoring relationships and contribute to creating a culture of mentoring in your organization.

Laura Gail Lunsford
Buies Creek and Wrightsville Beach, NC

Acknowledgments

Special thanks to:

the students who asked questions about mentoring: "Do tell!" and
colleagues who think mentoring is swell,
and those who shared their stories with me,
and my mentors who said: "A professor you must be"
or those who claimed "You can write!"
(how little did I know it would be such a delight),
and Art Padilla, who was always there,
and who fed and loved me with great care.

Chapter 1

Introduction

It is difficult to understand the universe if you only study one planet.
(Miyamoto Musashi, in Kaufman 2003, 12)

Mentoring has taken up a considerable portion of my professional life. Early in my career I was the alumni director at a top-ranked business school in the United States, Duke University's Fuqua School of Business. At Fuqua, I witnessed the positive outcomes of building effective networks of relationships. Later, at North Carolina State University, I spent more than a decade awarding millions of dollars from the generous trustees of the Park Foundation to talented undergraduates through the Park Scholarships. I developed a faculty–student mentoring program for these Park Scholars. Along the way, I have participated in mentoring relationships as both a protégé and a mentor. Most of the time, mentoring went well for me and for those in the formal mentoring programs that I oversaw. However, there were times when I questioned the effectiveness of these relationships. At other times I wondered if I or the participants were getting all that we could out of a relationship.

A friendly critic

As a scholar I developed a more critical view of mentoring, and as a practitioner I developed the skills to seek answers to my questions. Why did mentoring work so well for some people, and so poorly for others? Is a one-on-one relationship the only type of mentoring relationship? Does mentoring work the same way for people in different work settings or disciplines? I studied different types of helping relationships, how they develop, and what outcomes might be expected. In essence, I followed Musashi's advice in the epigraph to this chapter and studied other planets in the mentoring universe.

It is easy to be seduced by the popular literature on mentoring. Who doesn't want to be an "intelligent mentor" (Murrell et al. 2008) or a

DOI: 10.4324/9781003163862-1

"divine mentor" (Cordeiro 2008)? An internet search will provide lists of the traits of great mentors and protégés. According to various websites, mentors are knowledgeable, effective communicators who possess integrity, emotional intelligence, honesty, diplomacy, and compassion. They are personally and professionally successful, as well as accessible, available, confident, inquisitive, patient, objective, sensitive, supportive, and fair. I have never met anyone who possesses *all* of these qualities. (If you know someone who does have all these traits, please send me their name and contact information!) In fact, I continue to be surprised when I see program managers provide such lists as examples to mentoring participants.

This book will draw on the scholarly literature on mentoring. In it, I present a more nuanced view about mentoring and what it can do. Congratulations if you are already a mentoring skeptic; if not, I ask that you join me and adopt a skeptical view about mentoring in your practice. Such a view may help you to support others as they develop their mentoring relationships and to both improve mentoring and recognize its limitations. Mentoring is not for everyone, and some people do not benefit from mentoring experiences. Further, even great mentors and protégés have bad days. This book is written for practitioners of mentoring who are willing to accept mentoring as a flawed relationship engaged in by humans who have strengths and weaknesses, and as a sometimes neutral (or even negative) experience.

Of course, mentoring can provide a powerful and formative experience that transforms protégés, mentors, and organizations for the better. If I did not believe this, then I would not be writing this book. Consider me a friendly critic of mentoring who may be exactly the right person to write such a guide. You can read on with confidence that I have scrutinized modern research with a critical eye to distill what might be most useful and helpful for program managers.

Why focus on program managers?

Note I use the term "program manager" to refer to anyone with responsibility for a formal mentoring initiative. Your title might be "mentoring program director," "mentoring program coordinator," or "learning specialist." I selected one title for ease of writing and reading.

Over a decade ago I conducted my first workshop on mentoring titled "Creating Effective Mentoring Programs." It was scheduled as a four-hour, pre-conference activity for the Mentoring Institute held at the University of New Mexico. I found the organizers to be optimistic in their anticipation of 40 attendees. But soon we were adding chairs. I have conducted many workshops from program design to mentor effectiveness and have met hundreds of people who genuinely wish to help others through formal mentoring programs. Yet program managers were often unsure how to recruit, match, or orient participants, much less decide on the right mentoring program activities.

The idea for this book emerged in 2011 when I was recruited to design a mentoring network for math and science teachers in rural Arizona. There was sufficient material on how to be a good mentor or protégé but limited information for program managers on how to start or support a formal mentoring program. Most information on teacher mentoring in the United States can be traced back to the New Teacher Center, which was created as a nonprofit organization by faculty from the University of California, Santa Cruz. Yet their emphasis was on training mentors, rather than on supporting mentoring program managers. Later, I identified one handbook for mentoring program managers, written about workplace mentoring programs (Allen et al. 2009).

Mentoring program managers deserve to be informed practitioners. Experience is important, but it can lead us astray. I have encountered naysayers and well-intentioned but misinformed individuals who say things like: "Sure we can do a mentoring program – after all, it is not like it is going to hurt anyone," or "What's the big deal about mentoring? If the relationship is no good, why don't people just walk away?"

In other words, there is plenty of folk knowledge about mentoring that is downright wrong. This book draws on research to provide information about the bright and dark sides of mentoring; how to help mentors be "*aug*mentors" and not "*tor*mentors"; and how to think philosophically about the purpose of your mentoring program. (A list of mentoring resources is provided under "Resources" at the end of this chapter.)

Formal versus informal

This book focuses on formal mentoring relationships, although informal mentoring relationships also develop with some frequency and sometimes because of formal mentoring experiences (for example, see Case Study 11.1). There are two distinctions between formal and informal mentoring. First, formal mentoring implies providing assistance in connecting a mentor and a protégé. Second, formal mentoring programs are developed to achieve an organizational goal such as increasing diversity, retention, or developing future leaders. Formal mentoring programs are useful when it might be otherwise difficult for a protégé to connect with a mentor.

Terminology: "Protégé" versus "mentee"

The term "protégé" is used in this book to refer to the individual receiving mentoring. However, the term "mentee" may be substituted for protégé. Scholars in the United States often use the term "protégé," while scholars in other countries prefer the word "mentee." Some individuals object to the term "protégé" because it implies sponsorship or protection, which they feel is not appropriate in a mentoring relationship. One consistent term makes it easier to read, but there is no definitive reason why "protégé" is better than "mentee" – they are interchangeable terms here.

Purpose

The book has three aims:

1. create a single resource for program managers to reference;
2. advance the professionalization of the practice of mentoring by assembling evidence-based resources; and
3. make modern research on mentoring accessible to practitioners.

Mentoring has been around a long time, but attention to formal mentoring programs is relatively recent. At least in the United States, many formal mentoring programs grew out of lawsuits in the 1980s, where women and minorities did not have equal access to promotion and development opportunities. In Europe, mentoring is viewed more as a developmental relationship, rather than one focused on sponsorship (as in the United States). Perhaps this different emphasis has contributed to a greater effort in Europe to provide university coursework and certificates for mentoring program managers than is available in the United States or other countries.

The professionalization of mentoring and training for program managers is a relatively new idea, as is scholarship on mentoring. Universities and professional organizations in Australia and Europe now offer certification and training in mentoring. The United States has made a nascent effort in this regard, but colleges and universities have yet to offer much in the way of training, coursework, or professional development. See Table 1.1 for links to professional associations and related resources.

It is expensive to access journal articles unless you have an academic appointment, and, unfortunately, scholarly research often is written in a stilted academic style, using specialized language that may be difficult to interpret without advanced coursework in statistics. This book attempts to close the gap by translating research-to-practice in an easy-to-read format that hopefully will become well worn.

Who should read this book?

You may find this book to be helpful if you have responsibility for mentoring programs, activities, or initiatives. It is written for you if you are thinking about starting a mentoring program or if you are running an existing program. Further, the book may be useful to practitioners as well as graduate or advanced undergraduate students who desire to know more about mentoring. Your personal practice of mentoring as a mentor or protégé may be improved by reading Part III "Enriching and Strengthening the Process" – the chapters contained within it focus on the process of mentoring.

A mentoring program may range from a structured effort, which matches participants and has start and end dates, to a less structured activity (which still has organizational involvement or supervision) where participants find each other and engage over variable periods of time. Any mentoring initiative that is expected or supported in some way by the organization is a formal mentoring program.

Mentoring program activities vary according to their organizational context. Most scholars classify mentoring programs in these categories: youth mentoring, academic mentoring, and organizational mentoring. This book is written for program managers who work in any of these contexts. Tools are provided to help you think about what makes sense for your mentoring program, rather than a prescriptive list of the ten activities you must do. Thus, the *process* of starting, supporting, and sustaining formal mentoring has universal concepts, but the specific *content* may vary.

You may hold the title of "program manager," "program coordinator," or "program director." Perhaps managing a mentoring program is one of your many job responsibilities. For example, deans of graduate schools supervise the formal mentoring experiences of doctoral students, and vice-provosts of faculty affairs are charged with orienting and supporting faculty members. There may be professionals in human resource departments who are responsible for mentoring initiatives through leader development programming. I use the term "program manager" throughout this book to refer to anyone who has responsibility for a mentoring program.

This is not to suggest that all of the individuals listed here support mentoring activities. There are plenty of deans, vice-provosts, and human resource professionals who assume that mentoring is taking place and that it is best left to participants to arrange those relationships. There is a gray area between formal and informal mentoring. This book will be useful for individuals who seek to build on informal and formal mentoring to promote a mentoring culture in their institution or organization.

How to use this book?

There are two ways to read this book. If you are an experienced program manager or have a specific need, then you may wish to select the chapter(s) of interest to you. The stand-alone chapters will refer you to material and other chapters as needed. If you are new to the practice of mentoring, then you may wish to read the book from start to finish, because the chapters are also written to build on one another.

There are features of this book that may help you learn and use the material. Each chapter begins with an overview that highlights the main themes. Section summaries are provided to encourage you to pause and reflect on the main ideas in a section. Most of the chapters include case studies that provide examples of mentoring in practice. Reflection questions and key terms are listed at the end of each chapter to promote thinking about the themes and how they might apply to your mentoring program. Sample materials are provided in some chapters, which can be adapted for your program. There are also places to record your reflections to guide your development of a mentoring philosophy. Write in the book, fold down page corners for reference, and record your reflections as you read.

Contents

This book is arranged in four parts. In Part I, "Understanding Mentoring," Chapters 2 and 3 provide the foundation for program managers to understand what mentoring is and how to promote high-quality mentoring programs and activities.

In Part II, "Five Steps to Developing Mentoring Programs that Work," Chapters 4–8 present the steps to designing (or redesigning) and implementing a mentoring program. Chapter 4 helps to identify the purpose for a mentoring program. Chapter 5 describes how to uncover the assumptions and theories about why a mentoring program will achieve the desired goals. Chapter 6 explores how to recruit and prepare the right participants for mentorship. How to collect the right data is the focus in Chapter 7. Chapter 8 describes how to create your success story about mentoring to share with your stakeholders.

In Part III, "Enriching and Strengthening the Processes," Chapter 9 describes the stages of mentoring relationships and how program managers may educate participants to maximize activities at each relationship stage. Chapter 10 highlights how program managers may support participants and have critical conversations that advance their learning. Chapter 11 addresses diversity and inclusion in mentoring programs.

Part IV "Trends and Case Studies" presents three new chapters that highlight mentoring programs in specific settings. Chapter 12 focuses on alumni/industry mentoring programs in Canada and the United States. Chapter 13 describes two mentoring programs for first-generation students at a large public university and at a private, liberal arts university. Chapter 14 presents a new, global mentoring program focused on science, technology, engineering, mathematics, and medicine that is based out of Regensburg, Germany. Chapter 15 presents closing thoughts on mentoring programs and the practice of mentoring for program managers. You can make an important difference in creating a high-quality mentoring program that will help you develop your professional skills, increase learning for your participants, and benefit your organization through the outcomes accrued by the mentoring program.

This book is written in the first person, as if we might be having a conversation with one another. Please share your experiences with me, along with areas you hope might be included in future revisions. You may reach me through my website: leadmentordevelop.com. May you find this book to be a useful reference that you will keep on your desk.

Key terms

- Formal versus informal mentoring
- Mentoring program
- Program manager
- Professionalization of mentoring

Reflection questions

1. Where might you find free, high-quality resources to guide your practice of mentoring?
2. Which chapters appear most useful to you in starting, supporting, or sustaining your mentoring program?
3. How might you develop your professional skills in your role as a program manager?

Resources

Table 1.1 List of mentoring resources

Professional associations	Web site
International Mentoring Association	https://www.mentoringassociation.org
European Mentoring and Coaching Council	https://www.emccouncil.org
Resources	
Science of Effective Mentorship in STEMM	https://www.nap.edu/resource/25568/interactive/
University of New Mexico: The Mentoring Institute	https://mentor.unm.edu/
Wake Forest University Mentoring Resource Center	https://mentoring.opcd.wfu.edu/
New Teacher Center	https://www.newteachercenter.org
NMRN Net	https://nrmnet.net/
US Office of Juvenile Justice and Delinquency Prevention: Mentoring Resources	https://www.ojjdp.gov/programs/mentoring.html

References

Allen, T. D., Finkelstein, L. M., and Poteet, M. L. 2009. *Designing Workplace Mentoring Programs: An Evidence-based Approach.* Oxford, UK: Wiley-Blackwell.

Cordeiro, W. 2008. *The Divine Mentor: Growing Your Faith as You Sit at the Feet of the Savior.* Bloomington, MN: Bethany House.

Kaufman, S. F. 2003. *Musashi's Book of Five Rings: The Definitive Interpretation of Miyamoto Musashi's Classic Book of Strategy.* Boston, MA: Tuttle Publishing.

Murrell, A. J., Forte-Trammell, S., and Bing, D. 2008. *Intelligent Mentoring: How IBM Creates Value through People, Knowledge, and Relationships.* New York : IBM Press and Pearson.

Part I

Understanding mentoring

Chapter 2

Defining mentoring

> Minerva came close up to him in the likeness and with the voice of Mentor. "Telemachus," said she, "if you are made of the same stuff as your father you will be neither fool nor coward henceforward, for Ulysses never broke his word nor left his work half done." (The Odyssey, Homer, 1999)

Introduction

Defining mentoring is fundamental to the success of your mentoring program. After reading this chapter you will be able to define terms like "mentor," "mentoring," and "mentorship" and have a vocabulary about what mentoring is and is not. In this chapter you will learn about the origin of mentoring. Modern definitions of mentoring are presented, including a recognition of mentoring episodes and networks. The mentoring ecosystem is described to frame your thinking about what influences mentoring relationships. The purpose and outcomes of mentoring relationships are reviewed as well as the benefits and costs of mentoring. Reflect on your mentoring experiences and philosophy and think about how you can help others develop their own mentoring philosophy and practice.

Mentoring is often seen as a panacea that will solve social or organizational problems. For example, an internet search of news topics with the keyword "mentoring" turns up over a million results. One news story quoted US politician Jeb Bush, the former governor of Florida, who explained that the number of disaffected youth might be reduced with more mentoring.

> Kids in this country are aimlessly wandering around in their lives because they've never been told they were capable of learning. They've never been challenged to achieve far better. They've never really had the kind of mentoring and nurturing that gives them the sense their lives could be better.[1]

DOI: 10.4324/9781003163862-2

Other news stories highlight the importance of mentors in achieving elite performance in domains such as sports. Patrick Mouratoglou, "mentor to the stars," is attributed with helping the tennis Grand Slam champion Serena Williams "put together the most productive three-year stretch of her career."[2] These stories echo Roche's (1979) finding that most successful business executives reported having a mentor.

What makes mentoring different from other supportive relationships we might have? Does it mean to spend time together, to coach, to guide? Why does the term need defining anyway?

Given the oversized expectations reported in the news, it may be understandable that individuals who have responsibility for managing formal mentoring experiences may feel overwhelmed or underprepared. Participants also may have unrealistic expectations about what mentoring can or cannot do for them. Mentoring program managers are vested with and believe in the power of these special relationships, but there needs to be a shared understanding about what mentorship is and what it can do.

Origin of mentoring

Program managers (and those involved in mentoring) are often unaware of the origin of the term "mentor." Pause and consider – what language gave us the word mentor? Think about your description as the origins and archetypes for mentoring are described here.

Western tradition from the Greeks

Mentoring has deep roots in human history. Over 1,000 years ago the ancient Greeks transmitted the term to us through an epic poem. The poem chronicles Odysseus' heroic efforts to return home. During his absence he left his friend Mentor in charge of the household, including overseeing his son's (Telemachus) care and education. Mentor provided important advice and guidance to Telemachus. The Roman goddess Minerva, known as Athena in Greek mythology, took on Mentor's form when he gave advice to Telemachus.

Thus, the original mentor was an androgynous goddess who served in a parental role. For much of human history, fathers and mothers have provided personal and career guidance to their sons and daughters as part of their children's educational and professional development.

However, most scholars now accept that our modern conception of mentoring comes from Fénelon's eighteenth-century educational philosophies about Mentor and Telemachus. It was through his work that the term entered use in English and French. Garvey's (2017) critical analysis suggests the Mentor in Homer's *The Odyssey* accompanied themes of violence, male stereotypes of domination, and "failure of the original mentor (15)."

In contrast, Fénelon reinterpreted Mentor's relationship with Telemachus to involve independence, support, challenge, experiential learning, and trust, among other factors (Garvey, 2017). These ideas have permeated a Western understanding of mentoring relationships.

Asian archetypes of mentoring

Traditions around the world embody similar archetypes of an experienced elder who provides support and guidance to a younger, inexperienced person. For example, in Asia there is the Chinese ideal of Confucius and the Japanese term "sensei." People from Asian countries have a collective orientation where group goals and outcomes are paramount (Hofstede et al. 1990). The collectivist notion is embodied in their mentoring ideals. Confucius was born in the fifth century BCE. He became a famous philosopher, teacher, and mentor. He believed that mentors advance in life only through the work of their protégés.

The Japanese martial arts have the tradition of a sensei. A sensei teaches the practice of a martial art and budo, which is a way of living and conducting oneself (Funakoshi 1996). This sensei–student relationship is an example of what Bright (2005) calls "vertical relationships," which refer to an older, experienced person who assists a younger, less experienced person. Two kinds of vertical relationships in Japan are similar to the Western notion of mentoring (Bright 2005). The first is the *senpai–kohai* (senior–junior) relationship, which is common in organizational settings. The emphasis is on respect, a sense of obligation to the other, and a strong emotional bond. The second type of vertical relationship is *oyabu–kobun* (leader–subordinate), which is similar to an apprentice model of mentoring. The *oyabu–kobun* relationship occurs in settings characterized by trades or industries with laborers and is characterized by respect, a sense of obligation, and an emotional dimension, which may not be as strong as in the *senpai–kohai* relationship.

West African traditions

Characters in folk stories provide examples of mentor-like figures who, through their exploits, teach youth how to become responsible adults (Boateng 1983). The Ashanti people from West Africa share fables of Anansi, a folktale spider character, who provides mentor-like lessons. Anansi means spider in the Akan language, but Anansi is also a human figure and a trickster in these pedagogical stories. These stories impart knowledge and wisdom to young people. Anansi's stories serve as analogies for problem-solving (Brookins 2003) and thinking about the world in new ways – the kind of guidance that mentors provide.

Native American traditions: The Hopi

The Hopi, indigenous people in the southwestern part of the United States, also have a strong oral tradition. Their creation story involves Spider Woman, who is a wise sage and diety. One story chronicles the journey of a chief's son who wanted to explore the Grand Canyon. Spider Woman mentored him as he encountered various difficulties and counseled him when he first met the Snake people (Voth 1905). She guided the chief's son in how to act and behave in a new setting. "Spider Woman had whispered to him that they were now going to try him very hard, but that he should not be afraid to touch the snakes; and she gave him many instructions" (32).

Draw on local traditions

Knowing about these traditions may provide a stronger foundation on which to develop a mentoring program for your organization that honors the attitudes, motivations, and values of participants. Identify your local traditions related to mentoring that have a direct connection to your organization or program participants. Consider how you can share these traditions as a way to connect mentors and protégés to an established human practice.

Section summary

There are archetypes and traditions of mentoring that may guide how you and your organization conceptualize mentoring. The Greeks gave French and English speakers the word "mentor." However, an awareness of other mentor traditions and archetypes may broaden your understanding of the origin of mentoring and help you educate participants about how these traditions may relate to or inform their mentoring practices today.

The mentoring ecosystem

We tend to focus only on the people in the mentoring relationship: the mentor and the protégé. However, people – even deities – interact in environments, which influence their interactions. The mentoring ecosystem is made up of three elements: mentors, protégés, and the contexts. This theory highlights the process of mentoring (see Figure 2.1).

People are influenced by the systems in which they interact. The mentoring ecosystem is drawn from systems theory (Bronfenbrenner 1979). Bronfenbrenner describes it thusly, "The ecological environment is conceived as a set of nested structures, each inside the next, like a set of Russian dolls. At the inner-most level is the immediate setting containing the

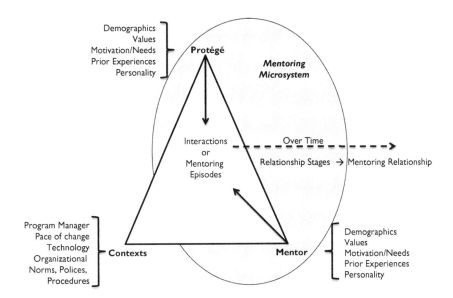

Figure 2.1 Mentoring ecosystem.

developing person" (3). Figure 2.1 illustrates such a system for mentoring relationships.

A setting such as home, work, or school is this innermost level. The set of direct interactions individuals have with others is their "micro" environment. The protégé and mentor dyad is part of this microsystem. Interactions between two people (dyads) are influenced by reciprocity, balance of power, and affective relation or caring.

In mentoring relationships characterized by sponsorship interactions, mentors have more power because of their greater status, experience, or knowledge. In contrast, peer mentoring relationship participants may be more equal on these dimensions.

> There is evidence to suggest that the optimal situation for learning and development is one in which the balance of power gradually shifts in favor of the developing person, on other words, when the latter is given increasing opportunity to exercise control over the situation. (Bronfenbrenner 1979, 58)

Psychosocial support characterizes the caring and affective aspects that are important for mentoring relationships to develop.

At the next level are the relationships between these settings or the "mesosystem." How you, the program manager, interact with individual mentors and protégés comprises this system. For example, a mentor may ask you for advice about a challenging interaction with a protégé. The mentor takes your advice, and thus you influence the protégé even though you never interacted directly with him or her. This system is represented by the contexts in Figure 2.1.

People in the organization may influence the mentoring relationship even though the mentor or protégé may never interact with these individuals. The third level of structures or "exosystem" refers, then, to events that influence the person even though the person is not present. A division manager may decide to provide monthly lunches when protégés and mentors could interact.

The mentoring ecosystem theory highlights your role as a replicator of organizational values through mentoring program activities and as an advocate for individual mentors or protégés. In systems theory, a basic unit is the dyad or two-person system. Yet $N + 2$ systems are important (triad, tetrads, organizational structures).

> [T]he capacity of a dyad to serve as an effective context for human development is crucially dependent on the presence and participation of third parties, such as spouses, relatives, friends, and neighbors. If such third parties are absent, or if they play a disruptive rather than a supportive role, the developmental process, considered as a system, breaks down; like a three-legged stool, it is more easily upset if one leg is broken, or shorter than the others. (Bronfenbrenner 1979, 5)

Your role as a program manager may be an important 'third leg' for developing effective mentoring relationships through formal programs.

The final contribution of systems theory is the importance it places on transitions in learning. These transitions refer to times when a person takes on a new role or enters a new setting. Individuals are often more motivated to engage in mentoring when they take on new roles. For example, people who are new to your organization or company or who are promoted to a new position may need mentoring. Similarly, as some individuals advance in their roles, they may experience a greater desire to give back to leave a legacy to their profession or company and also be motivated to participate in mentoring.

Mentor and protégé characteristics

Mentors and protégés have preferences and experiences that will influence how they enter into a mentoring relationship. These characteristics may even influence their likelihood of becoming a mentor or protégé. You cannot, and perhaps should not, take into account all of these differences, but you will want to be aware of certain tendencies and consider which characteristics may influence your mentoring program goals. As indicated in Figure 2.1, shared attitudes and values, motivation, prior mentoring experiences, and certain personality traits are associated with a greater likelihood of engaging successfully in a mentoring relationship.

Shared attitudes and values matter

Mentors and protégés who have similar attitudes, values, and beliefs, also known as "deep" level characteristics, are likely to report better mentoring relationships (Eby et al. 2013). Similar experiences in terms of background and education are determinants of career support. Career support refers to advice related to the types of challenging assignments to request or accept, how to network with others, and even protection from others.

There is little evidence that "surface" level characteristics like gender and ethnicity are important in mentoring relationships (Ensher and Murphy 1997). These characteristics will be covered more in Chapter 11.

Motivation and needs

Scholars suggest that mentoring works best when protégés and mentors have needs that are fulfilled by engaging in a mentoring relationship (Levinson 1978; Vaillant 1977). The extent to which protégés and mentors are motivated to learn and improve influences how much they interact and invest in the relationship. Protégés with a greater desire to advance in their career are more likely to experience successful outcomes from mentoring (Day and Allen 2004). Mentors are also more likely to engage in these relationships when they are more successful and express greater career aspirations (Emmerik et al. 2005).

Prior mentoring experiences

Prior mentoring experiences may influence how mentors and protégés interact with one another. Mentors who themselves had good mentors have been found to have high-quality relationships with protégés (Bozionelos 2004; Lunsford 2014). On the other hand, bad mentoring experiences appear to make people want to disengage from these relationships (Burk and Eby 2010). Chapter 3 presents more information on developing high-quality relationships and reducing dysfunctional ones.

Personality traits

Personality traits refer to relatively stable ways we act across our lives and in different settings. The Five Factor model of personality, also known as the Big Five, is one of the most accepted theories of personality (Judge et al.

2002). There are many freely available inventories on the internet you can use. The five traits are openness, conscientiousness, extroversion, agreeableness, and neuroticism (or emotional stability). Openness refers to curiosity, inquisitiveness, and creativity. Conscientiousness refers to the extent to which a person makes plans, is reliable, and is self-disciplined. Extraversion refers to the preference to interact with others, displaying high energy, and being action oriented. Agreeableness refers to sensitivity toward others, trust, cooperation, and altruism. Emotional stability refers to confidence and lack of anxiety or worry.

Individuals are more likely to be mentored if they are mid-range on openness, high on conscientious, high or low on extroversion, not extremely agreeable, and more emotionally stable (Bozionelos et al. 2014). Protégés who are low or high on openness do not receive as much mentoring. In other words, a protégé needs to be open to new ideas if he or she is going to be receptive to advice and guidance from a mentor. On the other hand, a protégé can be too open to new ideas if he or she is attracted (or distracted) by any new idea. A protégé can also be too agreeable to be mentored. People who report extremely high scores on agreeableness experience less mentoring. Introverts invest in a one-on-one relationship, and mentors will give the time and attention to introverts. Extraverts are highly visible and also attract mentors.

The research on mentors' personality is limited. Research suggests that personality has a more limited effect on mentors. The Big Five factor of openness appears to be associated with the likelihood of becoming a mentor.

Personality preferences may influence the amount of mentoring a protégé may receive. For example, more attention may be needed to ensure ambiverts are connecting with a mentor. Protégés who are low or too high on agreeableness and high or low on openness may be better served by other professional development activities than mentoring.

Contexts

The context refers to organizational features, such as pace of change and technology, that may affect mentoring programs.

In fast-paced industries a mentoring program may only last three to six months. Workplace mentoring programs appear to foster more interaction frequency than programs in other settings. This may be because employees might encounter one another through their job duties or social activities sponsored by work (Eby 2012). Mentoring programs in academic institutions have a longer duration than programs in other settings (Eby 2012). The semester schedule may result in programs lasting nine months or longer, for example over the duration of a degree program.

Case Study 2.1   "Curating" mentoring: Mentoring social entrepreneurs

Decker's interests highlight the changing landscape of mentoring and how mentoring administrators can be reflective practitioners to address these changes. This case illustrates the nuanced dimensions of mentoring and how one program coordinator evolved his role to recognize more complex needs for his mentoring program.

Traditional mentoring

Decker's early mentoring experiences were typical of informal, one-on-one, traditional mentoring relationships. During high school, he coached youth soccer. A father of one of his soccer kids offered him an internship at the Bank of America in Charlotte, North Carolina. He found his first mentors at the bank, which he calls his "mini-mentoring program." They helped him learn how to operate in the culture of banking and work, but some of his mentors also provided "thoughtful life advice and support as I decided what path to pursue."

He encountered another pivotal mentor during his first year of college. This time it was his North Carolina State University college T-shirt that attracted attention. Decker relates, "this dude rolls up on me and I thought 'scary old guy'!" The scary old guy asked if Decker attended North Carolina State University. Their banter turned into a mentorship. His mentor was an alumnus and served on the Alumni Board of Directors at North Carolina State University during a time of numerous leadership changes. Their conversations clarified how to identify organizational challenges through discussions about factors related to leadership turnover, tuition increases, and so on. "He became a mentor to me," says Decker.

Changing views of mentoring

A thoughtful mentoring practitioner, Decker has reflected on his mentoring experiences and how mentoring needs to evolve. He observes that "mentoring is not new, but we are in a space where we need to think about measuring the practices, strategies, and outcomes of it." He relates an analogy of youth mentoring to make his point. The old view of mentoring was to spend time with a young person, perhaps by going to a baseball game together. "Taking a kid to a baseball game is awesome," Decker says. "But in 2015, if all you do is go to the baseball game and your protégé does not pass math then the mentorship is a failure. Mentoring today needs to be focused on relationships that promote socio-emotional learning."

Curating mentors

He drew on his prior mentoring experiences to develop his mentoring philosophy when he worked with the Black Male Achievement (BMA) Fellows at Echoing Green,[4] a global nonprofit that develops social entrepreneurs. BMA Fellows were social entrepreneurs selected on the basis of their desire to start innovative, new organizations to support black male achievement. Decker worked with about 12–13 Fellows a year. He viewed his role as a mentor coordinator to be akin to a portfolio manager: "If you are trying to guide a company to market then you are giving the company all your resource to be ready. Cultivating and curating a community of learning."

His work was to identify the right mentors for the BMA Fellows so that these protégés could develop their organizations. Decker considered himself a matchmaker who identified protégés' needs as he looked for potential mentors with the right set of competencies and resources. However, Decker notes that "it isn't enough just to have access to a network." He saw his job as one where he "curated" resources for protégés. Emotional support was important for protégés, but they needed clarification of the nuts and bolts of what they were doing. "What does it mean to be productive and efficient as a social entrepreneur?" he asked. "We are moving from a time when mentoring involved providing *access* to teaching people *how* to operate within social networks."

Diversity

Decker is African American and worked with African American protégés. He notes that

> the traditional view on diversity is that it is difficult to have a mentor who doesn't understand 'my background, the pressures, and challenges I might face.' It is hard to interact with a mentor who wants to 'correct' certain protégé viewpoints if the mentor doesn't understand the protégé's challenges.

He asserts that mentors do not need to have the same experiences as their protégés, but they do need to demonstrate they can adopt a variety of perspectives in giving support and guidance. Effective mentors, says Decker, "need to understand structural bias and institutional bias that may limit protégé success." Mentors can support protégés by interacting in ways that empower protégés to select their actions rather than feeling they must conform to a certain pathway to achieve their aspirations. As Decker noted, "otherwise good advice might get lost if protégés don't see how it relates to their situation. Diversity in mentors encourages diversity of perspectives."

Benefits for protégés and mentors

Decker reflects on the benefits that accrue not only to protégés but also to mentors. The BMA Fellows gained a wider view of instigating change. Decker shared that one conversation with a mentor helped a protégé understand how some progress is better than no progress and that collaborating within a system is a way to change it.

Protégés enriched their mentors' skills and experiences as well. For example, mentors often had a traditional narrative on mentoring young African American men that was informed by a civil rights, baby boomer view of wanting to "fix these people." Yet protégés challenged these stereotypes and educated mentors about the structural challenges (rather than individual deficits) they faced. For example, a protégé might have all A's in school but lack access to transportation to attend community college. The mentors came to understand it was lack of access and opportunity, not lack of motivation, that presented challenges to protégé success.

Building mentoring infrastructure

Decker has moved from being in the trenches as a mentoring program coordinator (he would call it an agent, connector, or curator!) to a consultant role as he helps others think the structure of the philanthropic sector. He ponders questions such as:

- How can we make these kind of mentoring connections more possible?
- What will it take to support new leaders?
- How are philanthropic groups deploying resources in a more sustainable way?
- How can we best build communities and networks among young leaders?

There was a time when the value of mentors was the "sacred knowledge" they might share. In a time when information is more readily available, such as through internet searches, the role of an effective mentor has shifted to one where they help protégés use information well. What is the role of program coordinators in helping mentoring participants and organizations manage these changes in needs and expectations for mentoring?

Tackling big problems takes intense collaboration. One of Decker's new challenges is to help leaders in the social sector create the infrastructure to embrace how to mentor a new generation of diverse leaders. When Decker sees the protests related to cop shootings of African American men in the United States, he sees more potential for social entrepreneurs and local philanthropic organizations. These social issues "complicate how we used to talk about who might be a good mentor," he notes.

Source: Interview with Decker Ngongang, Senior Consultant,
Frontline Solutions.
https://echoinggreen.org/fellowship/

Technology is another factor that influences mentoring programs. Web conference and electronic communications have enabled organizations to match mentors and protégés who are not co-located. MentorNet[3] is an example of an e-mentoring program that pairs working professionals with students studying science, technology, engineering, or mathematics. MentorNet's aim is to support more women and minorities in science. The advantages of such arrangements provide greater access to mentoring and a decreased emphasis on surface characteristics. Further, these programs can be easier to monitor in terms of interaction frequency and can provide training. However, relationships can be slower to develop, as it may be more difficult to establish rapport and technological difficulties can hinder meeting frequency (Ensher and Murphy 2007).

Your organization has policies, procedures, and unwritten rules or norms that will influence your mentoring program. Identify the policies and procedures that will support (or hinder) your mentoring efforts. For example, do you need to meet with the department directors or managers to gain their endorsement before you start your program? Case Study 2.1 in this chapter highlights the need to develop an infrastructure to support mentoring in ways that achieve organizational goals.

Outcomes

Formal mentoring relationships are expected to result in individual and organizational outcomes, although connecting any one human resource activity to organizational-level outcomes is challenging (Baugh and Fagenson-Eland 2007). Outcomes occur at the individual and organizational levels. For example, you might expect that protégés will learn a new skill and as a result advance more quickly in the organization by achieving a degree or promotion. Mentors may fulfill psychological needs such as giving back to their profession. They may achieve status from their protégé's achievements or accrue psychological capital when they are seen as having the skills to develop others. Organizational outcomes such as retention of students or employees, talent or leader development, and revenues (at for-profit organizations) have been associated with formal mentoring programs.

Categorizing outcomes

Scholars have identified categories for mentoring outcomes, and it may be useful to you to have some familiarity with this taxonomy. Eby and colleagues' (2008) early work reported six categories, which they later narrowed to four categories: attitudinal, behavioral, career, and health (Eby et al. 2013). Descriptions of the four categories are presented here.

Attitudinal outcomes refer to satisfaction and affiliation. Satisfaction might include items related to a university, department, coursework, or professors as well as satisfaction with one's job or job attributes, such as one's supervisor, coworkers, pay, or benefits. Affiliation refers to items such as organizational commitment or sense of community.

Behavioral outcomes refer to both actual or intended behaviors. For example, professional or personal growth, team learning, knowledge, and academic or organizational socialization would be examples of behavioral outcomes. Time spent on a task, such as hours studying or working, would be other potential consequences of mentoring.

Career-related outcomes refer to compensation, perceived career success, and opportunities. Compensation may be measured in a variety of ways including starting salary, current salary, or raises received. Perceived career success is how one feels about career-related outcomes and refers to one's self-reported feelings about career success or attainment.

Health-related outcomes include measures related to strain and to self-efficacy – for example, measures of stress, job burnout, work–family conflict, depressed mood, and other psychological attributes associated with health. Self-efficacy measures refer to how a person feels about tasks at school or in their career.

Costs and benefits

Benefits, or positive outcomes, are assumed to accrue from mentoring programs. Yet all the participants may not experience a benefit. For example, perhaps not all the participants in a mentoring program designed to improve employee satisfaction (an attitudinal outcome) will experience an increase in work satisfaction. There are individual and organizational costs and benefits that need to be carefully considered before starting a mentoring program.

Costs to individuals may be associated with the psychosocial and career functions of mentoring. Psychosocial costs may include burnout, anger, and grief or loss (Lunsford et al., 2013). For example, a popular mentor may take on too many protégés, which may result in burnout and subsequent poor performance as a mentor. Difficult mentoring relationships, for example if a protégé fails to heed the guidance of a mentor, may lead to anger on the part of a mentor. Similarly, a protégé who is neglected, ignored, or taken advantage of may become angry at this poor treatment. Even close, effective relationships may result in cost to mentoring participants. If a mentor and protégé have worked together long enough to develop a close bond, they may experience a sense of loss when it is time for a protégé to move on to another position or to another organization.

Career costs may be categorized as reputational, productivity, and ethics. Reputational cost may occur when poor protégé performance is seen as a reflection of the mentor's skills or abilities. Productivity costs are related to burnout, such as if a mentor takes on too many protégés, then he or she may not be able to complete their work. For example, individuals may be asked to take on more protégés in times of budgetary constraints as have occurred recently in universities in the United States. Finally, ethical boundaries might become blurred if a mentor lacks competence in an area but provides guidance to a protégé anyway. Some mentors are also expected to protect professional norms, which may be challenging if a protégé's performance is unacceptable.

Organizational costs relate to time and money expended on the mentoring program. Time includes your time spent as the program manager as well as the time protégés and mentors invest in the relationship. Time invested in these relationships also means that time is not invested elsewhere, what economists refer to as opportunity costs. Some mentoring programs have budgets for a program manager, recruitment materials, and activities.

Section summary

The mentoring ecosystem helps you to recognize influences on formal mentoring programs from individual preferences and experiences, as well as your organization's unique characteristics. Consider how your organizational culture influences your mentoring program needs. Mentoring program outcomes fall into four categories: attitudinal, behavior, career, health. It is useful to understand the potential psychosocial and career costs of mentoring to participants and costs in time and money to organizations.

Defining mentoring

There are many popular works on mentoring, and most of these articles and books help the individuals (mentors or protégés) develop their mentoring skills. The universal assumption is we all need mentors. For example, the *Wall Street Journal* (Shellenbarger 2016) provides advice about "How to Cold Call Your Future Mentor."

The scholarly tradition is more recent. The work on mentoring has roots in scholarship from the 1970s on adult development (Levinson 1978; Vaillant 1977). A search using Google Scholar shows that research doubled from the 1970s to the 1980s and tripled by the decade of the 1990s – tripling again by the first decade of the twenty-first century.

A commonly accepted definition of mentoring is a "relationship between a younger adult and an older, more experience adult [who] helps the younger individual learn to navigate the adult world and the world of work" (Kram 1985, 2). This definition provides a broad umbrella that includes many helping behaviors. There is a lack of clarity on the use of terms such as a mentor, coach, teacher, co-mentoring, group mentoring, peer mentoring, and reverse mentoring.

The National Academies of Science, Engineering, and Medicine (NASEM) commissioned a two-year study on mentoring in science, technology, engineering, mathematics, and medicine (Byars-Winston and Dahlberg 2019). NASEM is a private, nonprofit organization in the United States that provides expert advice on pressing challenges. The organization commissioned its first study on mentorship because, even though it is seen as an essential relationship, "mentoring rarely receives the focused attention, evaluation, and recognition of other aspects of professional development such as teaching and research" (Byars-Winston and Dahlberg 2019, 1). The report provided a definition of mentoring that will be useful for most mentoring programs to use or refine (disclaimer: I was on the committee that authored the report).

> Mentorship is a professional, working alliance in which individuals work together over time to support the personal and professional growth, development, and success of the relational partners through the provision of career and psychosocial support. (Byars-Winston and Dahlberg 2019, 2)

The point is to clarify what you mean by "mentoring" in your mentoring program. There is no right or definitive answer; however, you also do not need to create your own definition. Mentoring is a term that includes certain behaviors and excludes others. If your use of the term "mentoring" is so broad as to include every relationship, then it will be difficult to communicate to program participants what you expect them to do.

I think about the people, processes, and behaviors involved in mentoring relationships. One researcher has noted the difference between mentoring as a relationship (people) versus a strategy (process) (Bright 2005). Thus, regardless of the definition you select you may want to also consider the people who participate in the relationship, the process of the interactions, and the behaviors involved.

People

People refer to the roles that are seen as providing mentoring. You may assume mentoring is taking place because someone has a responsibility to be an advisor or supervisor, or because he or she was assigned the role of mentor or protégé. The example of youth mentoring described by Decker in Case Study 2.1 demonstrates this point. Further, many mentoring programs seek to match individuals in one-on-one relationships, although an approach that supports for multiple mentors may be more successful and realistic.

Avoid trait approaches

There continues to be a concerning overreliance on personal characteristics in mentoring programs. Popular books and articles often take a trait approach. For example, *Inc. Magazine*[5] provides information about the "7 Key Qualities of an Effective Mentor." Being a good communicator, establishing successful personal and professional relationships, and having integrity, honesty, and other positive character traits are frequent items on such lists. There are similar lists for protégés, who should possess traits like loyalty, open-mindedness, enthusiasm, and confidence (Melanson 2008) or be respectful, motivated, and positive (according to *Happiness is Better*[6]). These approaches are like going to a fortune-teller; the advice is so vague as to be generally applicable to everyone without providing any real direction.

Successful mentors may not always have successful personal relationships or even possess all the key qualities or characteristics of effective mentors. Indeed, it might seem that protégés with all these ideal traits may not need a mentor. Possessing some of these traits may increase relationship satisfaction, but these traits have not been linked with other mentoring outcomes. As mentioned in the Prologue, even the best mentors (and protégés) have bad days when they may behave in manipulative or dysfunctional ways. A trait approach neglects a consideration of outcomes achieved by the mentor and protégé.

There are three reasons to take caution in an over-reliance on a trait approach. First, a long list of traits may turn off some mentors and protégés who may self-select out of participation. Second, providing a list of traits does not support individuals to develop the skills that might be helpful in mentoring relationships. Third, there are better ways to educate mentors and protégés to enter into successful relationships that involve a consideration of the behaviors of mentoring and the processes of developing an effective relationship.

Mentoring networks

Protégés, even when in a formal one-on-one mentoring program, often report multiple individuals they consider to provide mentor-like behaviors to them. It may be useful to broaden your concept of mentoring beyond a singular role of mentor–protégé to include mentoring networks, mentoring mosaics (Mullen 2009), or developmental networks (Higgins and Kram 2001). There are differences in these terms, which are briefly described here to help you think about the value of encouraging different types of mentoring networks in your program. Case Study 2.1 in this chapter highlights how program managers can navigate a changing landscape of mentoring by recognizing the importance of mentoring networks. "Mentoring networks" is the broad term that refers to the presence of multiple mentors. Mentoring mosaics include peer relationships where participants may alternate between the role of protégé and mentor.

Developmental networks are characterized along two dimensions: network diversity and relationship strength (Higgins and Kram 2001). Network diversity reflects the extent to which there is new information from members in the network. Individuals with several mentors who provide similar information would have low network diversity, whereas individuals with several mentors who provide different perspectives would have high network diversity. Relationship strength refers to the connectedness of the individuals. Strong relationships are characterized by strong emotional bonds and frequent and reciprocal interactions . A weak relationship is where the information flows only in one direction – for example, when the protégé receives advice and guidance. These two dimensions provide a typology of mentoring relationships with four categories: receptive, traditional, opportunistic, and entrepreneurial.

Protégés who have relationships with low diversity and weak ties would have a receptive network, while protégés with low diversity and strong ties would have a traditional network. The traditional network aligns with the common definition of mentoring as a one-on-one relationship. Protégés with high diversity and weak ties would have an opportunistic network, while protégés with high diversity and strong ties would have an entrepreneurial network.

Processes

Mentoring relationships develop over time. Imagine the start of your mentoring program. Just because an individual is assigned a mentor or protégé does not mean that mentoring has occurred. An understanding of mentoring episodes and relationship stages may help you design briefings and activities to support the processes of mentoring.

Mentoring episodes

Mentoring starts out in what has been called "mentoring episodes" (Allen and Poteet 2011). A mentoring episode is a single, mentor-like interaction. Over time, these interactions may develop such that the participants feel they are in a mentoring relationship. Figure 2.1 illustrates how, over time, mentoring episodes lead to mentoring relationships, which also move through stages.

For example, the first time a new employee asks a senior employee for advice about how to handle a situation may be viewed as advice-seeking (and receiving) behavior. Over time, their conversation may include building confidence and providing emotional support and career advice. After a certain number of interactions, the pair may consider each other as mentor and protégé. Mentoring relationships, like other relationships, develop in stages. Case Study 8.1 in Chapter 8 provides an example of how mentoring episodes develop into a mentoring relationship.

Relationship stages

Relationships develop in stages (see Chapter 9 for more details). One classic mentoring stage theory was proposed by Kathy Kram (1985). Kram (1985) identified four stages of mentoring relationships. Initiation is the first stage and refers to the time when the participants get to know one another. The second stage is cultivation. The real work of the relationship takes place during this stage. Cultivation is the time when mentors and protégés work on a project or idea together, give and receive feedback, and learn from the relationship. Separation is the third stage of mentoring relationships. The separation stage may be more obvious in a formal mentoring program, but even naturally occurring mentoring relationships evolve over time. Finally, redefinition is the fourth stage. During this period, the individuals redefine the relationship as colleagues or friends, or they may chose to end the relationship altogether.

Behaviors

Mentoring may also be defined by the behaviors of the participants. Kram (1985) studied 18 pairs of protégés and mentors and identified two kinds of behaviors that defined these relationships: career and psychosocial support. Career support refers to behaviors such providing protection, suggesting challenging assignments, coaching, and sponsoring. Psychosocial support refers to what we think of as friend-like behaviors, such as listening, acceptance, counseling, friendship, confidence building, and role modeling. Some studies find that role modeling is a separate kind of support; however, decades of research suggest that the two functions of career and psychosocial support define mentoring (Allen et al. 2004).

Researchers have measured these behaviors as a way to define mentoring in educational and organizational contexts. Three evidence-based measures of mentoring behaviors are described here. The measures show how the psychosocial and career functions, first identified by Kathy Kram, vary by settings – in this case, graduate school, undergraduate education, and business. For example, a career function in graduate school might be learning which conference to attend. While in a business setting, it might be identifying assignments that provide visibility and status. How the behaviors vary in different settings is described next.

Graduate school settings

The Advisory Working Alliance Inventory (AWAI) has been validated for use in graduate education. The AWAI contains 30 items that measure rapport (psychosocial support), apprenticeship (career support), and a third factor the authors titled identification-individual (Schlosser and Gelso 2001). The response scale is a Likert scale from 1 (strongly disagree) to 5 (strongly agree). Refer to Table 2.1 for the items. The same authors also developed a companion inventory to measure mentoring from the faculty member perspective (Schlosser and Gelso 2005). A shortened version of the AWAI was successfully used to measure mentoring (Lunsford 2012) among advanced doctoral students.

Undergraduate settings

The "College Student Mentoring Scale" was developed to assess mentoring received by undergraduates (Crisp 2009). The psychosocial and career mentoring functions are subdivided to reflect the needs of undergraduates. The psychosocial support subcategories are psychological and emotional support, and the existence of a role model. The career subcategories are degree and career support, and academic subject knowledge support. The response scale is a Likert scale from 1 (strongly disagree) to 5 (strongly agree). There is empirical evidence that this scale is reliable and measures mentoring received in college settings. It has also been tested on underrepresented students (refer to Resources for a link to the scale).

Business settings

Researchers have developed questionnaires and inventories to measure mentoring, as another way to ensure mentoring is taking place. There is an

Table 2.1 Advisor Working Alliance Inventory items

Items by function
Rapport
I get the feeling that my advisor does not like me very much.[*]
I do not think that my advisor believes in me.[*]
My advisor does not encourage my input into our discussions.[*]
My advisor is not kind when commenting about my work.[*]
I do not feel respected by my advisor in our work together.[*]
My advisor offers me encouragement for my accomplishments.[*]
My advisor welcomes my input into our discussions.[*]
My advisor takes my ideas seriously.
I do not think that my advisor has my best interests in mind.
I feel uncomfortable working with my advisor.
I am often intellectually "lost" during meetings with my advisor.
Apprenticeship
My advisor introduces me to professional activities (e.g., conferences, submitting articles for journal). My advisor helps me conduct my work within a plan.[*]
My advisor has invited me to be a responsible collaborator in his/her own work.[*]
My advisor helps me establish a timetable for the tasks of my graduate training.[*]
Meetings with my advisor are unproductive.[*]
My advisor helps me recognize areas where I can improve.[*]
My advisor facilitates my professional development through networking.[*]
I consistently implement suggestions made by my advisor.
I learn from my advisor by watching him/her.
I am an apprentice of my advisor.
My advisor does not help me stay on track in our meetings.
My advisor strives to make program requirements as rewarding as possible.
My advisor does not educate me about the process of graduate school.
My advisor is available when I need him/her.
Identification-individuation
I do not want to be like my advisor.
I tend to see things differently from my advisor.
I do not want to feel similar to my advisor in the process of conducting work.
My advisor and I have different interests.
I feel like my advisor expects too much from me.

[*] indicates items in the AWAI-r (Lunsford 2014).Source: Schlosser and Gelso 2001.
Note: Response scale is a Likert scale (from 1 = "strongly disagree" to 5 = "strongly agree." Reverse the scores for negative items.

increasing number of scholars who have developed proprietary measures of mentoring. A review of commercially available measures by Gilbreath et al. (2008) identified only the Alleman Mentoring Activities Questionnaire (Alleman and Clarke 2002) as being tested to make sure it measures mentoring. Many measures are lengthy, or it is unclear how other mentoring program managers might use them. Dreher and Ash (1990) created a free, short, well-studied scale to measure the behaviors of mentoring in work settings (see Table 2.2).

Table 2.2 Mentoring scale for business settings

Items

To what extent has a mentor:

Given or recommended you for challenging assignments that present opportunities to learn new skills?

Given or recommended you for assignments that required personal contact with managers in different parts of the company?

Given or recommended you for assignments that increased your contact with higher-level managers?

Given or recommended you for assignments that helped you meet new colleagues?

Helped you finish assignments/tasks or meet deadlines that otherwise would have been difficult to complete?

Protected you from working with other managers or work units before you knew about their likes/dislikes, opinions on controversial topics, and the nature of the political environment?

Gone out of his/her way to promote your career interests?

Kept you informed about what is going on at higher levels in the company or how external conditions are influencing the company?

Conveyed feelings of respect for you as an individual?

Conveyed empathy for the concerns and feelings you have discussed with him/her?

Encouraged you to talk openly about anxiety and fears that detract from your work?

Shared personal experiences as an alternative perspective to your problems?

Discussed your questions or concerns regarding feelings of competence, commitment to advancement, relationships with peers and supervisors or work/family conflicts?

Shared history of his/her career with you?

Encouraged you to prepare for advancement?

Encouraged you to try new ways of behaving on the job?

Served as a role model?

Displayed attitudes and values similar to your own?

Source: Dreher and Ash 1990.
Note: Response format is: 1 = "not at all"; 2 = "to a small extent"; 3 = "to some extent"; 4 = "to a large extent"; 5 = "to a very large extent".

Section summary

Define what mentoring means in your program. Mentoring involves people, processes, and behaviors. It is a special kind of relationship that involves career and psychosocial support. You can use existing measures to assess the extent to which mentor-like behaviors are taking place in your setting.

Conclusion

It is helpful to understand the origins of mentoring and its place in other cultures. This understanding can help you connect your formal mentoring program with an effective practice that is culturally sensitive. The mentoring ecosystem presented in Figure 2.1 illustrates a framework for thinking about the influences on your mentoring participants and programs. There are many ways to define mentoring through roles, behaviors, and processes. There is no correct definition of mentoring. You do need to define what mentoring means in your program. This chapter provides you with a vocabulary to create a shared understanding about the role of mentoring in your organization.

Key terms

- Costs and benefits: individual and organizational
- Mentoring ecosystem: dyad, microsystem
- Mentoring episodes
- Mentoring functions: psychosocial and career support
- Mentoring networks: mosaics, developmental networks
- Outcomes: attitudinal, behavioral, career, health
- Relationship stages: initiation/goals, cultivation, separation, termination

Check your learning

1. What archetypes of mentoring are relevant to your mentoring program?
2. What people, processes, and behaviors are important for your mentoring program?
3. What outcomes do you expect from your mentoring program for participants and for your organization?
4. Write a short statement about your mentoring philosophy, given what you now know about mentoring.

Resources

College Student Mentoring Scale: http://www.gloriacrisp.com/mentoring-scale.html

Extensive, free materials about the dimensions of national cultures and organizations are available at the Hofstede Centre website: https://geerthofstede.com/ and clicking on the 'culture' tab.

Download the Ten Item Personality Inventory (TIPI) from the Goz Lab in at least 23 languages from Catalan to Urdu: https://gosling.psy.utexas.edu/scales-weve-developed/ten-item-personality-measure-tipi/

Notes

1 http://thinkprogress.org/election/2015/06/29/3675488/jeb-bush-says-baltimore-ferguson-protests-caused-lack-mentoring/
2 http://www.nytimes.com/2015/06/28/sports/tennis/serena-williams-and-le-coach-seek-a-new-wimbledon-triumph.html?_r=0

3 http://mentornet.org
4 http://www.echoinggreen.org
5 http://www.inc.com/jayson-demers/7-key-qualities-of-an-effective-mentor.html
6 http://happinessisbetter.com/2009/03/30/10-things-to-look-for-in-a-mentor/

References

Alleman, E., and D. Clarke. 2002. *Alleman Mentoring Activities Questionnaire.* Sharon, OH: Silver Wood Associates.

Allen, T. D., L. T. Eby, M. L. Poteet, E. Lentz, and L. Lima. 2004. "Career Benefits Associated with Mentoring for Protégés: A Meta-Analytic Review." *Journal of Applied Psychology* 89(1): 127–136.

Allen, T. D., and M. L. Poteet. 2011. "Enhancing Our Knowledge of Mentoring with a Person-Centric Approach." *Industrial and Organizational Psychology* 4(1): 126–130.

Baugh, S. G., and E. A. Fagenson-Eland. 2007. "Formal Mentoring Programs." In *The Handbook of Mentoring at Work: Theory, Research, and Practice,* edited by B. R. Ragins and K. E. Kram, 249–271. Los Angeles, CA: Sage Publications.

Boateng, F. 1983. "African Traditional Education: A Method of Disseminating Cultural Values." *Journal of Black Studies* 13(3): 321–336.

Bozionelos, N. 2004. "Mentoring Provided: Relation to Mentor's Career Success, Personality, and Mentoring Received." *Journal of Vocational Behavior* 64(1): 24–46.

Bozionelos, N., G. Bozionelos, P. Polychroniou, and K. Kostopoulos. 2014. "Mentoring Receipt and Personality: Evidence for Non-Linear Relationships." *Journal of Business Research* 67(2): 171–181.

Bright, M. I. 2005. "Can Japanese Mentoring Enhance Understanding of Western Mentoring?" *Employee Relations* 27(4): 325–339.

Bronfenbrenner, U. 1979. *The Ecology of Human Development: Experiments by Nature and Design.* Cambridge, MA: Harvard University Press.

Brookins, C. 2003. "Anansi and How the Moon Got Put in the Sky." *American Journal of Community Psychology* 32(3): 283–284.

Burk, H. G., and L. T. Eby. 2010. "What Keeps People in Mentoring Relationships When Bad Things Happen? A Field Study from the Protégé's Perspective." *Journal of Vocational Behavior* 77(3): 437–446.

Byars-Winston, A., and M. Dahlberg. 2019. *The Science of Effective Mentorship in STEMM.* Washington, DC: The National Academies Press. 10.17226/25568.

Clutterbuck, D. 2007. "An International Perspective on Mentoring." In *The Handbook of Mentoring at Work: Theory, Research, and Practice,* edited by B. R. Ragins and K. E. Kram, 633–655. Los Angeles, CA: Sage Publications.

Crisp, G. 2009. "Conceptualization and Initial Validation of the College Student Mentoring Scale." *Journal of College Student Development* 50(2): 177–194.

Day, R., and T. D. Allen. 2004. "The Relationship between Career Motivation and Self-Efficacy with Protégé Career Success." *Journal of Vocational Behavior* 64(1): 72–91.

Dreher, G. F., and R. A. Ash. 1990. "A Comparative Study of Mentoring among Men and Women in Managerial, Professional, and Technical Positions." *Journal of Applied Psychology* 75(5): 539–546.

Eby, L. T. 2012. "Workplace Mentoring: Past, Present, and Future Perspectives." In *Oxford Library of Psychology. The Oxford Handbook of Organizational Psychology, Vol. 1*, edited by S. W. J. Kozlowski, 615–642. Oxford, UK: Oxford University Press.

Eby, L. T., T. D. Allen, S. C. Evans, T. Ng, and D. L. DuBois. 2008. "Does Mentoring Matter? A Multidisciplinary Meta-Analysis Comparing Mentored and Non-Mentored Individuals." *Journal of Vocational Behavior* 72(2): 254–267.

Eby, L. T., T. D. Allen, B. J. Hoffman, L. E. Baranik, J. B. Sauer, S. Baldwin, M.A. Morrison, K. M. Kinkade, C. P. Maher, and S. Curtis. 2013. "An Interdisciplinary Meta-Analysis of the Potential Antecedents, Correlates, and Consequences of Protégé Perceptions of Mentoring." *Psychological Bulletin* 139(2): 1–36.

Emmerik, H., S. Baugh, and M. Euwema. 2005. "Who Wants to Be a Mentor? An Examination of Attitudinal, Instrumental, and Social Motivational Components." *Career Development International* 10(4): 310–324.

Ensher, E. A., and S. E. Murphy. 1997. "Effects of Race, Gender, Perceived Similarity, and Contact on Mentor Relationships." *Journal of Vocational Behavior* 50(3): 460–481.

Ensher, E. A., and S. E. Murphy. 2007. "E-mentoring: Next-Generation Research Strategies and Suggestions." In *The Handbook of Mentoring at Work: Theory, Research, and Practice*, edited by B. R. Ragins and K. E. Kram, 299–322. Los Angeles, CA: Sage Publications.

Funakoshi, G. 1996. *Karate-Do Kyo-han: The Master Text*. Tokyo: Kodansha America LLC.

Garvey, R. 2017. "Philosophical Origins of Mentoring." In *The Sage Handbook of Mentoring*, edited by D. Clutterbuck, N. Dominguez, F. Kochan, B. Smith, J. Haddock-Millar, and L. G. Lunsford, 15–33. Los Angeles, CA: Sage Publications.

Gilbreath, B., G. L. Rose, and K. E. Dietrich. 2008. "Assessing Mentoring in Organizations: An Evaluation of Commercial Mentoring Instruments." *Mentoring & Tutoring: Partnership in Learning* 16(4): 379–393.

Higgins, M. C., and K. E. Kram. 2001. "Reconceptualizing Mentoring at Work: A Developmental Network Perspective." *Academy of Management Review* 26(2): 264–288.

Hofstede, G., B. Neuijen, D. D. Ohayv, and G. Sanders. 1990. "Measuring Organizational Cultures: A Qualitative and Quantitative Study across Twenty Cases." *Administrative Science Quarterly* 35(2): 286–316.

Homer. 1999. The Odyssey. Translated by S. Butler. Project Gutenberg. https://www.gutenberg.org/files/1727/1727-h/1727-h.htm.

Judge, T. A., J. E. Bono, R. Ilies, and M. W. Gerhardt. 2002. "Personality and Leadership: A Qualitative and Quantitative Review." *Journal of Applied Psychology* 87(4): 765–780.

Kram, K. E. 1985. *Mentoring at Work: Developmental Relationships in Organizational Life*. Glenview, IL: Scott, Foresman, and Company.

Levinson, D. 1978. *The Seasons of a Man's Life*. New York: Knopf.

Lunsford, L. G. 2012. "Doctoral Advising or Mentoring: Effects on Student Outcomes." *Mentoring & Tutoring: Partnership in Learning* 20(2): 251–270.

Lunsford, L. G. 2014. "Mentors, Tormentors, and No Mentors: Mentoring Scientists." *International Journal of Mentoring and Coaching* 3(1): 4–17.

Lunsford, L. G., V. Baker, K. A. Griffin and W. B., Johnson. 2013. "Mentoring: A typology of costs for higher education faculty." *Mentoring – Tutoring: Partnership in Learning* 21(2): 126–149.

Melanson, M. 2008. "Qualities of the Ideal Protégé." *US Army Medical Department Journal* (October–December), 44–46.

Mullen, C. A. 2009. "Reimagining the Human Dimension of Mentoring: A Framework for Research Administration and the Academy." *Journal of Research Administration* 40(1): 10–31.

Roche, G. R. 1979. "Much Ado about Mentors." *Harvard Business* 57, 14–25.

Rose, G. 2003. "Enhancement of Mentor Selection Using the Ideal Mentor Scale." *Research in Higher Education* 44(4): 473–494.

Schlosser, L., and C. Gelso. 2001. "Measuring the Working Alliance in Advisor–Advisee Relationships in Graduate School." *Journal of Counseling Psychology* 48(2): 157–167.

Schlosser, L., and C. Gelso. 2005. "The Advisor Working Alliance Inventory: Scale Development and Validation." *Journal of Counseling Psychology* 52(4): 650–654.

Shellenbarger, S. 2016. "How to Cold Call Your Future Mentor." *Wall Street Journal*. Available online at https://www.wsj.com/articles/how-to-cold-call-your-future-mentor-1476813053 (accessed April 11, 2021).

Vaillant, G. E. 1977. *Adaptation to Life*. Boston, MA: Little, Brown.

Voth, H. R. 1905. *The Traditions of the Hopi*. Chicago, IL: Field Columbian Museum. Available online at www.sacred-texts.com/nam/hopi/toth/toth009.htm (accessed February 15, 2016).

Chapter 3

Promoting high-quality mentoring

Introduction

North Carolina State University has produced more generals and flag officers, outside of military service academies and corps of cadet programs (Ryals 2012), than any public or private university or college in the United States. Technology companies in Silicon Valley, named for the silicon chips that are made there, are the envy of the world. These companies attract more than their fair share of talented employees from the best universities in the world (Lev-Ram 2014). These are just two examples of what Zuckerman (1977) called "evocative environments." Her study of Nobel Laureates highlighted a fact known by scientists and chief executive officers: Some environments produce more discoveries or new companies than would be expected. She attributed the creation of these learning spaces to excellent mentors.

Episcopal High School (EHS), founded in 1839 in the US state of Virginia, is one such evocative environment for adolescents. EHS is an elite institution with numerous prominent alumni. Among them is US Senator John McCain. By McCain's own account, he was a difficult and challenging teenager. Yet one of his high school teachers, Mr. Ravenel, saw potential in the young McCain.

Mr. Ravenel, says McCain, gave him "moorings and a compass. He was a man of such admirable qualities. You wanted to be like him. And it wasn't just me, but the other boys as well" (Harvard T.H. Chan School of Public Health n.d.). McCain noted that he was an inspirational man:

> I wasn't the only one that he inspired. His influence over my life, while perhaps not apparent to most who have observed its progress, was more important and more benevolent than that of any other person save members of my family. (McCain, in Harvard T.H. Chan School of Public Health n.d.)

These examples illustrate a narrative of mentoring as a positive experience. Many successful individuals, as illustrated in the previous quotes, attribute

DOI: 10.4324/9781003163862-3

part of their achievements to a mentor's influence. Can formal mentoring programs provide similar benefits as the informal mentoring relationships reported here?

This chapter draws on the mentoring ecosystem presented in Chapter 2 to focus on both the relationship between mentors and protégés (the microsystem) and the organizational context. Research from positive organizational scholarship is described. This chapter reviews sources of dysfunctional relationships and how you might minimize their occurrence. Ethical obligations provide the compass for mentoring; common ethical tensions are examined. Characteristics of high-quality mentoring programs are presented as a segue to the organizational contexts that support a culture of mentoring. The chapter concludes with suggestions on how to develop high-quality mentoring relationships and programs.

High-quality relationships

Ragins et al. (2000) wondered if "all mentoring relationships are created equal?" (1177). They note the variability in the quality of mentoring relationships and in the design of mentoring programs that support mentoring relationships (Ragins et al. 2000). Relational quality falls along a continuum, where most relationships are in the middle: neither great nor horrible. There is an opportunity to focus more on the bright side of mentoring and encourage high-quality relationships.

Defining a high-quality relationship

A quick thought experiment demonstrates the importance of high-quality relationships. Imagine a friend or colleague whom you enjoy seeing. Imagine a recent encounter with this person. How did you feel as you approach this person? What was it that this person said or did? Recall how they talked with you and what their body language communicated. What three adjectives best describe this person? Now, imagine someone whom you do not like and try to avoid. This is a person about whom you might say, "if you never saw him or her again it would still be too soon!" How did you feel as you approach this person? What three adjectives best describe this person?

This thought exercise illustrates the power of high-quality connections. Most people have no difficulty imagining a person for each scenario, and the adjectives generated are easily categorized. The positive individual is approachable, pleasant, smiles, uses humor, or otherwise invites you to interact and draws on positive emotions to make that interaction a positive one. The adjectives for the person you wish to avoid involve terms such as distracted, gruff, verbally abusive, clingy, narcissistic, mean, and self-absorbed.

The first person is "heliotropic" (Rogers and Fraser 2003). This term comes from biology and explains why flowers, plants, and trees grow toward the sun. They are attracted by the life-giving energy the sun provides. Similarly, individuals are attracted to people who provide psychic energy through positive interactions. Such people energize others, and we want to be around them.

Scholars have taken an interest in work relationships. Their research provides a road map for what matters in high-quality mentoring relationships. Scholars have begun to connect relationship quality to mentoring outcomes (Xu and Payne 2013; Lunsford et al. 2018). Dutton and Heaphy (2003) identified three defining features of high-quality connections: emotional carrying capacity, tensility, and degree of connectivity.

Emotional carrying capacity refers to the expression of a range of positive and negative emotions. For example, a mentor who recognizes the success of the protégé through a celebratory lunch or note has a relationship with a higher emotional carrying capacity. Similarly, a protégé who notes how their mentor helps him or her work through frustrations is an example of expressing negative emotions.

Mentors seem more reluctant than are their protégés to share stories about when an action or decision did not go well (Lunsford et al. 2018). Sometimes, mentors are concerned that a negative story suggests a lack of competence. Yet sharing such emotional events (positive and negative) strengthens the mentoring relationship.

Tensility refers to the ability of the relational partners to come back together after difficult or challenging interactions. For example, consider a graduate student who is comfortable returning to her PhD supervisor even after receiving critical feedback on her work. She feels she can depend on that relationship, even if she perceived a challenging and unpleasant interaction.

Michele Tam (see Case Study 11.1) provides an example of tensility when her mentor asked her some sensitive questions about her personal and professional goals. At the time she replied: "I am not comfortable pursuing this line of questioning." As she recounts: "I appreciated the questions and get more value when people ask me to be reflective. I needed someone to encourage me to take risks and get out of my comfort zone."

Finally, degree of connectivity refers to connecting individuals to new people and new ideas. Relationships marked by a high degree of connectivity increase access to people (and ideas) who may broaden their horizons. For example, a mentor "sponsors" their protégé when she introduces her protégé to other professionals in her network. Such opportunities provide the protégé with new occasions for learning.

Researchers are beginning to develop measures of relationship quality (Lunsford et al. 2018). One such example that aligns with these characteristics is listed in Table 3.1. Findings suggest that higher relationship quality predicts better outcomes such as job satisfaction.

Table 3.1 Relationship quality measure

Items

I can express my feelings (good or bad) to my mentor/protégés.
I can count on my mentor/protégés even after difficult conversations.
I think about new ideas as a result of interactions with my mentor/protégés.

Source: Lunsford et al. 2018.
Note: Responses from 1 to 5: never, rarely, sometimes, often, all the time.

The power of positive interactions

Research on emotions highlights two areas of attention in developing high-quality relationships. First, negative emotions, and the interactions associated with them, hold more emotional weight that disproportionately influences future interactions. Vivid recall of bad experiences enabled our survival (Eby et al. 2010). Emotions like fear narrowed our attention to a threat and instructed us to take appropriate action. For example, "the lion is coming, run!" It makes sense that you need to remember where that lion lives to avoid future injury or death. Instigating quick, life-saving actions are the evolutionary function of negative emotions.

For relationships to flourish, the ratio is about 3:1 of positive to negative interactions needed from a relational partner (Fredrickson and Losada 2005). The "positivity ratio" has been documented in professional settings (e.g., teams) and personal settings (e.g., couples who stay married versus get divorced) (Gottman 2014; Losada 1999). Losada and Heaphy (2004) studied interactions among 60 low-, medium-, and high-performing teams. They found a 5:1 ratio of positive to negative interactions characterizing the highest performing teams. Medium performing teams had a ratio of 2:1. Overall, the evidence suggests that a positivity ratio between 3:1 and 5:1 may also be important in mentoring relationships.

This ratio is not a prescriptive one, but it provides important guidelines. Negative interactions are part of organizational and relational life. We need to engage in more positive interactions to even out one negative interaction. Interactions need to be genuine and meaningful to count. Make sure you highlight the importance of positive interactions in your mentoring program materials. An understanding of the positivity ratio may help relational partners develop tensility to remain in relationships, especially if there is an early negative interaction.

Second, positive emotions appear to undo the physiological effect of negative emotions so that we can broaden our attentional span. Positive emotions are associated with creativity and learning. Fredrickson's "broaden and build theory" recognizes the fleeting nature of positive emotions that occur as a result of positive interactions (Fredrickson 2013). Positive emotions build resources for individuals on which they can draw later

(Fredrickson 1998; Fredrickson and Losada 2005). Positive interactions may be short-lived, but they create psychological resources that endure. These psychological resources include increased intelligence, curiosity, and exploration. All of these attributes promote learning and flourishing – both of which are related to positive outcomes for mentoring relationships and programs. Fredrickson (2013) presents ten well-researched positive emotions that influence how we interpret events: joy, gratitude, serenity, interest, hope, pride, amusement, inspiration, awe, and love. Most of these emotions can and should be expressed frequently in mentoring relationships as a means to encourage the risk-taking needed for learning.

Mentoring memes

The interactions between mentors and protégés involve the transmission of values, beliefs, and practices, also known as memes. Nakamura et al. (2009) have examined how the memes of good mentoring are passed down from one generation to another, which is another element of sustaining high-quality mentoring. They note the importance of contexts in these relationships in terms of the culture and social aspects of the field and society.

Nakamura et al. (2009) report that these mentoring memes were passed on to protégés from their mentors through verbal conversation, role modeling, observational learning, and the learning environment created by the mentor. It was just as important what the mentors (who passed on good memes) did not do. They did not engage in certain kinds of verbal interactions. For example:

> Neither the lineage heads nor their former students mentioned the kind of hectoring that characterizes some advisor-student relationships – the "guilt trips, harsh yelling, insults or subtle jabs" that are part of the necessary arsenal of [some] graduate advisors. (Nakamura et al. 2009, 160)

Avoid dysfunction

High-quality relationships are marked by a relative absence of dysfunctional behaviors. The goal is to manage (not eliminate) dysfunction, as well as to recognize and put in place policies and procedures to reduce dysfunctional mentoring.

Fortunately, truly dysfunctional relationships occur infrequently. However, there is sufficient evidence that many mentors and protégés experience negative interactions in their mentoring relationships, which can be derailing for both protégés and mentors. Remember, these negative incidents are experienced more intensely and are more memorable than are positive ones (Eby et al. 2010).

Doctoral education provides a cautionary example. This setting is one where good mentoring is assumed to take place. The heart of the doctoral experience is the mentoring students receive from their faculty advisors or supervisors on their dissertation. There are substantial university resources dedicated to supporting this mentoring relationship and mentoring as a part of the role of the faculty member. Yet a study by Lunsford (2012) reported that a sizable minority of advanced doctoral students did not consider their advisor to be a mentor even after being in that relationship for at least three years. Further, negative interactions with mentors or protégés stand out for individuals even many years later (Lunsford 2014).

Learn to recognize sources of dysfunction and educate mentoring participants to be aware of these potential barriers. There are five main sources of dysfunction for mentoring relationships, which are listed here:

1. mismatch;
2. distancing behavior;
3. manipulative behavior;
4. lack of competence; and
5. general dysfunction.

Mismatch refers to relationship partners who do not share values, working styles, or who have a personality conflict. The dissonance in personal preferences makes it difficult for the individuals to initiate their relationship. Mismatch in the dyad is one of the top two reasons for relational dysfunction (Eby et al. 2000). Recognizing mismatch in the dyad is even more important for formal mentoring programs where a third party facilitates the match (Hamlin and Sage 2011).

Distancing behavior refers to mentors who neglect or fail to include their protégés in activities. This is the other most common source of dysfunction in mentoring relationships (Eby et al. 2000). Protégés may engage in distancing behavior by "forgetting" to attend meetings. Another common distancing behavior is "being too busy" to meet.

Manipulation refers to two types of behaviors: position power and political power. Mentors who are misusing position power may over- or under-delegate work to protégés. Mentors who are misusing their political power may take credit for their protégés' work or engage in outright deceit. For example, a faculty mentor who claims inappropriate authorship on a protégé's paper would be engaging in manipulative behavior. These mentors – sometimes referred to as "tormentors" – engage in tyrannical and deceitful behavior.

Lack of competence or expertise refers to interpersonal or career skills. The dysfunction arises when a protégé expects to learn a particular skill from a mentor who lacks competence in that area, or a protégé may lack skills the mentor assumed she possessed. Perhaps the mentor or protégé lacks the interpersonal skills to initiate or maintain the relationship.

General dysfunction refers to individuals whose personal problems interfere with their ability to engage in the relationship. Mentors or protégés with poor attitudes about their organization also display general dysfunction.

Awareness of the sources of dysfunction may help to limit its damage in two ways. First, program managers may establish processes and procedures to identify and minimize dysfunctional interactions. For example, you might include information about sources of dysfunction in briefing sessions. A check-in with protégés within a month of starting a program is a procedure that may also help to identify early problems in the relationship. Mentoring partners who are experiencing general dysfunction or manipulation may need to be reassigned to someone else.

Second, relationship partners can increase their awareness of potential dysfunctional interactions early on and ask for assistance in resolving potential problems or transitioning early to another mentoring relationship. For example, mentors and protégés who are aware of the sources of dysfunction may better be able to identify if he or she is not well matched. In these cases, program coordinators may orchestrate a change in mentoring partners. The information on sources of dysfunction suggests the importance of early monitoring of relationship interactions (Eby et al. 2000). Case Study 3.1 outlines an example of how a protégé's proactive behavior, and skilled intervention by a program manager, can transform what could have been a dysfunctional experience into a positive learning opportunity.

Ethics

Ethics is rarely an area of concern I hear voiced by program managers. This section reviews the ethical concerns formal mentorship presents and suggests guiding ethical principles for program managers. Three common ethical tensions that arise in mentorships are discussed. These principles and tensions can be included in briefings and mentorship education, which are discussed in Chapter 6.

Professional societies for mentorship advocate a focus on ethics. The European Mentoring and Coaching Council (EMCC) and the Association for Coaching recently created the Global Code of Ethics, with signatories like the International Mentoring Association and the Mentoring Institute. The code of ethics pertains to working with clients, professional conduct, and excellent practice.

Case Study 3.1   Program managers who create learning opportunities

SAS is a business analytics company that consistently tops the lists of the best companies to work for in the United States and in the world. The company regularly places in *Fortune Magazine*'s top spots on rankings of "Best Companies to Work For." A subsidized cafeteria, free state-of-the-art workout facilities, free on-site health care, and other services such as a salon, dry cleaning, and jewelry repair contribute to making SAS a great place to work. Wait, but there is more: The company's progressive human resources programs, including mentoring, also add to SAS's reputation as a place that values their people resources. These factors contribute to a low 3.6 percent employee turnover rate (compared to an industry average of 18 percent).

Mentoring emerging leaders

Brian Germano, a learning and development specialist, is a skilled program manager of an emerging leaders mentoring program. As part of the program, new protégés are paired with experienced mentors who have successfully mentored other employees. The small size of this program enables the program manager to know the participants and ensure a high success rate in pairing mentors and protégés. Matching is based on a combination of the program manager's knowledge of the individuals' personalities, competencies, and goals. The program's success rate is high, as measured by end-of-program surveys.

Learning opportunity

This high success rate doesn't mean there are no relational problems – it means the program manager knows how to intervene to get relationships on track. For example, in one case, despite several meetings, a protégé was struggling in a relationship with her mentor. Their conversations never seemed to go anywhere. The protégé felt the mentor was "showboating," and she did not perceive a value out of the time she was investing in the relationship. As the program manager observed: "Her needs seemed to be neglected in the relationship."

Early on the protégé contacted the program manager about her concerns. He displayed effective management of mentoring and relational challenges in three ways:

1.   he acknowledged and thanked the protégé for sharing her feelings;
2.   he encouraged her to talk to her mentor; and
3.   he lined up another potential mentor.

The protégé was understandably worried about upsetting her mentor and felt she should maintain her connection with him to avoid any negative repercussions for both of them. The program manager coached her on how to talk with her mentor about ending the relationship and remembers how worried and stressed she was about having the conversation. Meanwhile, the program manager consulted his list of alternate mentors and contacted one who was willing to meet at least once or twice with the protégé.

Effective transitions

The protégé finally had the needed conversation with her assigned mentor. She felt good about how it went and made a successful transition, with the program manager's encouragement and support. The new mentor was hesitant about the time commitment but agreed to meet a few times with the protégé. The relationship started well, and they continued to meet regularly, with positive reports to the program manager from both individuals.

Perhaps even more importantly, the program manager helped the protégé learn the skill of navigating a difficult relationship successfully. She reported positive interactions with her original mentor in work-related meetings. The presence of a proactive and involved program manager made the difference in moving a talented employee to a positive mentoring experience. Without the program manager she would likely have suffered for five more months in a difficult relationship. The lesson here is to be approachable for protégés (or mentors) to let you know when the relationship is not working.

Source: Interview with Brian Germano, learning and development specialist, SAS Institute, Inc., and program manager of the Emerging Leadership program.

The ethical concerns about the mentoring process fall into four categories (NcubeandWasburn 2006; Moberg and Velasquez 2004; McDonald and Hite 2005):

1.   access to mentoring;
2.   transmission of organizational ethics and values;
3.   mistreatment in the relationship; and
4.   power inequities in the relationship.

Program managers have direct influence on the first two categories, access and transmission. Mentors tend to select protégés who are similar to them (Johnson 2002). Thus, mentoring programs must ensure equal access to mentoring opportunities for individuals from underrepresented groups. For example, equal access could be ensured in undergraduate mentoring if a faculty member encourages all students in their classes to consider such an opportunity. My former students have shared with me that such encouragement was why they joined my lab, an activity they would otherwise have felt unqualified to pursue (Lunsford and Ochoa 2014).

Program managers can assist in the matching process to make sure there is equitable access. Ensuring multiple mentoring opportunities, through alternative forms of mentoring such as peer mentorship, is another way equal access to mentoring can be available.

Mentorship is an important relationship in transmitting professional and organizational norms. Thus, mentoring programs should be created only after an organizational scan to ensure that the formal mentoring programs will transmit ethics that are beneficial to all parties, and align with good organizational practice (McDonald and Hite 2005).

The sources of dysfunction discussed earlier in this chapter highlight the need for an ethical consideration of mistreatment in the relationship. Such mistreatment can be invisible to others. Thus, making mentoring participants aware of sources of dysfunction through education and having a trusted person, such as a program manager, may minimize mistreatment.

Most mentorships involve a more senior person working a less powerful junior person. Thus, power inequities can create an environment where problems occur in mentoring relationships. For example, a male mentor may initiate inappropriate sexual overtures to their female protégé or a mentor may take credit for a protégé's idea. Mentorship education may minimize such problems, along with regular check-ins on the relationship progress.

Guiding ethical principles

Mentorship education should include information on ethical obligations of mentors and protégés. Johnson (2017) suggests eight ethical principles for mentorships (see Table 3.2: autonomy, beneficence, boundaries, competence, justice, non-malfeasance, privacy, and transparency). These principles were developed from his early work on ethics and mentoring doctoral students in psychology (Johnson and Nelson 1999).

Autonomy promotes independence and knowledge. Mentors help protégés identify projects that will show their competence rather than asking them to work on projects that will benefit only the mentor's agenda. Autonomy also relates to providing appropriate support when protégés take on tasks that require them to engage in new roles. Mentoring programs need to be set up to promote independence rather than dependence.

This principle suggests that mentors encourage protégés to solve their own problems rather than being rescued from them.

Table 3.2 Ethical principles

Principle	Definition
Autonomy	Promote independence and knowledge
Beneficence	Increases well-being
Boundaries	Awareness of role conflicts
Competence	Developing mentorship skills
Justice	Equal opportunities and treatment
Non-malfeasance	No harm
Privacy	Keeping confidences
Transparency	Open communication and expectations

Source: Adapted from Johnson and Nelson 1999.

Beneficence focuses on the welfare of protégés and mentors. It relates to how the relationship increases the well-being of the participants. Participants have an ethical responsibility to interact in ways that energize and support their learning and psychological well-being.

Engaging in multiple relationships can present concerns related to role boundaries. A protégé may be uncomfortable sharing an obstacle with a mentor who is also their supervisor. Boundaries refers to being aware of entering into new relationships with a protégé that may not be beneficial to the protégé. For example, entering a romantic or sexual relationship with a protégé, even if consensual, may hurt the protégé. If other employees learn of the relationship, then they may have the perception of unwarranted favoritism that goes beyond a mentor–protégé relationship. There may be reputational costs to the protégé. Unfortunately, such romantic advances are not uncommon. For example, the civilian head of the Pentagon's Missile Defense agency was charged with "subjecting one woman to unwanted attention and photographing her buttocks and massaging another woman during a 'mentoring' session."[1]

Competence refers to the willingness of the mentor to continue developing skills that will add to their mentoring expertise. Becoming a better mentor through education, reflection, and work with colleagues is one way to demonstrate competence in mentoring.

Justice refers to providing equal opportunity and treatment, regardless of the person's background or demographic characteristics. If a mentor regularly recommends protégés for awards or opportunities only if they seem to be a good 'fit' (and they are always from a majority background), then the justice principle may have been violated. Ensure that all mentoring participants have equal access to program resources.

Non-malfeasance means no harm should come to the participants in the relationship. Harm can and does occur in mentoring relationships through neglect, abandonment, or manipulative behavior (Johnson and Nelson 1999). Further, it must be clearly stated that mentors and protégés should not engage in sexual intimacies when they are participating in the formal mentoring program.

Privacy refers to keeping appropriate confidences. In some settings, mentors might be expected to provide referrals to employee assistance programs or mental health centers. In other settings, there may be a legal obligation to share information about an individual in distress. Privacy means that individuals are aware of any such expectations before information about them is shared.

Transparency refers to having clear communication about expectations and being open about their mentorships. Mentors should avoid unspoken expectations they have of their protégé or the relationship. Transparency includes sharing information about how much time can be devoted to the relationship and other commitments that might take time away from a mentorship.

Ethical tensions

Three ethical tensions are common in mentoring relationships:

- integration-separation;
- stability-change; and
- expression-privacy.

Support mentoring participants to think about their ethical obligations in negotiating these tensions.

Integration-separation refers to the tension between developing rapport and connection versus a supporting autonomy. This tension may be most important at the beginning and end of mentorships. At the start of a relationship mentors need to encourage and support protégés but not so much so that the protégé constantly looks to the mentor for affirmation. Toward the end of mentorships, mentors and protégés may have a shared project they are bringing to completion. A mentor might envision the next step in this work, but a protégé may wish to go in a different direction.

Stability-change refers to the tension between developing the habits and conventions of working together versus supporting creativity and discovery. Hopefully, as the relationship matures the protégé and mentor can move from a more hierarchal relationship to one that is closer to colleagueship.

Expression-privacy refers to the tension between appropriate self-disclosure and intimacy and concealing certain feelings or thoughts. This tension becomes stronger as dyads have lengthier relationships. Self-disclosure is one way to develop the rapport needed for mentorships to flourish. For example, it can be helpful for mentors to share when their work may not have gone well. However, concealment may also be needed. For example, a mentor may feel attracted to a protégé and yet should conceal those natural feelings. It would be unfair to burden a protégé with that information.

Complicating factors

Relationship quality is complicated by two factors: time and perspective. First, even great mentors and protégés may have a bad day where they engage in less optimal interactions. Second, mentors and protégés do not often perceive their relationship in the same way. Thus, is a relationship poor if only one person thinks it so?

Mentoring relationships develop out of a series of mentor-like interactions, or what some researchers call "mentoring episodes" (Fletcher and Ragins 2007). It takes time for mentoring relationships to develop, and it can be difficult to know when is the right time to determine their effectiveness. High-quality relationships can be distinguished from average- or low-quality relationships when, over time, the majority of the mentoring episodes promotes learning that leads to desired outcomes.

A second factor is the difference in mentors' and protégés' perspectives about their relationships. Mentors and protégés may not have the same view about being in a mentoring relationship, much less about assessing the relationship quality. Researchers who study informal relationships found that protégés identified individuals as mentors (who had also agreed with this designation) only 43 percent of the time and that mentors were only somewhat better at identifying their protégés (who had also agreed with this designation) – 54 percent of the time (Welsh et al. 2012). Attempts to measure relationship quality suggest that protégés rate the relationship higher than do mentors, on all three dimensions of relationship quality (Lunsford et al. 2018). Thus, relationship quality may vary depending on the perspective assessed.

Section summary

High-quality relationships are marked by three characteristics: emotional carrying capacity, tensility, and degree of connectivity. Attention to a ratio of interactions where there are more positive interactions than negative ones may contribute to flourishing relationships. Procedures can be put in place to recognize and reduce the common sources of dysfunction. Consider how to prepare participants to consider their ethical obligations. Remember high-quality mentoring requires time and attention and that even great relationships sometimes have bad moments.

High-quality programs

Organizations invest in a formal mentoring program when informal mentoring opportunities are perceived as insufficient or unavailable. Scholars have studied the characteristics of formal mentoring programs associated with improved program outcomes (Dubois et al. 2011; Giscombe 2007; Wanberg et al. 2003). These characteristics can be grouped into four categories (see Table 3.3) that relate to:

1. recruiting the right participants;
2. orienting participants to the program goals;
3. supporting participants; and
4. assessing progress.

First, effective programs have a process to screen or select participants and to match mentors and protégés. This process might involve self-selection as well as input from participants about the best match. Effective matches depend on some similarity so that participants can build rapport. (More details on matching are presented in Chapter 6.) The process of how participants are recruited, selected, and matched is well-defined and aligned with the program objectives.

Second, effective programs orient participants to the program goals and expectations. There might be a face-to-face briefing session or online training that ensures participants understand the program goals, expectations, and activities. There are guidelines on what participants are expected to do or produce together. For example, in an organizational setting mentors and protégés may develop a written mentoring plan.

Third, ongoing support is available for mentor and protégé skill development. This support might include workshops or on-demand skill development modules. The perceived availability of the program manager is

Table 3.3 Characteristics of effective mentoring programs

Characteristic	Related activities
Recruit participants	Recruiting participants, Selecting/screening, interested participants, Participant input into matching
Orient participants to the program	Providing briefings, Sharing guidelines about meeting frequency, Participants can describe program outcomes
Support participants	Program manager monitors relationship progress, Participants know who to contact about relationship problems, Providing workshops for mentorship skill development
Assess progress	Establishing standards for mentor–protégé activities, Evaluating achievement of program outcomes

important for mentoring participants who encounter relational challenges. (Case Study 3.1 is an example of such support.)

Fourth, effective programs have standards for accountability for both the mentors and protégés, and for the program. These standards include tracking and assessment of program activities and outcomes. Ensure that individuals are achieving their goals and/or desired program benchmarks, i.e., meeting frequency or professional conduct.

Section summary

Effective mentoring programs recruit and select the right participants. Communicate expectations by orienting participants to the formal mentoring program goals. Provide ongoing support for mentors and protégés to develop their skills in mentoring and to deal with relational challenges. A sustained effort to assess participant progress and program outcomes is important.

Hallmarks of a mentoring culture

If asked, most people will agree that having access to a high-quality mentoring program is a good idea – yet few people can describe the organizational features that support such a program. Indeed, the assumption is that mentoring programs, much like mentoring relationships, are effective.

A mentoring culture is present when an organization supports mentor-like episodes in day-to-day interactions (Zachary 2011). For example, Nakamura et al. (2009) reported on the importance of the lab environment in good mentoring in graduate school. The environment established by the mentor provided resources to protégés through the knowledge and role models provided by other students. In fact, these authors noted that:

> Some lab heads may not fully appreciate how much the environment affects the work that takes place in labs. Some may recognize the importance of the lab environment, but design theirs with goals other than the students' welfare in mind. (168)

In contrast, good mentors, "were keenly aware of the contribution made by the lab environment or training program to the student's education is a scientist"(168).

A mentoring culture fosters organizational learning, where innovation and productivity are enhanced (Carmeli et al. 2009). The Mentoring Ecosystem (see Figure 2.1) provides a framework that emphasizes the role of organizational context. Zachary (2011) describes the context more specifically by delineating eight hallmarks of a mentoring culture:

1. accountability;
2. alignment;
3. communication;
4. demand;
5. education and training;
6. multiple mentoring opportunities;
7. safety net; and
8. value and visibility.

Table 3.4 provides an overview of the hallmarks. The hallmarks may guide your efforts to leverage mentoring programs to develop a mentoring culture in your organization. It is useful to consider how these hallmarks reflect formal organizational processes and procedures, as well as the informal expectations.

Table 3.4 Mentor culture hallmarks: Formal and informal examples

Hallmark	Formal	Informal
Accountability	Share expectations and goals; documentation of progress.	Promotes shared responsibility.
Alignment	Mentoring aligns with organizational values.	Not seen as an "add-on" or one more thing to do.
Communication	Messages targeted at stakeholders; feedback guides process improvements.	Increases interest in learning.
Demand	Valued professional development.	Desire to be in multiple mentoring relationships.
Education and training	Integrated into organization's training and development activities.	People share best practices and enhance peer learning.
Opportunities	Organization supports different types of mentoring.	Availability of informal mentoring individually and in groups.
Safety net	Procedures to identify challenges.	Individual resilience.
Value and visibility	Leaders allocate resources for and make it a priority.	Leaders share mentoring stories.

Source: Adapted from Zachary 2011.

Formal characteristics

Formal characteristics refer to visible support from those in charge of the organization, available resources, processes, and procedures. The presence of a program manager is an example of a formal mentoring characteristic. The eight hallmarks of a mentoring culture have both formal and informal elements. This section reviews the formal aspects of the hallmarks and how program managers can establish them.

Accountability is about the mentor and protégé agreeing they have an obligation to one another. Program managers may support accountability by developing role descriptions for mentors and protégés, suggesting forms to capture desired relational outcomes, and reporting about the frequency of meeting or progress on outcomes.

Alignment refers to mentoring activities that support the organization's mission and strategic plans. Program managers can support alignment by ensuring there is a shared, common vocabulary about mentoring that all employees know and use. For example, onboarding or orientation sessions would include information about mentoring opportunities. Some organizations may decide to use certain terms (e.g., mentor versus protégé) or develop special designations for excellent mentors like "Master Mentor." Alignment suggests that mentoring is seen as part of the process and procedures in the organization. For example, annual reviews might include a category related to mentoring.

Communication involves stakeholders in the mentoring activities and ensures they are in the feedback loop to improve mentoring. Program managers may develop outlets (e.g., newsletters or e-mail updates) to communicate about mentoring activities, progress, and periodic improvements.

Demand refers to the recognition of mentoring as a valued professional development activity. In universities, for example, mentoring students is seen as part of the job responsibilities of faculty members. Demand means that students want to be in those relationships.

Regarding education and training, human resource offices or other professional training departments might include sessions on mentoring in their offerings. Education and training might involve exchanging best practices and experiences and ways to promote peer networking.

As for multiple mentoring opportunities, organizations with a mentoring culture have more mentoring "opportunities" than a formal, one-on-one mentoring program. Such organizations would also have opportunities for different forms of mentoring such as e-mentoring, peer mentoring, or group mentoring. Peer mentoring occurs when people at similar levels in the organization provide mentoring support to one another. Group mentoring involves multiple individuals, perhaps co-mentors and several protégés or one mentor with several protégés.

A safety net refers to reducing dysfunctional mentoring. This means there is an individual (a resource) who can provide confidential support counseling about how to handle unsuccessful mentoring experiences. Program managers might check in with mentors and protégés to make sure they have connected, are meeting, and are in a productive relationship.

Value and visibility refer to leaders who ensure there are resources and tools to support mentoring activities. Resources include the time, money, and space for a program coordinator to run and operate the program. Leaders who provide visibility for mentoring may issue letters of invitation to participate or sign certificates recognizing participation in the mentoring program.

Informal characteristics

The hallmarks also occur informally. Informal environmental characteristics refer to the unwritten rules about how people interact.

Regarding accountability, mentoring is a voluntary activity, even in formal programs that require participation of a particular group (e.g., new employees). Accountability includes informal agreements between mentors and protégés, which reflect how they may interact and what they hope to achieve in their time together. Through their shared interactions, they become responsible to one another outside of formal obligations. This accountability is supported by others in the organization. A mentor who is seen as derelict in his or her duties might receive informal feedback from colleagues about his or her neglect or misdeeds, rather than from a program coordinator.

As for alignment, participants view mentoring activities that are "aligned" as a good use of time rather than an unnecessary burden. When mentoring is seen as desired and valued, even by those who are not participating in mentoring, it is aligned with the organization's culture and mission. Alignment means mentoring is not considered "one more thing" people have to do.

Informally, communication refers to the development of trust and open dialogue in the relationship. Trust flows from the psychosocial function of mentoring, which involves confidence building, encouragement, and listening. A focus on shared values and goals helps mentors and protégés develop productive communication styles. A communication style that promotes reflection and critical thinking, rather than dictating or telling, fosters learning (Crasborn et al. 2011).

Demand indicates there is a motivation and desire to engage in mentoring. People might assume both the roles of mentor and protégé in organizations with high demand.

Education and training also occur informally when a mentoring culture is present. Mentors and protégés share their experiences or turn to trusted colleagues for advice about mentoring challenges. For example, a mentor may ask a colleague for advice after a disappointing conversation with a protégé.

Multiple mentoring opportunities exist informally in organizations with a mentoring culture. For example, peers may develop a peer mentoring network that meets informally over lunch periodically or new employees may develop a support group where mentoring takes place. The opportunity to meet potential mentors and protégés outside their usual sphere is also important. Research shows that protégés with mentors in departments other than their own were more satisfied with the mentoring relationship (Ragins et al. 2000).

The presence of a safety net reflects the level of resiliency and responsibility individuals possess. When mentoring challenges are faced, individuals who can communicate about those challenges, and are supported to do so, experience resiliency in overcoming them. Further, in a mentoring culture there is a felt responsibility to resolve challenges related to mentoring. Informally this takes place when it is accepted that changes must sometimes be made in mentoring relationships or there is a process that supports termination of mentoring relationships.

Value and visibility refer to leaders' willingness to share their stories about mentoring and the extent to which they encourage mentoring. This informal aspect highlights the extent to which stories about mentoring are valued, told, and shared in the organization. Allison McWilliams provides a compelling example of this and other hallmarks of a mentoring culture in Case Study 3.2.

Fostering sustainability

Excellent mentoring programs may end when the program champion leaves the organization or is promoted to another position. Mentoring programs that are disconnected from an organizations' goals or mission are unlikely to continue; therefore, the hallmarks of a mentoring culture are important guides for program directors who wish to develop and support sustainable mentoring efforts.

There are three strategies you can employ to leverage your mentoring program to foster an organizational culture of mentoring:

1.   become a mentoring champion;
2.   develop processes and procedures; and
3.   cultivate a focus on high-quality mentoring.

First, become a champion of your mentoring program and recruit other champions. Educate organizational leaders by providing regular updates about program activities and successes. Public recognition of the mentoring program through internal newsletters, formal letters of recognition, or verbal thanks to participants may enlist the support of organizational leaders.

Second, develop processes and procedures. Establishing advisory committees may extend institutional knowledge about your program so that it may continue after you. (Chapter 10 provides information about how to establish an advisory committee.) Some programs fail when all the institutional knowledge leaves if you, the program manager, take a new position.

Case Study 3.2 Creating a mentoring culture at Wake Forest University

The Mentoring Resource Center (MRC) developed out of Wake Forest University's 2007 strategic plan. Mentoring has always been at the heart of the university's mission and values. However, there was a desire to place more strategic, focused emphasis on mentoring as a core institutional value. The Office of Personal and Career Development was created, and the new vice president was charged with creating the MRC. By placing the MRC within this office, the university demonstrated a belief that mentoring was a key skill and experience of a lifelong developmental process. Part of the office's vision was to equip students with the tools, knowledge, and resources to cultivate lives of meaning and connection, which included an emphasis on mentoring.

The MRC was made possible by support at all levels of the university. The top-down support started with the university president and trustees. They communicated the importance of mentoring across the university. Great support from the university vice president ensured funding to do the work with relative autonomy. The MRC is a collaborative effort and simply would not and could not exist without the support of campus partners.

Before

Like many schools, Wake Forest University had several stand-alone mentoring programs in different departments, which were administered by dedicated people (faculty and staff) on top of their normal job duties. There was a strong culture and history of informal mentoring, particularly within the academic departments, through research and advising. However, there was an opportunity to provide resources to help these individuals serve in these roles more effectively.

After

Five years later, the number of formal mentoring programs has quadrupled from less than 5 to more than 20. More importantly, people now use the same language around the importance of intentional conversations, giving and receiving feedback, and being reflective about choices, decisions, and lessons learned. The students see the value of developmental networks and why they need to build them, not just while they are at Wake Forest University, but after they graduate as well. The MRC enables people by placing more tools and resources at their disposal to do the work effectively.

Key characteristics

A decentralized model of mentoring, supported by the MRC, is one of its unique features. The director, Allison McWilliams, does not run any mentoring programs out of her office. She does not match people. Instead, she and her staff operate as on-campus consultants to the university community. They provide (a) guidance about what effective mentoring practices look like and (b) support to mentors, mentees, and mentoring programs to deploy those practices. The MRC provides training and resources, like handbooks, tool kits, worksheets, and videos, to individuals and program directors. The MRC staff will also help develop and implement programs, and provide guidance on matching, ongoing support, and assessment. McWilliams states: "It is critical that the oversight of the actual programs remain with the programs themselves, and not in our office. That way, we can have a broader reach to more students, and ensure continuity of the programs over time."

Advice

McWilliams' advice for others who want to support mentoring in their organization starts with noting that you must have "support from the administration with a clear demonstration that this work is important; freedom to do the work; and, strong campus partnerships." Mentoring is a strategic initiative, and like any strategic process it is important to have clear goals, an action plan for achieving those goals, and a plan to tie those goals and actions back to the mission and vision of the organization. That is how anyone can make the case for mentoring as the right strategy.

McWilliams asserts that "people need to be supported in this work." The ability of the center to provide training, orientation, and ongoing support to help individuals develop and support mentoring is critical. Sometimes, the director added, "that's as simple as sending a check-in email or a suggested conversation topic." The MRC also has to be clear about staff roles and expectations. For example, the MRC will not run a mentoring program. The decentralized consulting model has been successful at Wake Forest University in creating a culture of mentoring.

Mentoring Resource Center: http://mentoring.opcd.wfu.edu
Source: Interview with Allison McWilliams, Director, MRC, Wake
Forest University.

Third, in the last decade, researchers have acknowledged the variability in the quality of work relationships. As shown previously in Case Study 3.2, Wake Forest University provides an example of how to cultivate a culture of mentoring through creating an MRC. This university essentially created a repository of resources and consulting support to help individuals throughout the institution star, support, and sustain high-quality mentoring programs. The MRC does not run programs but rather consults with other program managers. This is an efficient and effective model that facilitates sharing of information across and between programs.

Section summary

High-quality mentoring programs are sustainable when they are supported by an organization that is committed to learning. You may use mentoring activities to promote the development of a mentoring culture, which has the eight hallmarks described here. These hallmarks exist formally and informally in organizations. You can be an advocate for sustainable, high-quality mentoring programs by becoming a champion of mentoring, developing infrastructure to support mentoring, and intentionally emphasizing relationship quality.

Conclusion

This chapter advocates an intentional focus on relationship quality and a culture of mentoring. The presumption is that mentoring is a positive experience. However, the reality is that most mentoring relationships are neutral and a minority are dysfunctional. Having an intentional focus on helping your relational partners know what high-quality mentoring is may help increase the chances that mentors and protégés develop such relationships.

Implement policies and procedures that enable both you and mentoring participants to recognize and reduce dysfunctional relationships. Dysfunctional mentoring relationships may be derailing experiences for both protégés and mentors.

How will you know when a mentoring culture is present in your organization that supports both high-quality mentoring relationships and programs? Rate your organization on the hallmarks of a mentoring culture to identify where resources might be allocated to enhance mentoring. Organizations with a culture of mentoring are marked by frequent positive and energizing learning conversations that take place informally and formally.

Key terms

- Degree of connectivity
- Emotional carrying capacity
- Ethics
- Hallmarks of mentoring: accountability, alignment, communication, demand, education and training, opportunities, safety net, value and visibility
- Heliotropic
- Mentoring memes
- Positivity ratio of 3:1 positive to negative interactions
- Sources of dysfunction: mismatch, distancing behavior, manipulation, lack of competence, and general dysfunction
- Sustainability
- Tensility

Check your learning

1. Describe the three characteristics of high-quality mentoring relationships and how you might recognize these characteristics.
2. Provide examples of each of the five sources of dysfunction in mentoring relationships.
3. Compare the four characteristics of effective mentoring programs to your program's current characteristics.
4. What procedures can you implement to promote high-quality mentoring relationships and reduce dysfunctional ones?
5. Rate your organization's mentoring culture using the eight hallmarks of a mentoring culture.

Resources

Harvard College, *Who Mentored You?* http://www.hsph.harvard.edu/chc/wmy/who-mentored-you/intro.html.

The Chronicle of Evidence Based Mentoring: https://www.evidencebasedmentoring.org/.

The European Mentoring and Coaching Council Global Code of Ethics: https://www.globalcodeofethics.org/.

Note

1 https://www.usatoday.com/story/news/politics/2020/09/16/top-pentagon-official-sexually-harassed-women-seven-years-ig-says/5819604002/.

References

Carmeli, A., D. Brueller, and J. E. Dutton. 2009. "Learning Behaviours in the Workplace: The Role of High-quality Interpersonal Relationships and Psychological Safety." *Systems Research and Behavioral Science* 26(1): 81–98.

Crasborn, F., P. Hennisnen, N. Brouwer, F. Korthagen, and T. Bergen. 2011. "Exploring a Two-Dimensional Model of Mentor Teacher Roles in Mentoring Dialogues." *Teaching and Teacher Education* 27(2): 320–331.

DuBois, D. L., N. Portillo, J. E. Rhodes, N. Silverthorn, & J. C. Valentine (2011). "How Effective Are Mentoring Programs for Youth? A Systematic Assessment of the Evidence." *Psychological Science in the Public Interest* 12(2): 57–91.

Dutton, J. E., and E. D. Heaphy. 2003. "The Power of High-Quality Connections." In *Positive Organizational Scholarship*, edited by K. Cameron, J. E. Dutton and R. E. Quinn, 263–278. San Francisco, CA: Berrett-Koehler.

Eby, L. T., M. Butts, J. Durley, and B. R. Ragins. 2010. "Are Bad Experiences Stronger than Good Ones in Mentoring Relationships? Evidence from the Protégé and Mentor Perspective."*Journal of Vocational Behavior* 77(1): 81–92.

Eby, L. T., S. E. McManus, S. A. Simon, and J. E. A. Russell. 2000. "The Protege's Perspective Regarding Negative Mentoring Experiences: The Development of a Taxonomy." *Journal of Vocational Behavior* 57(1): 1–21.

Fletcher, J. K., and B. R. Ragins. 2007. "Stone Center Relational Cultural Theory." In *The Handbook of Mentoring at Work: Theory, Research, and Practice*, edited by B. R. Ragins and K. E. Kram, 373–399. Los Angeles, CA: Sage Publications.

Fredrickson, B. L. 1998. "What Good Are Positive Emotions?" *Review of General Psychology* 2(3): 300–319.

Fredrickson, B.L. 2013. "Positive Emotions Broaden and Build." In *Advances in Experimental Social Psychology* 47: 1–53. 10.1016/B978-0-12-407236-7.00001-2.

Fredrickson, B. L., and M. R. Losada. 2005. "Positive Affect and the Complex Dynamics of Human Flourishing." *American Psychologist* 60(7): 678–686.

Giscombe, K. 2007. "Advancing Women through the Glass Ceiling with Formal Mentoring." In *The Handbook of Mentoring at Work: Theory, Research, and Practice*, edited by B. R. Ragins and K. E. Kram, 549–571. Los Angeles, CA: Sage Publications.

Gottman, J. M. 2014. *What Predicts Divorce? The Relationship between Marital Processes and Marital Outcomes*. New York: Psychology Press.

Johnson, W.B., 2002. "The Intentional Mentor: Strategies and Guidelines for the Practice of Mentoring." *Professional Psychology: Research and Practice* 33(1): 88–96. https://doi.org/10.1037/0735-7028.33.1.88.

Hamlin, R. G., and L. Sage. 2011. "Behavioural Criteria of Perceived Mentoring Effectiveness: An Empirical Study of Effective and Ineffective Mentor and Mentee Behaviour within Formal Mentoring Relationships." *Journal of European Industrial Training* 35(8): 752–778.

Harvard T.H. Chan School of Public Health (n.d.). *Senator John McCain*. https:// sites.sph.harvard.edu/wmy/celebrities/senator-john-mccain/.

Johnson, W. B. 2017. "Ethical Considerations for Mentors: Toward a Mentoring Code of Ethics." In *The Sage Handbook of Mentoring*, edited by D.A. Clutterbuck, F. K. Kochan, L.G. Lunsford, N. Dominguez and J. Haddock-Millar, 105–118. Thousand Oaks, CA: Sage Publications.

Johnson, W. B., and N. Nelson. 1999. "Mentor–Protégé Relationships in Graduate Training: Some Ethical Concerns." *Ethics & Behavior* 9(3): 189–210.

Lev-Ram, M. (2014, September 4). *The global talent crunch*. Fortune. http:// fortune.com/2014/09/04/the-global-talent-crunch.

Losada, M. 1999. "The Complex Dynamics of High Performance Teams." *Mathematical and Computer Modelling* 30(9): 179–192.

Losada, M., and E. Heaphy. 2004. "The Role of Positivity and Connectivity in the Performance of Business Teams: A Nonlinear Dynamics Model." *American Behavioral Scientist* 47(6): 740–765.

Lunsford, L. G. 2012. "Doctoral Advising or Mentoring: Effects on Student Outcomes." *Mentoring & Tutoring: Partnership in Learning* 20(2): 251–270.

Lunsford, L. G. 2014. "Mentors, Tormentors, and No Mentors: Mentoring Scientists." *International Journal of Mentoring and Coaching* 3(1): 4–17.

Lunsford, L. G., V. Baker, and M. Pifer. 2018. "Faculty Mentoring Faculty: Career Stages, Relationship Quality, and Job Satisfaction." *International Journal of Mentoring and Coaching in Education* 7(2): 139–154. 10.1108/IJMCE-08-2017-0055.

Lunsford, L. G. and E. Ochoa. 2014. "Cultural Competency and Mentoring on the Border. In *Uncovering the Hidden Cultural Dynamics in Mentoring Programs and Relationships: Enhancing Practice and Research*, Vol. 4 edited by F. Kochan, A. Kent, and A. Green, Perspectives in Mentoring Series. Information Age Publishing.

McDonald, K. S. and L. M. Hite. 2005. "Ethical Issues in Mentoring: The Role of HRD." *Advances in Developing Human Resources* 7(4): 569–582.

Moberg, D. J. and M. Velasquez. 2004. "The Ethics of Mentoring." *Business Ethics Quarterly* 14(1): 95–122.

Nakamura, J., D. J. Shernoff, and C. H. Hooker. 2009. *Good Mentoring: Fostering Excellent Practice in Higher Education*. New York: John Wiley & Sons.

Ncube, L. B. and M. H. Wasburn. 2006. "Strategic Collaboration for Ethical Leadership: A Mentoring Framework for Business and Organizational Decision Making." *Journal of Leadership & Organizational Studies* 13(1): 77–92.

Ragins, B. R., J. L. Cotton, and J. S. Miller. 2000. "Marginal Mentoring: The Effects of Type of Mentor, Quality of Relationship, and Program Design on Work and Career Attitudes." *Academy of Management Journal* 43(6): 1177–1194.

Rogers, P. J., and D. Fraser. 2003. "Appreciating Appreciative Inquiry." *New Directions for Evaluation* 2003(100): 75–83.

Ryals, J. (2012, September 26). *Leaders from the Pack*. NCSU News. https:// news.ncsu.edu/2012/09/leaders-from-the-pack/.

Wanberg, C. R., E. T. Welsh, and S. A. Hezlett. 2003. "Mentoring Research: A Review and Dynamic Process Model." In *Research in Personnel and Human Resources Management*, Vol. 22, edited by C. R. Wanberg, E. T. Welsh and S. A. Hezlett, 39–124. Bingley, UK: Emerald Group Publishing.

Welsh, E. T., D. Bhave, and K. Y. Kim. 2012. "Are You My Mentor? Informal Mentoring Mutual Identification." *Career Development International* 17(2): 137–148.

Xu, X., and S. C. Payne. 2013. "Quantity, Quality, and Satisfaction with Mentoring: What Matters Most?" *Journal of Career Development* 41(6): 507–525.

Zachary, L. J. 2011. *Creating a Mentoring Culture: The Organization's Guide.* San Francisco, CA: Jossey-Bass.

Zuckerman, H. 1977. *Scientific Elite: Nobel Laureates in the United States.* New York: The Free Press.

Part II

Five steps to build a mentoring program

Chapter 4

Step 1: Identify the why

If America is going to remain on top in the evolving world economy, we must be dedicated to encouraging innovation and entrepreneurship, while simultaneously cultivating a scientifically and technologically astute future workforce.[1] (Honorable Ralph Hall from Texas)

Introduction

In August 2007, US President Bush signed into law the America Competes Act, which was reauthorized and signed into law by President Obama. This law sought to stimulate the economy through providing resources to support scientific innovation and entrepreneurship. Title VII of the law focused on the National Science Foundation and authorized its funding (along with a goal to double funding). Section 7008 of the law included a requirement for a mentoring plan for Postdoctoral Research Fellows funded by the National Science Foundation. Section 7010 mandated reporting on how this requirement was met in all funded proposals as of January 4, 2010. I visited the National Science Foundation in the summer of 2010, and no one knew exactly what a mentoring plan should look like or how it might be evaluated. Unfortunately, it is not uncommon that organizations mandate mentoring without providing much guidance about how program activities are to achieve desired organizational outcomes.

America competes act

SEC. 7008. POSTDOCTORAL RESEARCH FELLOWS.

a. MENTORING. – The Director shall require that all grant applications that include funding to support postdoctoral researchers include a description of the mentoring activities that will be provided for such individuals, and shall ensure that this part of the application is evaluated under the Foundation's broader impacts merit review criterion. Mentoring activities may include career counseling, training in preparing grant applications, guidance on ways to improve teaching skills, and training in research ethics.[2]

DOI: 10.4324/9781003163862-4

Scholars have noted that the first step to start a formal mentoring program is to conduct a needs assessment (Allen et al. 2011); yet the example of the newly required mentoring plan for the National Science Foundation is more typical of how many formal mentoring programs begin. Organizations start a mentoring program because another entity such as the US Congress has required it, an organizational leader believes it worked effectively elsewhere and has championed it for your organization, or it is seen as a way to address an organizational need.

If you are reading this chapter, you have been tasked to start a mentoring initiative or you have inherited an existing mentoring program. Managing a mentoring program may even be one of many job duties you have. If you are in the program design phase, you will need to develop a consensus around the purpose of the program while resolving logistical questions: How will you recruit participants? What will they do together? Most importantly, how will you know if it is successful?

It can be challenging to redesign an existing program that you have inherited. A new program manager usually arrives when the program is already underway. It may be difficult to redesign a program if there is inadequate documentation about the program's purpose or history or if records are missing about who is participating in the program.

The first step in designing (or redesigning) a mentoring program is to determine why it is needed. Before you continue reading, please take a moment to record your responses to the prompts in Table 4.1.

- First, write down the goals of your mentoring program. Your response may be based on what you have been told or what you believe are the right goals.
- Second, list your assumptions about what resources you can access and how the mentoring program will achieve the stated goals. For example, do you assume you will have access to a sufficient number of mentors?

Table 4.1 Goals and assumptions

My program goal(s) is/are:
1.
2.
3.
I assume I will have access to:
1.
2.
3.
I assume mentoring will accomplish my goals because:
1.
2.
3.

This chapter will equip you with the knowledge to design or redesign a mentoring program efficiently and effectively. This chapter focuses on the first step, identify your why, of a five-step process.

- Step 1: Identify why the program is needed
- Step 2: Map your theory of change (Chapter 5)
- Step 3: Recruit and prepare the right participants (Chapter 6)
- Step 4: Collect the right data (Chapter 7)
- Step 5: Create your success story (Chapter 8)

Identify goals and outcomes

Mentoring programs are formal efforts to connect protégés with mentors to achieve a desired outcome. Thus, "identifying your why" means you need to define expected goals and outcomes. In other words, resources (including you) are being allocated in expectation of some different outcome than might normally occur. What is this desired outcome?

Goals reflect assumptions held by you, your organization, and/or your stakeholders. It is critical to clarify these goals, as they will guide what activities your mentoring program will expect and support. Further, goals provide the foundation for how you (and others) will allocate time and resources. Clarifying the program goals will provide a foundation for how to design an effective evaluation plan.

The goal paradox is that you may hold different goals from your stakeholders, which may lead to conflict, lack of program support, or ineffective mentoring. The case study on faculty mentoring highlights such a paradox (see Case Study 4.1). Engaging in a short reflection activity called "The Power of Why" can help to resolve misalignment.

Case Study 4.1 Paradox of conflicting goals

An evaluation team on behalf of the National Science Foundation visited a large, public university to review a grant program designed to support women faculty. One critique from the team was that the proposed mentoring program had not materialized. The director of the grant was asked to address this critique. The vice provost for faculty affairs was contacted, and a joint effort was started to pilot a faculty mentoring program for early career faculty. I was recruited to consult with this group, and a program coordinator was hired to run the mentoring program.

The immediate institutional goal was to address the critique from the National Science Foundation. Another goal was to develop sustainable support for female faculty members. The goal of the program coordinator was to provide quality mentoring for new faculty that could be sustained in future years. These goals were not necessarily in conflict; however, the pilot mentoring program was in competition with other priorities charged to the provost's staff.

The grant program director worked out of the president's office, while the program coordinator was funded temporarily. Funding was temporarily available for mini-grants for the protégé–mentor pairs. The mentoring program was not continued after the conclusion of the yearlong pilot program, even though there were successful evaluation results from the protégés and mentors (Thomas et al. 2015). The goals for the mentoring program enabled it to be successful for the pilot year, but it was not continued. With my support, the program director submitted a white paper to the provost and the grant program director that included evaluation results and recommendations for the future.

The faculty affairs office has since developed other mentoring initiatives, presumably more in line with their perceived goals and resources. In 2014, this included a daylong seminar on mentoring for faculty to attend.

In this scenario, whose responsibility was it to align the mentoring programs' goals? Was it a failure that the program ended after so much was invested to get it started? Or was it a success because it raised awareness about mentoring with a greater emphasis on informal mentoring in future years?

Source: Author's experience.

"The power of why"

Goal clarification is an important first step in designing a mentoring program (and in mentoring relationships!). It is not uncommon that stakeholders may hold different ideas about the program's goals. "The Power of Why" (Friedman et al. 2006) was developed for program evaluators and is useful for mentoring program managers. This questioning technique will help you:

1. clarify the program's goals;
2. establish consensus among stakeholders;
3. guide an effective evaluation plan.

This technique requires you to ask three questions to stakeholders representing different interests (management team, participants, advisory board). It is likely you will need to probe responses to get a full answer. The three questions are listed and described further here, along with suggested probes.

"The power of why?"

1. What is the goal of our mentoring program?
2. Why is this goal important to you?
3. How do you think the program should go about achieving these goals?

Who to ask?

Consider who the stakeholders are in your program. Collect responses from people in each of your categories of stakeholders. For example, the program funder or your boss might answer these questions as well as representative, potential program participants. You should include yourself, as the program manager, in this exercise.

One way to collect this information is to schedule brief meetings, in-person or virtual, with the manager or leader who will oversee your work and hold two 20-minute focus groups with potential mentors and protégés. Finally, answer the questions yourself, and if you have an advisory board, ask them for their responses. You should be able to collect this information within a few weeks. It will be time well spent to design and pre-advertise your program.

What is the goal?

This first question – "What is the goal of our mentoring program?" – will help you to identify what people believe is the ultimate goal of your mentoring program. However, people may give generic, positive responses such as "make the organization better," "support our employees," or "help students." Many activities could accomplish these rather general goals – your job is to probe their generic responses to arrive at specific reasons for the mentoring program.

Another way to help individuals think about this question is to ask a follow-up question about ultimate outcomes. For example, you might inquire: "How will you know the program was successful?" In the case of the response "make the organization better," you need to explore how mentoring will do that. Will mentoring make the organization better because people will feel more valued and will stay there? Mentoring could be seen as a way to pass on the knowledge of experience from people who will soon retire. (Case Study 4.2 illustrates how asking why helps you to identify your mentoring program goal(s).)

As another example, someone might reply that a goal is for mentors and protégés to get together and do good things. Thoughtful probing will help you understand why do they need to get together at all, how often do they need to get together, and what kind of "good things" are expected. In other words, there are many ways the organization can be made better and many ways mentoring might support such improvements. Your objective is to gain an understanding of the specific goal related to the organization and how a mentoring program might achieve it.

Case Study 4.2   The power of "why"

> For seeking leadership ... the ordinary won't cut it, you have to strive for the extraordinary. (Peter Lougheed)

Has a vision but needs goals

Kelly Hobson (pronouns: they/them) had a legacy to live up to when they were selected to coordinate the mentorship program in the Peter Lougheed Leadership College (PLLC) at the University of Alberta.

Reading about Lougheed gives you a sense of his legacy and how a PLLC mentorship program must embody his values. Lougheed was "one of the most beloved alumni of the University of Alberta…, he was a remarkable campus leader: president of the Students' Union, sports editor for the Gateway, leader in his fraternity and a Golden Bear football player." It doesn't stop there. After becoming a successful businessman, he entered politics and was elected as the tenth premier of Alberta from 1971 to 1985.

> As premier of Alberta, the Honourable Peter Lougheed's capacity to attract and inspire creative and productive teams and communities; to imagine a future that differed from the present; and to translate plans and vision into reality characterized by his power as a leader. His passionate defense of the province's interests and his visionary thinking set the province on the path to longterm economic, cultural and social success.

Hobson attended my workshop on mentoring programs with a clear sense of the vision of PLLC and of the mentorship program.

However, our "why" exercise made Hobson recognize the need to clearly map the program vision to the goals for the mentoring program.

Here are excerpts from our post-workshop email exchange that may help you better determine your "why." Hobson starts with a vision but needs to craft the program goals. Then, they engage in discovery with stakeholders before transforming the program with a clear set of goals participants can understand and that can be used to assess success.

Discovery

Hobson – April 8, 2019
…After going through Chapter 4 of your handbook and asking our board what the goal of the program is, why it's important and so on, the best draft I can come up with for our program goals are:

- Support PLLC scholars in their personal and professional development as they explore their aspirations and enhance their leadership practice.
- Add value to the PLLC community by building a rich network of high-quality mentor–mentee relationships.

I have a note for myself from your evaluation session that says goals should be specific – there should be no ambiguity about what they mean. Phrases like "leadership practice" and "add value" and "high quality" seem too vague to me. Do you have any suggestion for how I might bright more clarity to these goals?

Lunsford – April 8, 2019
…On the first bullet – it might help if you could provide an example (to me at least) of what you mean by "support their personal and professional development." In other words, how will you know that happened? Do mentees fill out a report at the end or develop a professional plan?

On the second bullet – it seems redundant – we will have a mentoring program so we have more mentors and mentees? *What* do you think might happen in the community by having more mentor–mentee relationships, e.g., might there be more informal mentoring or contribution to a culture of mentoring?

I think you are almost there. Clarity will help your participants know what is expected.

Hobson – April 8, 2019

...One thing that comes up a lot in conversation about our program is confidence – that we want mentorship and our leadership program as a whole to build more confidence in our students. I've been agonizing over research trying to figure out whether increased confidence would be a behavioural or attitudinal measure, or perhaps both. If it's attitudinal we could certainly do a baseline survey and follow up with another survey to see if self-reported confidence improved over time. But if confidence is behavioural, do you have any ideas how we might measure it?

Lunsford – April 8, 2019

...Confidence to do WHAT?

Transformation

Hobson – April 11, 2019

Okay, I chewed on it and came up with four goals:

- Challenge PLLC scholars to develop their self-awareness, so they know who they are and can identify what they need.
- Help PLLC scholars cultivate the self-confidence required to turn their ambitions into realities.
- Engage external leaders through the Mentor Team, enhancing PLLC's reputation of excellence in the community.
- Offer Mentor Team members an opportunity to hone their leadership practice through coaching and collaboration.

Thank you for the prompts that helped me dig into what we're trying to do – what are your thoughts on this new round of revisions?

Lunsford – April 17, 2019

...I made a few edits to clarify your goals (underlined or crossed-out). At the end of the program PLLC scholars should be able to:

- Describe an increase in their self-awareness about their personal preferences and areas to develop, so they know who they are and can identify what they need.
- Identify 3–5 personal and professional goals to achieve in the next year. Help PLLC scholars cultivate the self-confidence required to turn their ambitions into realities.

The program will:

- Engage external leaders through the Mentor Team, <u>which will also</u> enhance PLLC's reputation of excellence in the community.
- Support Mentor Team members in honing their leadership practice through coaching and collaboration.

https://www.ualberta.ca/lougheed-leadership-college/about-us/peter-lougheed-leadership-history.html
https://www.alberta.ca/aoe-peter-lougheed.aspx
Source: Kelly Hobson, Team Lead, Student Engagement & Partnerships, University of Alberta.

Why is this goal important?

The second question – "Why is this goal important to you?" – will help you identify the motivation and passion behind creating a mentoring program. What is so important that a mentoring program, versus other solutions or programs, is the best answer? For example, someone might say: "The boss told me to start a mentoring program" or "The boss strongly suggested that I participate in the optional program." Careful probing will help you understand if there is any other motivation other than "I was told to do it." It might be helpful to better understand the boss' motivations and how these motivations might be better communicated to others. Successful mentoring initiatives need a motivated person to coordinate it. Your passion and excitement will be communicated to participants who will quickly recognize a perfunctory, required activity versus a meaningful one.

However, like the example that begins this chapter, the reality may be that the goal is important because otherwise your organization will lose access to resources (funding, people, and so on). In this case, you may need to help others think about ways this "required importance" may also help the organization to meet its goals.

For example, the America Competes Act has led to the development of thoughtful mentoring plans for postdoctoral researchers.[3] Career and professional development activities are core components of these plans. One might argue that these activities were taking place informally or should have been taking place already. However, faculty members who thoughtfully approached this goal have developed formal plans that have been shared with other faculty members.

How should the program achieve these goals?

The third question – "How do you think the program should go about achieving these goals?" – can help you identify how participants might engage with one another. Answers to this question may suggest the kinds of activities your program might sponsor or encourage for mentors and protégés. For example:

- Will people be expected to meet or might they communicate by email?
- How often do participants need to connect to achieve the desired outcomes?
- Do people need to be in the same geographic location to participate, or may they engage through video conferencing or email?

How to probe for assumptions

Imagine yourself as a nonjudgmental explorer as you ask the questions. Your job is to understand before you bring about consensus; therefore, you need as much detail and specific examples as people can provide. Encourage respondents to be as specific as possible in their answers: Most people find it difficult to answer these seemingly simple questions, usually because they have not thought much about them.

Probing questions help clarify answers and promote participants to think more about their responses. Good probes include items such as:

- Why do you feel so strongly that mentoring is a good option for us?
- Why do you care so much that we have good mentors for our protégés?
- Can mentors and protégés meet as infrequently as they want?
- Will it be a success if mentors and protégés simply meet three or four times?

Examine assumptions behind the answers you receive:

- Do you expect your participants to meet on a regular basis, or is it fine if they communicate by email, texting, or telephone?
- What kind of information do you expect to be transmitted between participants?
- How do you expect your participants to be different at the conclusion of your program?

Examining your assumptions may help you to identify constraints or challenges you or your participants might face. Knowing about these challenges will help you communicate them to your participants and develop resources for participants to overcome these challenges. For example, you might expect that mentors and protégés have time to meet during the workday. However, in some departments mentors and protégés can work different shifts and are not at work at the same time. This situation would require the program coordinator to support mentors and protégés to communicate virtually or to coordinate some overlapping times in work shifts.

Report and resolve responses

After you have collected responses to these questions, you will want to provide a summary of them to program stakeholders. It is at this point you may need to integrate goals and to identify areas of potential conflict. Your role is to identify commonalities and conflicts in these goals. Then, conflicting goals must then be reviewed with your boss or advisory board for making a decision about which goals your mentoring program will have – which you then must communicate to your program's stakeholders.

Goals and outcomes

After your exploration and inquiry, you will be well prepared to describe the mentoring program goals and outcomes. Goals and outcomes are different. In fact, you could say that goals drive your outcomes. Outcomes allow you to achieve your goals, but they are not the goals.

Some examples illustrate the difference between goals and outcomes:

- My goal might be to earn a college degree – passing certain classes are the outcomes that will allow me to earn a degree.
- A mentoring program for new teachers might have a goal to increase teacher retention – the program outcome might be to increase the knowledge and self-efficacy of new teachers, which may then increase teacher retention.
- A faculty–student mentoring program for underrepresented undergraduates has a goal to increase the number of underrepresented students who attend graduate school – the program outcome might be for students to gain undergraduate research experience and take the Graduate Record Examination.
- A company starts a mentoring program for emerging leaders, with the goal to prepare future leaders for the organization – the outcome of a yearlong mentoring program might be for protégés to develop their leadership skills or learn more about the organization.

All of these outcomes can lead to the goals, but notice that the goals are different from the program outcomes.

Fortunately, researchers have identified categories of mentoring outcomes. Chapter 2 presented four such categories of outcomes associated with changes for protégés. These categories may help you to identify appropriate outcomes for your mentoring program. The categories are attitudinal, behavioral, career-related, and health (Eby et al. 2013). These categories provide a useful guide to consider the outcomes for your mentoring program. (See Table 4.2 for a list of the categories and examples of ways to measure them.)

Table 4.2 Mentoring program outcomes and related measures

Outcome	Measure
Attitudinal	Increased satisfaction (career, job, university, academic experience), sense of community, organizational commitment
Behavioral	Increased performance: research productivity, sales, academic achievement (grades), citizenship behaviors (helping others, mentoring, community service)Decreased deviance or withdrawal: absenteeism, school or job attrition, intent to leave organization, aggression
Career	Increased recognition/success: awards, promotion, pay, prestige of first job Increased skill development: communication, work knowledge, problem-solving, goal setting
Health	Increased self-perceptions: stress, self-efficacy, locus of control Decreased psychological strain: stress, anxiety, work strain, role conflict, depression

Source: Adapted from Eby et al. 2013.

Examples of outcomes

Attitudinal outcomes refer to satisfaction and affiliation. A mentoring program with attitudinal outcomes might include employee satisfaction or a sense of belonging at work. Usually, attitudes are measured through surveys asking participants how satisfied they feel about a person or setting. It is harder to measure attitudes, as they cannot be observed. Thus, measures of attitudinal outcomes ask individuals to self-report their attitudes. Attitudes change more quickly than the other categories; thus, if you select a career-related goal, you may consider including an associated attitudinal outcome. For example, let's assume the goal of your mentoring program is to increase the number of women promoted from mid-level to senior positions. You might measure the number of promotions (career-related) and their satisfaction with being recognized for their career efforts (attitudinal).

Behaviors are observable. Behavioral outcomes include increasing performance behaviors or reducing dysfunctional behaviors. Work or school records might be examined for changes in behaviors (e.g., absenteeism). Participants may also be asked how frequently they engage in a particular behavior: For example, in graduate school, a mentor might be expected to help a protégé publish articles and complete their dissertation (productivity). A behavioral outcome for a Master Gardener mentoring program might be to help the Master Gardeners answer questions on the gardening hotline quickly and correctly.

Career outcomes refer to quantifiable outcomes like compensation and promotions and perceived career success and career prospects. Mentoring programs that have increased career recognition as one outcome might support mentors and protégés to be considered for outside awards, be quoted more frequently in the media, or obtain higher-status jobs. For example, the University of Arizona's Office of Research started a series of workshops under their mentoring activities to help new faculty apply for (and hopefully receive) an Early Career Award from the National Science Foundation. Career outcomes may include skill acquisition. An under-graduate mentoring program might focus on helping protégés to clarify their career interests and build a professional network. The skills would involve learning how to identify and set career goals and how to develop professional relationships.

Health outcomes reflect mental and physical health behaviors and atti-tudes. Mentoring programs may seek to increase self-perceptions and reduce psychological strain or substance abuse. For example, a mentoring program might aim to reduce substance use, decrease absenteeism due to sickness, or reduce perceived stress or strain. Mentoring programs that reduce work conflict might have an outcome to reduce work stress and strain.

Review your responses in Table 4.1 and revise any outcomes. Think about the categories of outcomes that relate to the mentoring program goals. These categories might also give you ideas for other outcomes that relate to your mentoring program goals.

Section summary

Step 1 is to identify the goals of your mentoring program and the related outcomes that will help you to achieve those goals. Use "The Power of Why?" to check assumptions and clarify your goals and outcomes. Outcomes support achievement of mentoring program goals. Make sure you have identified goals and outcomes.

A few words on redesign

If you are new to mentoring, it may be helpful to adopt a mindset that your program is always under construction. Effective mentoring programs are always in the process of a redesign. This perspective means you do not have to make all the changes at one time, nor is your program ever its final version. Encourage your program participants and other stakeholders to share this view, and they will be more likely to provide feedback and support to you on how to redesign and improve the program.

It is natural to become attached to activities in which you invest a lot of time. This inclination is why a critical perspective is crucial when it comes to mentoring programs. Your prior mentoring experiences, however good they are, may not be the best basis on which to develop a formal mentoring program. Commit to the idea that an activity or process will be eliminated, made more efficient, or done differently next time.

Redesign is also an effort to improve the mentoring program. This chapter provided you the template or guide to start your program and the benchmarks for assessing and improving it. (Chapters 7 and 8 provide more detailed information about evaluating and improving your mentoring program.)

Conclusion

The three-step process described here is useful to review on an annual basis as part of any redesign effort. Revisit and redesign your program to adjust to changing individual and organizational goals. These changes may require a change in the mentoring program goals as well, so build in time to redesign.

There are three strategies you can use over time to redesign a mentoring program. First, use your annual review period as motivating to review the mentoring program goals. This reflection provides an opportunity to consider any organizational goals which have changed in ways that may influence the goals of the mentoring program. For example, if your organization has a new initiative to start a new division, it might be warranted to adjust a mentoring program to meet the needs of new hires in the coming year. Similarly, if your organization just sent out a report noting that many senior people are retiring soon, then this may be a time to orient a mentoring program such that the knowledge of these employees can be shared with potential protégés in the coming year.

Second, communicate annually, or on some time frame that aligns with the end of your program, with program participants to share the program goals and outcomes. As part of this communication you may ask stakeholders to share comments or suggestions on areas of improvement based on their recent experiences.

Third, appoint an advisory board (refer to Chapter 8) that meets once or twice a year, which can serve as a sounding board, to review your evidence for effectiveness. The board members may also share their own experiences (if they are participants) to help you think about parts of the program that need to be redesigned.

The main point is to build in time to reflect on the mentoring program activities and processes at least annually. Creating time to redesign the program, based on changing individual and organizational needs, will keep it relevant and useful.

Key terms

- Goals
- Outcomes: attitudinal, behavioral, career-related, and health
- Stakeholders
- "The Power of Why"

Check your learning

1. Why is it important to "identify your why"?
2. Which stakeholders can you identify to ask "The Power of Why" questions?
3. Describe the difference between a goal and an outcome.
4. In which category or categories do your mentoring program outcomes belong?

Notes

1 Hall, R. 2010. From Opening Statement on America Competes Act, January 20, 2010. Available online at https://www.nsf.gov/statistics/about/BILLS-111hr511 6enr.pdf (accessed April 16, 2021).
2 Government of the United States of America, 2007. America Competes Act of 2007, 100th Congress, 20 USC 980. Available online at https://www.congress.gov/110/plaws/publ69/PLAW-110publ69.pdf (accessed April 16, 2021).
3 See, for example, https://www.nationalpostdoc.org/page/MentoringPlans (accessed April 16, 2021).

References

Allen, T. D., L. M. Finkelstein, and M. L. Poteet. 2011. *Designing Workplace Mentoring Programs: An Evidence-Based Approach*, 2nd ed. Oxford: John Wiley & Sons.

Eby, L. T., T. D. Allen, B. J. Hoffman, L. E. Baranik, J. B. Sauer, S. Baldwin, M.A. Morrison, K. M. Kinkade, C. P. Maher, and S. Curtis. 2013. "An Interdisciplinary Meta-Analysis of the Potential Antecedents, Correlates, and Consequences of Protégé Perceptions of Mentoring." *Psychological Bulletin* 139(2): 1–36.

Friedman, V., J. Rothman, and B. Withers. 2006. "The Power of Why: Engaging the Goal Paradox in Program Evaluation." *American Journal of Evaluation* 27(2): 201–218.

Thomas, J. D., Lunsford, L. G., & Rodrigues, H. A. (2015). "Early Career Academic Staff Support: Evaluating Mentoring Networks." *Journal of Higher Education Policy and Management*, 37, 320–329. 10.1080/1360080x.2015.1034426.

Chapter 5

Step 2: Map your theory of change

Program effectiveness

If your participants are happy with their mentoring experiences, then why does it matter why mentoring worked or even if the mentoring program will be successful in the future? First, most funders or bosses will want some evidence of program effectiveness if you and others continue to devote resources to it. Second, making a judgment about if your mentoring program was an effective one requires you to answer a few questions.

- What constituted mentoring in your program?
- Did everyone have a similar experience?
- Were the mentoring activities related to your program goals?

Think of effectiveness as falling into three categories: apparent, demonstrated, and proven (Brest 2010). Apparently effective programs present anecdotal evidence of success. For example, you might have testimonials or refer to your personal experience. Many program managers rely on apparent effectiveness to determine the effectiveness of the mentoring program.

Demonstrated effectiveness is shown by systematic evidence of success. Systematic evidence means it is collected in an organized, and repeatable, manner from a representative sample of participants and stakeholders. Demonstrated effectiveness requires more than anecdotal evidence. An example of demonstrated effectiveness would be pre- and post-surveys that show attitudinal or behavioral change in participants. Another example would be a program manager who holds a series of focus groups with a representative group of participants and stakeholders toward the end of the mentoring program. The key point is that you collect evidence using a method that others can replicate. Further, the evidence presents information about how your program contributed to the participants' or organization's outcomes.

Proven effectiveness presents documented evidence, over time, that shows success relative to other interventions. This type of effectiveness means you have:

DOI: 10.4324/9781003163862-5

- more than one year of data;
- data from multiple sources; and
- data collected in more than one way.

For example, a survey that is administered every year provides information about program effectiveness over time. If the survey is given to mentors and mentees, then you have information from multiple sources about the program's effectiveness. Proven effectiveness also requires you to collect data in more than one way. Thus, in addition to a survey you might conduct a focus group with participants. Or you might examine written records of the mentoring activities – for example, a mentoring contract – and compare that with survey data. Chapter 7 provides information about methods you to collect data.

Theories of change

To know if your mentoring program is effective, you need to think through your beliefs or theories about how your mentoring program will change people. A theory of change lays out the underlying beliefs and assumptions you have that will result in behavior change. Chapter 4 helps you to complete Step 1 by identifying the goals and outcomes of your mentoring program, while this chapter, Step 2, helps you outline the processes of mentoring. Mentoring programs are created with the aim to change participants in some way that will also benefit the organization. Program coordinators often focus on changes for protégés, but remember that mentors and organizations may also change. Identifying your theory of change will make it easier to develop program expectations, provide informational materials for participants, collect the right data, and create your success story.

Step 2 is often the most difficult because it requires you to be specific about your beliefs of how mentoring is connected to your goals. For example, you may feel that mentors need to provide more emotional support to mentees in your program. It is likely you have a good idea about what emotional support means, but it is a general term that could be interpreted differently by participants. Does emotional support mean to build confidence or provide a role model or only to listen well. Your participants need to share your idea about what is expected, and you need to link the mentoring support provided to the program goals.

Map your theory of change

A logic model is an effective and visually appealing technique to capture your assumptions and beliefs about how mentoring works in your program. This framework provides an intuitive way to examine your mentoring program. After you have created a logic model, you will find it easy to explain your mentoring program to others and, if needed, make the case as to why your program needs resources. Logic models are on one page and capture the essence of your program activities and goals.

Logic models may seem complicated at first. However, people find it difficult when they are not clear about how mentoring is working in their program. Give it some time and share it with others and you will find, like many other program managers with whom I have worked, that it suddenly clicks and makes future decisions easier.

If you are unfamiliar with logic models you may wish to refer to information, including a workbook, on logic models developed by the Kellogg Foundation (Kellogg 2004). Logic models enable you to make the connections between the resources that you have to operate your mentoring program, the activities in which you expect your mentors and protégés to engage, and your program's outcomes and goals. Logic models show how your goals are related to desired outcomes. Further, a logic model may help you identify the resources you need to achieve your goals. Mentoring programs take resources to operate, and these might include time (yours and the participants), money, space, or incentives for participation.

Logic model overview

There are different ways to present a logic model. However, all logic models have five elements: resources, activities, outputs, outcomes, and impact (see Figure 5.1). Logic models are read from left to right. The left side of the model refers to your planned activities (items 1–2 in Figure 5.1), while the right side of the model shows the results of these activities (items 3–5 in Figure 5.1). As you read about each element, use the example in Figure 5.1 to create a logic model for your mentoring program.

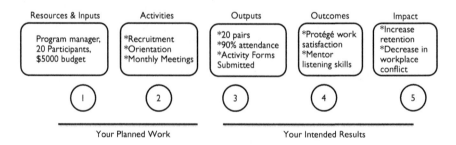

Figure 5.1 Logic model example.

Resources

Resources and inputs (1 in Figure 5.1) refer to what you and your participants will need as well as what resource limits might exist. The most common resources are time and money. For example, many individuals are not full-time program managers; participants are not full-time mentors or protégés either. How much time will be needed for a coordinator to manage the mentoring program? Do participants need to meet during the workday or in person? What kind of meeting facilities are needed, and is there a cost associated with them? Other resources might include development of a web page, funds to prepare recruitment materials, or access to an organization's newsletter to promote the mentoring program.

Use your logic model to determine the needed resources for your program. Successful mentoring programs are well supported by the organization. Discern available resources and how to manage limits on these resources. Most resources can be grouped into these categories: participants, program operations, and visible organization support.

Asking yourself "Who will most benefit from participating in the mentoring program?" will help identify your participant resources. Which individuals would make the best mentors and how might these individuals be recruited to participate in the program? Similarly, who will most benefit as a protégé from participating in the mentoring program, and how might they be recruited? Consider your organizational norms, practices, and calendar in developing your recruitment strategies. A university might use an already scheduled orientation period to recruit student mentors or use an email invitation. In contrast, a company might rely on their monthly newsletter to invite potential participants.

Program operations refer to what you will need to operate the program. Will you need office supplies or access to technology through computers and a website? Think about all the resources you will need to make your program successful and then identify who can provide access to these resources.

Consider how you can document and recognize participation as part of your program activities. Faculty members might benefit from a thank you letter than could be included in their tenure file to show their service work. Students might benefit from a letter of recognition that could then be listed as a line item on their resume. Employees will benefit from written recognition that can be part of their annual performance appraisal that documents team work, collaboration, or an interest in professional development.

Your time, as program manager, is a resource that also needs to be considered. How much of your time can be devoted to the mentoring program? Are there certain times of the year the mentoring program might need more or less of your time and effort? Document how you can allocate your time effectively to starting and supporting the mentoring program, and ensure you have the mental and physical time and attention to provide.

Successful mentoring programs are part of an organization's human resource strategies or professional development activities. Mentoring programs that are embedded in organizational strategy are more likely to be well supported and received. Consider how you can enlist organizational leaders to publicize the program. In workplace mentoring programs managers may need to provide support for employees to meet their mentors or protégés. Think about whom you need to enlist to show organizational commitment to the mentoring effort.

Activities

Activities (2 in Figure 5.1) refer to planned or expected events or interactions. Common mentoring program activities include an orientation and mentorship briefing, monthly group meetings, and an end-of-program reception. Participants might be expected to engage with one another on a particular project or have discussions on specific topics. There may be optional activities, such as attending certain events or professional development activities together. Activities also refer to expected interactions between mentors and protégés, even if they are unstructured meetings or email contacts. It is important to list all the expected activities of mentors and protégés.

You might think of activities as falling into activities you plan and activities you expect of participants. For example, your activities might include recruitment efforts of participants, a program orientation, and professional development for the participants to develop their mentorship skills. Participants might be expected to meet once a month, to attend special interest meetings, and to complete a mentoring compact.

There are two common errors I see when working with program managers to outline their activities. The first is a lack of specificity. For example, rather than have an activity listed as "student events," you would want to state the number and type of events. How many events will you support, or do you expect participants to attend?

The second error relates a misalignment of activities with outcomes and impact. If you see that you have an activity that does not relate to outcomes or impact, then it should be omitted from the program or you need to clarify how it is related. Alternatively, if there are no activities that support an outcome or impact, you need to rethink your activities. For example, you might have "increased knowledge" as an outcome that relates to the impact of higher passing rate on a professional exam. Yet in this program the manager realized there were no activities or expectations that mentors address professional knowledge. In this case, it would be important to make sure that in individual meetings the participants discuss professional knowledge.

Outputs

Outputs (3 in Figure 5.1) are the direct results from the activities. Outputs let you know if the activities took place as planned. Consider the previous activities in establishing an output for each one. For example, your participant recruitment efforts might be expected to result in an output of 15 mentoring dyads or 5 peer mentoring groups. An output from an orientation session might be participant attendance (percentage of participants) and a participant survey about the session. Be realistic about outputs; expecting 100 percent attendance is unlikely, so make it 90 or 95 percent.

Activities of participants could be measured by asking them to report on how many times they met during the program. Some programs ask participants to submit a short summary after they meet, which is another way to measure an output of mentoring frequency. If mentors and protégés are expected to collaborate on a project, then an output might be how often they met to discuss it and ultimately if they produced the project.

Outcomes

Outcomes (4 in Figure 5.1) are covered in greater detail in Chapter 4. Outcomes refer to the benefits that accrue from participating in the program activities. For example, mentors might learn how to develop rapport with protégés from attending a mentoring program orientation session.

Outcomes are arranged by time periods. There will be short-, mid-, and long-term outcomes. Short-term outcomes can be expected in a year or less. Mid-term outcomes may occur in two to three years, while long-term outcomes may happen in three years or more. Consider a workplace mentoring program with one goal of socializing talented new employees to the different divisions in the company. A short-term outcome might be that the protégés can name all the divisions on a three-month survey of the program. A mid-term outcome might be that the protégés have visited each division, and a long-term outcome might be a reduction in work delays because protégés know whom to contact in each division.

Outcomes relate to the program activities. For example, if you expect participants to meet a certain number of times, you also have some expectation about what they are doing or discussing during those sessions. An outcome of attending professional development might be improved skills to build rapport or communicate well in the mentorship. An outcome of regular meetings might be an increase in the sense of belonging or professional identity.

Be as specific as possible in describing your program outputs and outcomes (Allen and Poteet 2011). For example, a statement that your mentoring program will increase retention by 5 percent is better than a general statement that the mentoring program will increase retention. The more specific and measurable your outputs and outcomes, the easier it will be to know the right data to collect and how to create your success story.

Select outputs that are realistic and achievable. For example, if you have an activity that is a three-hour orientation, you should consider what is the percent of people who need to attend. If you select 100 percent attendance as a related output, then you need to have an option for people who might be sick that day. Perhaps you can record the orientation for later viewing within one week or hold a second orientation session.

Impact

Finally, impact (5 in Figure 5.1) presents the goals of your mentoring program. The impact refers to how your organization will be different as a result of participant changes. Perhaps you expect that employees will be more satisfied at work and therefore more likely to stay in the organization as a result of having a mentor. In this case, the impact would be increased employee retention, as well as financial savings to the organization through a reduction in job searches and employee turnover. Another impact might be that mentors develop skills in transmitting institutional knowledge to the next generation of organizational leaders and thereby help maintain the organization's competitiveness.

Section summary

Formal mentoring programs seek to promote change in participants and their organizations or communities. A logic model helps you prepare a one-page illustration to show the process by which this change will occur. Logic models identify how resources support program activities, which are related to specific outputs. The outcomes indicate how the mentoring program will support the program goals and ultimately the program impact. Be as specific as you can in describing each element. The logic model will serve as a guide for your data collection plan.

Tips

You may find two tips helpful. First, consider piloting your mentoring program if it is new. Start with 10–15 pairs or groups. Calling it a pilot program will signal that you are in design mode, which makes participants more patient with problems. Tell participants you want their feedback as you test out the program and activities. Starting small is an effective strategy for new programs, especially if there are significant limitations on resources. For example, if you do not have sufficient time to devote to the program throughout the year, you might need to scale down expectations about certain activities. Use the pilot program to work out logistical or organizational problems. It is better to have small failures with a few people than with a lot of people.

Failing big may have reputational costs that can affect the long-term success of a mentoring program. One program I worked with started big with hundreds of protégés in the first year. The program included briefing information for all participants, but not all of the participants were able to attend. It was not clear that all of the participants even wanted to participate, and many never reached out or met with their assigned mentor. As a result, many mentors, in the post-program survey, indicated they did not want to participate again because they did not feel the protégés followed through on their commitments. The program coordinator realized she had a problem because she had been counting on mentors to serve a second year as mentors and many did not wish to do so. In this case, starting big created a problem that might have been recognized earlier or even avoided if there had been less pairs to oversee.

Second, consider putting your logic model in a spreadsheet and color coding what activities relate to each output, outcome, and impact. This approach will help you to identify areas of disconnect in your program. Take a look at your model and consider the following questions.

- Have you identified all the needed resources for the activities?
- Does every activity have an associated output?
- Is there at least one output that is related to each outcome?
- Is there at least one outcome that will support achievement of each impact?
- Are there items on the logic model that are not related to impact and should be eliminated?
- Is there an impact that has no associated activity that will support it (in which case you need to change your activities)?

Section summary

Use your logic model to determine what resources you will need to start, support, and sustain a formal mentoring program. Think broadly about available resources and consider these categories: people, program operations, and organizational visibility.

Key terms

- Activities
- Impact
- Logic model
- Outcomes

- Outputs
- Resources

Check your learning

1. What resources do you need for your mentoring program?
2. Identify an output for each activity in your logic model.
3. Design a logic model to connect your program activities to individual and organizational outcomes and impact.

References

Allen, T. D., and M. L. Poteet. 2011. "Enhancing Our Knowledge of Mentoring with a Person-Centric Approach." *Industrial and Organizational Psychology* 4(1): 126–130.

Brest, Paul. 2010. "The Power of Theories of Change." *Stanford Social Innovation Review* 8(2): 47–51.

Kellogg. 2004. *Using Logic Models to Bring Together Planning, Evaluation, and Action Logic Model Development Guide.* Technical Report, Battle Creek, MI: W. K. Kellogg Foundation. https://www.wkkf.org/resource-directory/resources/2004/01/logic-model-development-guide.

Chapter 6

Step 3: Recruit and prepare the right participants

The more we get together the happier we'll be.

For your friends are my friends and my friends are your friends.
(The More We Get Together, traditional British folksong)

Introduction

You are responsible for facilitating how people "get together" as the British folksong quoted here suggests. Through most of human history, how we get together has been determined by our proximity, or physical location, to one another. Social psychologists tell us being near someone is the greatest predictor of whom we will marry, choose as friends, or mentor. Mentoring programs facilitate a matching process by making connections that might otherwise take longer to happen or fail to occur.

The pressure to get a program going often means that busy people are given a pass on participating in orientation or information sessions. Further, protégés are rarely included in such sessions. Having attended many such sessions (and having given some of them), I understand why mentors and protégés may not wish to attend them.

However, briefings may help support mentors and protégés to engage in more effective mentoring practices. There is an opportunity for you to create interactive and meaningful briefing sessions that mirror the skills you hope mentors and protégés might develop. You can (and should) avoid tedious, boring seminars or lectures full of PowerPoint slides. How you title and market the session and how you conduct a briefing session sets the expectations for how mentors and protégés will interact with each other and with you, the program coordinator.

The first section of this chapter deals with best practices on recruiting and matching processes for mentors and protégés. The second section of the chapter focuses on briefings. The four elements of effective briefings are presented. The chapter concludes with suggestions on how to facilitate

DOI: 10.4324/9781003163862-6

briefings in ways that reflect the best practices for adult learning and that model good mentoring practices. Table 6.1 presents a checklist of items to consider in recruiting, matching, and briefing your program participants.

Table 6.1 Checklist for recruiting, matching, and briefing

Decisions	Checklist	Options
Recruitment:		
Participation	Is participation required or voluntary?	Mentors required; protégés required; mentors and protégés required; mentors and protégés voluntary.
Content	What information needs to be in recruitment materials?	Program goals, expectations, requirements, and benefits.
Process	What communication medium will be effective?	Email, message board, letter, newsletter, in-person appeals at events.
Matching:		
Characteristics	What are the three to five relevant characteristics?	Demographic, values, attitudes, competencies, and/or needs.
Amount of input	How much input will you have in creating protégé–mentor matches?	100 percent; mixer events with participant rankings/input; mentors and protégés select.
Briefings:		
Audience	Who will attend?	Mentors, protégés, or both
Content	What will be covered?	Ethical principles; Emphasis on high-quality program goals and expectations
Format	How to deliver a briefing? How to check participant learning?	In person, online, videotape? Include questions/quiz.

Recruit the right participants

You will need to educate participants about program goals and expectations. The literature is mixed on if it is better to have voluntary or required participation (Allen et al. 2011). It appears requiring protégés to participate does not reduce the effectiveness of a mentoring program (Wanberg et al. 2003, 103). The consensus is that mentoring programs report better outcomes if participants have some input in the matching process.

As you read the rest of this section, refer either to the logic model you developed in Chapter 5 or to your mentoring program document that outlines the program's activities and goals. These materials will provide the information you need for a successful recruitment effort. There are two guiding principles to consider in designing your recruitment strategy: what to provide and how to provide it.

Required versus voluntary participation

There are times when mentoring is required as part of a job or degree program. In these contexts, mentoring programs may be perceived differently. There may be times when new cohorts of employees or students are required to participate in a mentoring program to orient them to the organization. In these cases, it is important to provide a rationale for the required participation along with the "what to provide" information described here. Even in required programs, mentoring is a voluntary activity. Individuals find reasons not to participate if they do not perceive a value from their involvement.

There are many occasions where mentoring may be required. For example, the US Army has a policy on mentoring as part of their doctrine (6–22) on leadership (US Department of the Army 2019). These regulations state that leaders are expected to use mentoring as one of the tools to develop those junior to them. Similarly, graduate students in doctoral programs around the world engage in mentor-like relationships with the faculty supervisor or advisor who oversees their doctoral dissertation. Simply by being in a doctoral program the student has agreed to be a protégé to a faculty member, who in turn is expected to mentor the student through the doctoral dissertation requirement (Lunsford 2012).

If your mentoring program involves voluntary participation, then you need to recruit participants. Recruiting is more than sending out an email to announce your program and to invite participants. The aim is to recruit the right mentors and protégés. Having the right participants will increase the chances of achieving optical outcomes for the individuals and for your organization. How do you determine who the "right" people are? The right people are those who see the program as meeting their needs or who are interested in achieving your stated program goals. Case Study 6.1 illustrates the effectiveness of a required mentoring program for new hires. In addition, the case highlights the importance of screening mentors and using mentoring to build a professional network that benefits the individual and the company.

What to provide

The best recruitment materials enable potential mentors and protégés to self-select into your program. Materials need to communicate your goals, expectations, requirements, and benefits of participation. Present the goals of the mentoring program concisely and clearly. If possible, a short description explaining the relationship of the mentoring program goals to organizational needs, strategies, or plans is helpful. Your mentoring participants need to know the goal of your mentoring program if you hope to achieve it.

Case Study 6.1   Leadership mentoring for new hires

Isaac Owolabi had the opportunity to be formally and informally mentored before Eaton Corporation recruited him for an engineering position. As part of his job offer he asked to participate in the three-year Leadership Development Program (LDP), where formal mentoring was a central activity.

Owolabi came from a home that was "very much a cross between cultures." His parents emigrated from Nigeria, and he was assimilated as a first-generation American. His father was a role model for how to engage in lasting mentoring relationships. He notes that his father's mentors from his graduate school days "became my white grandparents. My dad stayed in their home, saw their kids, saw their families. Their families have influenced him. My dad was really good at building those relationships and he was also a good mentor."

A network of mentoring

Each year Owolabi was expected to rotate to a new position with one of the company's approved manager-mentors and attend a weeklong summer professional development conference with other LDP participants. A talent development officer in human resources served as the program manager and helped Owolabi navigate each year's career (and physical) move. Only managers with high performance ratings were eligible to serve as a manager-mentor for LDP candidates. "Some managers were older and some were high achieving – they all worked hard and embodied the values of Eaton," Owolabi observed. The program matched people with input from the protégés and potential mentors. Owolabi notes: "You would interview with different managers and they interviewed you and the talent development manager facilitated the best match. I would rank my preferences and the program manager would help negotiate the best match." As a result, Owolabi was exposed to a range of sectors in the company and to different plants and locations.

The program provided a network of mentoring opportunities. Owolabi notes that between his job and the summer conference he found "I was getting mentored by my manager at a specific site and I was being mentored by my peers." His peers provided support and information. The summer conference provided a time for them to learn and to network with one another. Owolabi notes that as a result he "probably mentored thirty to forty employees who came through that program. It is a cool cycle and it makes me more excited about staying with this company because of the huge network I have. If I was to get promoted now I feel like I know more people."

During his LDP experience he noted he benefited, "but I also get to pay it forward." For example, he went on to start an organization to support African American employees at Eaton Corporation. He says, "We have monthly calls and invite organizational leaders to come speak."

Mentor feedback

Although Owolabi is of African descent, he observed that having relationships with people who are an underrepresented minority was often a powerful learning experience: They provided role models as good leaders. He said: "They were very competent with stellar backgrounds." His mentors gave him more responsibilities as he showed interest and energy to take on those tasks.

At each site Owolabi was asked about his goals, needs to achieve those goals, and thoughts about tracking his professional development path. A month or so before his transition to another rotation he would be asked to reflect about his needs. Owolabi says, "I would come in with a plan and the managers appreciated that." The mentors critiqued his progress. He said that at each site he was asked to quit the LDP and remain at that worksite. However, his last mentor helped him decide to take on a more technical role, a path he has embraced.

Protégés were expected to have one job with supervisory responsibilities, usually during their third rotation. Supervision presented a challenge, as he had to oversee employees, as a young adult, who were of his grandparents' generation. His mentor pulled him aside to provide feedback with Owolabi, who had learned to say: "I will take that, thank you."

Program management roles

The program manager facilitated the protégé matches to a new mentor each year. In addition, the program manager was available for support as needed. Isaac observes:

> [A]t one point when I had some significant challenges to overcome and she [the program manager] put me in touch with a vice president. He was able to provide really good advice. Anyone at that level has had to deal with some crisis and he was a good third

party on how to manage perception from your employees and also how to manage up. Their goal is that you are in charge of your career and they want to give you the tools. They don't want to rescue you every time you have a problem. They want you to solve it.

Source: Interview with Isaac Owolabi, Lead Project Engineer, Fuel & Motion Control Division, Eaton Corporation.

Expectations refer to what participants are expected to do and might take the form of a bulleted list: These include the duration of the commitment, frequency of interaction, and any products or outcomes. Potential participants need to know the expectations before the start of the mentoring program to be sure they can properly meet them. For example, will mentors and protégés be expected to meet weekly, monthly, or quarterly? Must they meet in person or are video or conference calls sufficient? Are certain skills or competencies needed for mentors or protégés? A mismatch in expectations is a common source of dysfunctional relationships. For example, a protégé who expects to learn a new skill from a mentor who lacks such experience is likely to be frustrated.

Your recruitment materials need to include information about program requirements. Requirements include any activity that is viewed as an essential aspect of the mentoring experience: These might include events, frequency of meetings between protégés and mentors, and activity reports or end-of-program surveys. Be sure to include the details of requirements in the recruitment materials. For example, list events along with their date, time, and location. You might provide a link or time estimate to activity reports or when surveys are administered.

It is a good practice to include the benefits of participation to prospective mentors and protégés. Benefits for mentoring programs across all settings include skill acquisition, developing a network of personal contacts, and learning about unwritten organizational rules. Other benefits may include recognition of criteria that are considered for promotion or advancement in an organization. Mentors may also benefit by leaving a legacy to their profession or organization through the knowledge they share. Further, mentors may meet other people in the organization at mentoring program events they would not have otherwise encountered. These benefits are not always considered and therefore are important to highlight in your materials.

Providing this content will help you recruit the right people who will be active participants. You want to help individuals who will most benefit from your mentoring program make good decisions about self-selecting into it. Excellent recruitment information increases the chances that people will engage in the activities you view as essential to accomplishing the program goals. I have heard numerous program managers complain that no one attends an event; yet often the date and times were not provided in advance. People are busy, and mentoring is a small part of their daily lives. Calendar conflicts are reduced when people know dates early and can place them on their calendar. These materials set participant expectations about what you need to support and sustain them and the mentoring program.

How to recruit

You need to consider the process of recruitment as well. The main points are to target your efforts using three factors:

1. program eligibility criteria;
2. the organization's communication practices; and
3. the natural calendar of events.

It is usually easier to recruit protégés than it is to recruit mentors, because there simply are fewer experienced individuals to serve as mentors.

If your mentoring program has certain eligibility requirements, then consider how to reach individuals who meet those requirements. I worked with a faculty mentoring program that targeted early career faculty members. We could have sent an invitation email to all faculty members, but that would have been inefficient and even annoying to some faculty who were not eligible. Instead, we targeted new faculty hires by mailing them an invitation from the provost of faculty affairs the summer before they started their job. There was some concern that faculty members might be moving and may not receive a letter. Therefore, the potential protégés were sent two follow-up emails with the letter attached. Mentors were recruited one-on-one by the provost's office because of their known competencies and experiences.

Some organizations may screen potential protégés or mentors as part of the recruitment and matching effort (Allen et al. 2011). Consider the goals of your mentoring program along with your available resources to determine the extent to which you must filter potential participants using eligibility requirements.

Think about your audience and organizational norms. How do people communicate in your organization? If your company newsletter is popular, then you might place a short article in the newsletter with an invitation to contact you, the program manager. Announcing the program at an event where desired protégés or mentors attend may be an effective method. For example, a program manager of a student–faculty mentoring program might attend first-year orientation events and hand out flyers to recruit students. Sometimes, email invitations are effective, but only if the potential participants communicate and respond using email.

The organizational calendar also provides a guide as to how to recruit participants. All organizations have natural ebbs and flows in the calendar year when people are more or less busy. The main point is to consider the starting and ending times in your organizational calendar.

Consider, for example, a mentoring program initiated by a large accounting firm. A recruitment email is likely to be ignored by employees in the United States if it arrives a month before the April 15 tax deadline or by employees in the United Kingdom if it arrives a month before the January 31 tax deadline. Schools and universities also have calendars that greatly influence participation rates and mentoring programs. A mentoring program that sends an invitation to undergraduates during an examination period would likely be quite unsuccessful.

Section summary

Recruit the right participants by communicating clearly your goals, expectations, requirements, and benefits of participation. Select an efficient process of recruitment that draws on your organizational communication practices and is sensitive to the ebb and flow of work demands in your organization.

Match

There are two guiding questions that may assist you in matching protégés and mentors.

1. What characteristics are relevant to achieve your mentoring program goals?
2. How much input will you and/or participants provide to make a match?

Characteristics

How can you decide which characteristics are relevant to achieving your program goals? Consider selecting a small set of attributes (three to five) that are relevant to the goals of the mentoring program, and use these in your matching process. A small set of attributes is manageable, whereas a long list of characteristics is not. Further, people may not wish to provide a lot of personal information as a prerequisite to participation in the mentoring program. Examine your goals and determine what experiences, personal characteristics, or skills are most important to achieve the mentoring program goals. Then, solicit this information from potential protégés and mentors.

The context and goals of the mentoring program will influence the characteristics on which protégés and mentors might be matched. For example, the literature on mentoring programs for teachers suggests that being in a similar subject and in close proximity were the characteristics protégés most valued in their mentors (Marable and Raimondi 2007). In contrast, shared attitudes and values appear to be an important characteristic for mentoring programs for undergraduates (Ensher and Murphy 1997). Other works suggest that mentoring dyads for graduate students and faculty work best when they orient around needs and competencies (Lunsford 2011; Thomas et al. 2015) and that collaboration is an important activity for successful matches.

You may wish to consider moderation in matching on too many similar characteristics. There is substantial literature on the importance of similarity of mentors to protégés on building effective relationships (Allen et al. 2011; Ensher and Murphy 1997; Wanberg, et al. 2003, 104). This research suggests that similarity in terms of values, attitudes, and work habits is associated with a good mentoring relationship. When people have something in common, they are more likely to form a bond with one another, called "rapport." For example, if protégés and mentors attended the same school or grew up in the same area, then they are more likely to have a topic to discuss that builds rapport and leads to a positive relationship.

However, mentoring relationships are learning relationships that expose participants to new ways of thinking and learning. If the protégé and mentor share too many characteristics, they may lack the opportunity to learn from their differences in approach or thinking. Overall, it appears that having some similarities, which are relevant to achieving the program goals, is useful – but you may not wish to pair people who are too similar, as that may inhibit opportunities to learn from differences.

Input into the match

The literature is unclear about the right amount of input program managers should have in matching protégés and mentors in informal mentoring programs. The method used to match participants also does not seem to influence program outcome (Wanberg et al. 2003, 89). Consider your program resources and goals as you make these decisions. Do provide participants some input into the matching process, through either an application process or a face-to-face meeting (Allen et al. 2011). The most haphazard (and not recommended) matching process is to provide a list and let people select one another on criteria they select. If you are 100 percent responsible for the match, then you need information about the participants, related to the program goals, to assign protégés and mentors to one another. Other options include supporting a mixer event where potential protégés and mentors meet one another and rank with whom they might like to be paired.

If your organization has the resources, it might be possible to develop software or use existing mentoring software to enable participants to review online profiles and propose who might be the best match. Case Study 6.2 describes two companies that rely on technology and research to help program managers match participants and monitor the relationship progress.

Case Study 6.2 Mentoring software to recruit and prepare

Wisdom Share and Xinspire are examples of resources program managers may use to match participants and run their program. Wisdom Share is a research-based software program used to match mentors and protégés and provides management tools to program managers. It is a turnkey solution with everything a program manager might need to launch a formal mentoring program. The software is unique in that it takes into account experiences, relevant personality factors, and communication styles in suggesting a match. It has a 99.8 percent success rate in matching participants. The program was developed by Mentor Resources Inc., one of the oldest companies in this sector. The software is available in several languages. The philosophy behind the matching was developed to promote mentoring dyads where people enjoy interacting and learning from one another. Mentoring programs that match students with alumni mentors are among the many success stories the company touts. The program has been used by businesses for employees in university settings, such as Cornell University for their faculty mentoring program.

Xinspire is an intuitive mentoring web application that enables program administrators to focus on the most important part of any mentoring program – the quality of the mentoring relationships. The software focuses on institutions (universities, professional associations, and companies) that want to run a managed mentoring program. The software provides the administrator with tools such as comprehensive follow-up plans, detailed logging of interactions, reporting, and flexibility to accommodate diverse program models (one of their strongest features). The application can be adjusted to meet the needs of an institution's program "on the fly."

Mentees benefit from not needing to cold call potential mentors; all participants go through a registration process with the understanding that they are in the system for the specific purpose of mentoring. Having such a structure in place encourages mentees to connect with potential mentors. From a user experience, the software streamlines registration, the search-and-match process, and communications.

The Stanford Alumni Mentoring Program used Xinspire to make approximately 2,500 matches since 2008. Its program is a search-request-match system; so students register for a mentoring session, search for a mentor, and request. The student and the alumnus are anonymous until the request is accepted, after which they are encouraged to meet in person.

Wheaton College has approximately 4,000 mentors and approximately 500 mentees enrolled in their system. The college uses it as an online search and communication platform with faculty and career services roles included. The former program director, Emily George DeLew, notes:

Wheaton College's *Wheaton in Network* [*WiN*] program has transformed how students prepare for life after college. *WiN* has proven to be a critical tool for strengthening the entire college community and providing significant opportunities for alumni to get involved and give back to the College.

Source: Mentor Resources: (http://www.mentorresources.com) and Xinspire: (http://xinspire.com).

Section summary

Consider your mentoring program goals and select the relevant three to five characteristics protégés and mentors need to exhibit. Match individuals on these characteristics and where possible give mentoring participants some input in the match. If you have resources, there are companies that can provide software to help you match participants and assess their progress.

Prepare participants

Briefings provide information about the program goals, the principles of good mentoring, and opportunities for participants to share information about mentoring practices. However, mentors in informal relationships do not attend briefings, so why should mentors, or protégés, be expected to attend a briefing for a mentoring program? Some individuals are skilled mentors because they had good role models or worked on developing their mentoring skills. Mentors generally want to be available to their protégés. For example, they have noted a desire of "being available for any advice" (Thomas et al. 2015, 326).

Yet we know that about half of mentoring participants report at least one negative mentoring interaction (Wanberg et al. 2003, 52). Briefings provide an opportunity to increase participants' skills in building rapport, listening, framing reflective questions, and setting goals. Briefings may also inoculate mentors and protégés against bad habits they may have acquired, such as endorsing sink-or-swim attitudes related to mentoring.

What is in a name?

I prefer the word "briefing" or mentorship education rather than "orientation," "training," or "information sessions." Your program activities set expectations for participants, and the title of these sessions convey your expectations. This book advocates a developmental, learning process that you model in every activity and communication.

An "orientation" sounds like you are orienting a person to an experience or activity. Experienced mentors may not perceive any value in attending an orientation. Training sometimes conveys technical skill acquisition rather than developing a relationship. The word "training" can be off-putting for some individuals, especially in university settings where learning is valued over training. "Information sessions" imply a unidirectional flow of information from the speaker to the audience. In contrast, a briefing suggests an interactive experience where the latest information about mentoring will be provided, along with needed instructional materials about expectations.

The benefits of briefings

Briefings are beneficial to participants who will be more prepared to engage in effective mentorships. They also provide you an opportunity to receive feedback about your program. Briefings benefit participants in three ways. First, mentors and protégés benefit from understanding the goal(s) of the mentoring program and thinking about how they may shape interactions and activities to support these goals.

Second, briefings may provide opportunities for participants to develop their mentoring communication skills further and share what has worked well in the past. It is important that participants understand what good mentoring is, including how relationships develop, what interactions are important at different relationship stages, and the characteristics of high- and low-quality interactions. The hope is that this information will promote high-quality interactions and empower mentors to work with program coordinators to minimize dysfunctional relationships.

Third, even experienced mentors and protégés may benefit from the opportunity to reflect and develop their mentoring philosophy. Briefings provide a forum where experienced participants may share their knowledge with others.

Briefings as eligibility requirements

Consider making your briefing sessions an eligibility requirement for participation. If you believe your briefing is optional, then why have it? The individuals who may most need support rarely attend these opportunities (if they did, they might become better mentors!). You want mentors who will have the time and interest in improving their mentoring skills. Further, if some mentors or protégés do not need the information, then it might be time to reconsider the content of your briefings. Include dates of briefings in your recruitment materials.

Technology enables you to offer briefings in different formats, not just in-person meetings. It might be appropriate to have different sessions for new versus returning participants, where the briefing seminar might be more of a review for experienced individuals. It might also be the case that you could develop an online briefing module for participants who need a refresher or review.

Who should attend?

Who will attend your briefing? Will mentors and protégés attend together? Will new and experienced mentors attend the same session? One strategy may be to design the content for your briefing seminar and then adapt it as needed to your audience.

Some programs hold joint sessions where mentors and their protégés attend together. Attending briefings together is a way mentors and protégés may initiate their relationship, especially if role-playing exercises are included in the briefing. However, there may be times when it is impractical or impossible to have mentors and protégés attend the same briefing. In these cases, you can use your core briefing material to tailor each session to protégés and to mentors.

What to include?

Briefings need to be interactive and provide opportunities for participants to reflect on and practice what they are learning. Active involvement of participants will increase their retention of the information. A suggested briefing template of topics, methods to cover the information, and the role of the program manager are presented in Table 6.2. Effective briefings include information in four areas:

1. program goals and expectations;
2. mentoring principles;
3. ethical, policy, and legal considerations; and
4. diversity and inclusion.

For example, faculty members at the University of Wisconsin–Madison developed an eight-session seminar for faculty members to learn about mentoring researchers in science called "Entering Mentoring." This evidence-based seminar provides a multi-session, interactive mentorship education. Its goal is to help faculty members learn effective mentoring practices. An important element of the seminar is the development of a mentoring philosophy. A link to these materials is provided in the "Resources" section at the end of this chapter.

Table 6.2 Briefing template

Topic	Method	Program manager role
Program goals and expectations	Survey participants about program goals and expectations. Participants identify a plan for first contact.	Clarify missing information. Indicate guidelines on meeting frequency and expected activities.
Principles of good mentoring	Fishbowl to demonstrate listening and communication skills.	Solicit participants to describe what worked well, what they might do differently.
Ethical, policy, and legal obligations	Discuss ethical dilemmas. Role-play scenarios.	Collect participant responses and discuss how responses align with obligations.
Diversity and inclusion	Case discussions: how appreciating differences may enhance relationship development.	Highlight points about diversity and inclusion relevant to your context.

Program goals and expectations

The briefing starts before anyone shows up for it. Participants should have already received information about program goals and expectations in recruitment materials. A sample email reminder is presented in the following box. Ask participants to review the program goals, mentoring expectations, and requirements in advance of the briefing.

Sample Email reminder for briefings
SUBJECT LINE: REMINDER – Mentoring Briefing at TIME, DAY – LOCATION
Greetings,
This is a gentle reminder that our mentoring briefing session is on DAY at TIME in LOCATION. Review our program goals and expectations again <u>before</u> attending. The interactive session will be an opportunity to check your understanding and provide you with more information to be effective in your relationship. I encourage you to come with your mentoring partner, as a first step to get to know each other.
Sincerely,
Name of Program Manager

Open a briefing session by asking attendees to describe the program goals and expectations. Your contribution to the briefing will be to summarize their comments by indicating where they line up with the program goals and expectations while clarifying any misinformation. Ensure that your participants understand the organizational goals in addition to their individual expectations of mentoring.

The program expectations refer to what the participants might actually do together that will help the organization achieve the desired goal. Providing a timeline for your program and activities is one way to communicate this information. Share:

1. how often participants are expected to meet;
2. what kind of activities are appropriate;
3. what forms that need to be completed; or
4. what event attendance is expected.

Principles of good mentoring

Emphasize an intentional focus on high-quality mentoring. Mentoring participants need to know the relationship's progress through stages and that different activities are warranted at each stage. (The stages are covered in more detail in Chapter 9.) The critical knowledge to impart is for mentors and protégés to understand that initiation, the first stage, is when trust and rapport need the most attention.

RELATIONSHIP QUALITY

An emphasis on relationship quality may promote better relationships. I often ask people to imagine a person with whom they enjoy interacting and to describe the qualities of that individual. They report feeling energized when interacting with that person and describe personal qualities that imply listening, confidence building, and humor. This exercise can be a useful jumping off point to ask people to describe the characteristics of high-quality relationships. You might then share the three qualities (described in Chapter 3) of high-quality relationships: emotional carrying capacity, tensility, and degree of connectivity.

You can increase participants' awareness of the common sources of dysfunction in relationships. I often ask participants to share examples they have experienced or heard about related to "tormentors" or poor mentoring relationships. Then it is possible to match these experiences to the five sources of dysfunction. The five categories are mismatch in the dyad, distancing behavior, general dysfunction, lack of competency, and manipulative behavior (refer to Chapter 3 for more detail). Such an activity may increase awareness that mentoring relationships are not always beneficial or positive.

Ethical, policy, and legal obligations

An essential element of briefings to discuss are ethical, policy, and legal considerations. Mentoring relationships may develop into close, intimate relationships where relationship boundaries may become blurred. It is important to state (and not assume it is known) what is ethically acceptable in a mentoring relationship. These obligations are especially important when organizations support and encourage formal mentoring efforts that might not have otherwise formed, because there may be legal consequences for some negative behaviors.

An effective segue to this topic is to present an ethical dilemma for participants to discuss. You can draw on the ethical tensions discussed in Chapter 3 to design an appropriate case study. Give the participants time to discuss their responses and then ask a few participants to share their responses. Then the facilitator can share the core ethical principles (refer to Table 3.2 in Chapter 3) and tie them into the discussion about the ethical dilemma.

Role-playing of ethical challenges helps participants understand why ethics are important. Suggested prompts are presented here.

1. <u>Summer undergraduate research mentoring</u>: A faculty mentor is mentoring an undergraduate on a research project, which involves analysis of the mentor's existing data set. The mentor runs the statistical analysis for the protégé and provides her the results. The protégé presents the results, which were significant, on a poster session. When another professor asks her about these results, she is unsure exactly why the analysis was done in that way. The protégé realizes that the analysis was not run correctly. The protégé, after some encouragement from another professor, shares her concerns with her faculty mentor. The faculty mentor acknowledges that another student also found the mistake, and the mentor agrees the analysis was not correct. What ethical principles were violated by the mentor or protégé? How would you have handled this if you were the mentor or protégé? (based on author's experience).

2. <u>Business</u>: Armando's mentor is the vice president of sales in a Fortune 500 company. He has benefited from working with his mentor over the last six months, including having sought out more high-profile assignments that developed his skills. Recently, he asked his mentor if he could use him as a reference for a different position in the company that would be a promotion. His mentor enthusiastically agreed even though he has doubts about Armando's ability to be successful in that position. What ethical principles would come to bear on this situation?

3. <u>Tech mentoring</u>: Ellie, a Stanford University undergraduate, was assigned a high-powered mentor in the technology industry through her course on technology entrepreneurship. She was one of only a few women who

attended industry events and had to fend off some of the men. However, her mentor was helpful through email. In fact, she felt lucky to have such a knowledgeable and successful entrepreneur as her mentor. He suggested they meet at a local bar the next time he was in Palo Alto, California, to learn more about her career interests. She accepts the offer, thinking this is part of how you network with others. Informal contexts such as these are common ways for mentors and protégés to interact. What ethical principles might influence the mentor's decision to make that request or for the protégé to accept it? (This scenario is based on an actual story that led to dating, then allegations of rape (Bazelon, 2015)).

Verify that participants are aware of institutional or organizational policies relevant to mentorship. For example, on university campuses in the United States there are policy requirements to share information about a student who may be a danger to himself or herself or to others. Mentors and protégés need to have a shared understand when seemingly private information may not be private. If mentors have a gatekeeping role for the profession, for example, in graduate studies or professions with strict accreditation requirements, then this role needs to be explained to protégés. External checks and balances need to be put in place to ensure that mentors are maintaining a proper gatekeeping role.

There may also be legal obligations that participants need to know. You may wish to check in annually with your organization's human resources office to review any laws and policies in your state or country that may influence the mentoring program. Case Study 6.3 provides an example of one such set of laws in the United States that relates to sexual harassment.

Diversity and inclusion

The globalization of companies and increased immigration have contributed to greater diversity in our institutions and organizations. Mentoring is seen as one way to support more women and minorities to advance to the C-suite or to pathways leading to advanced professional education. (In Chapter 11 there is more information about welcoming diversity.) Context also matters. Diversity and inclusion discussions will be different in a multinational company as they might focus on discussions around cultural differences. Such discussions might focus on gender, in fields where women are underrepresented. In the United States, there may be a need to discuss diversity in terms of ethnicity if mentees are underrepresented on that characteristic. Concerns about social justice have increased in the United States, which reflects one of the ethical obligations of program managers to ensure that the mentoring program is not perpetuating the status quo it seeks to change (refer to Chapter 3 for more information).

Case Study 6.3   What mentors (and protégés) need to know

A heightened duty

Mentors have access to a wealth of information that protégés hope to learn. However, mentors may need to know more about their legal obligations so they do not put their organization at risk. The current legal climate in the United States gives greater weight to some mentoring conversations in the country, which may have important implications for mentors and for protégés. As Mary Beth Tucker, executive director at the Office of Institutional Equity at the University of Arizona, notes, "there is a duty to be responsive to the law while fostering trust filled relationships."

US Federal Law

The US Federal Government explicitly forbids sex discrimination in the 23,500+ institutions or organizations that receive federal funding. There have been renewed efforts to educate students and employees about sex discrimination, which includes sexual harassment. Title VII (the Civil Rights Act of 1964), Title IX of the 1972 Education Amendments, and the 1990 American with Disabilities Act cover race, national origin, religion, and sex. Further, Title IX covers the entire employee population, including graduate students who may report sexual harassment in their laboratory.

Who is responsible?

Is a director of a public museum, the principal of a high school, or even the president of a university responsible for what a protégé may say to an employee who is a mentor? The courts say yes, if the conversation suggests any sex discrimination has taken place. The question before the US Supreme Court was to decide if an employer was responsible even if the president or CEO never knew sex discrimination had occurred. In 1998, the US Supreme Court ruled in two cases, *Faragher v. City of Boca Raton* and *Burlington Industries, Inc. v. Ellerth*, that if a student or employee tells another employee, who is in a responsible position, then the organization cannot legally claim it did not know about the sex discrimination. In other words, organizations are responsible for the climate at the institution; must have policies in place that prevent harassment and discrimination; and provide a mechanism for raising concerns or complaining. Thus, an organization has knowledge of sex discrimination if, for example, a student protégé shared information about sex discrimination with a trusted faculty mentor, even if this faculty member did not report the event.

What if?

For example, the University of Arizona is a big place, but the president of the university is to be held accountable if someone in the organization knew of the problem. Who is in the position to know? It may be faculty members, supervisors, or faculty mentors. Every mentor is required to report any form of harassment, discrimination, or retaliation that is disclosed to him or her. Different organizations may have different policies about who is required to report. At the University of Arizona, the policy is one of mandatory reporting for all employees, including student employees. The policy states:

Employees or agents of the university who (a) supervise other employees, graduate or undergraduate students, contractors, or agents; (b) teach or advise students or groups; or (c) have management authority related to a university-sponsored program or activity are required to:

- engage in appropriate measures to prevent violations of this policy; and
- upon receiving a report or having a reasonable basis to suspect that potential discrimination, harassment, or retaliation has occurred or is occurring, promptly notify and provide all available information and documentation either to the Dean of Students Office if the alleged policy violator is a student, or to the Office of Institutional Equity for all other matters.

What if a protégé described any of these scenarios to their mentor:

- a series of events about another faculty member who was making inappropriate comments in a classroom or tutoring session;
- sexual misconduct allegations that he or she was sexually assaulted in their dorm room last semester; or
- the protégé's partner or spouse hit him or her?

If an employee, even in their role as a mentor, becomes aware of *any form* of sex-based mistreatment, discrimination on protected classes, or retaliation from having complained about them, then he or she is required to share the information with the Office of Institutional Equity (if the matter involves an employee) or the dean of students (if the matter involves a student). How might knowing about a partner or spouse relate to institutional climate? It is relevant if the spouse or partner is also a student at the university. In such a case, the dean of students may have jurisdiction over the situation because two students would be involved.

Tips for briefings

It is essential that program managers consult with their organization's human resources to determine if there are policies that need to be shared with mentors and protégés. Briefing materials need to provide options for mentoring participants on how to handle conversations that may have legal implications. In the case of the United States and the scenarios described previously, there are different ways program coordinators can ensure mentors and protégés are prepared for these conversations. Mentors might discuss these requirements at their first meeting with a protégé. Another approach might be for program materials to state these obligations. A third approach might be to deal with it as needed. Program managers can educate mentors about the cues that indicate a protégé might begin to share such information. For example, he or she may ask, "can I close the door?" or "this is confidential right?" At that point, the mentor needs to say "let me talk to you about my responsibilities first."

The point is program managers need to prepare mentors to appropriately handle any reporting responsibilities. Program coordinators have an important role in educating mentors to "do no harm" and protect students, so they can work in a safe environment to complete their classes or research.

Title VII: http://www.eeoc.gov/laws/statutes/titlevii.cfm

U.S. Department of Education: Title IX and Sex Discrimination: http://www2.ed.gov/about/offices/list/ocr/docs/tix_dis.html

Source: Interview with Mary Beth Tucker, Executive Director, Office of Institutional Equity, University of Arizona.

Some program managers are reluctant or nervous about discussing diversity at the beginning of the program. There are three reasons to include information about welcoming diversity in your briefings. First, one of the differences in mentoring outcomes by race and gender is related to compensation. Female protégés have been found to have less average compensation than male protégés. There is evidence that protégés who have Caucasian male mentors experience greater individual benefits, as measured by promotion and compensation. It might be the case that these mentors have greater status in the organization and can connect their protégés with greater opportunities. These findings suggest two strategies:

1. raise awareness of the importance of identifying possible activities that will give female protégés opportunities for promotion; and
2. examine selection or screening processes for mentors and work to provide additional resources to protégés who may have mentors with less organizational status or knowledge in the organization.

The goal is to be aware of inequities and to design a mentoring program that does not replicate these inequities.

Second, cultural diversity is important to consider for companies and educational organizations. International students have reported feeling greater vulnerability in their mentoring relationships because of a concern for their visa status. Cultural norms may also influence formal mentoring programs in multinational companies. (More information is provided in Chapter 11 about how cultural differences may be considered.)

Third, diversity is a broad concept that is greater than "race" or "gender." Work with stakeholders and human resources to determine how your organization addresses diversity and inclusion. You need to provide information about welcoming differences and reducing inequities in ways that are consistent with your national laws (as in Case Study 6.3) and organizational practices.

Section summary

Engage participants in briefings by using frequent questions, role-playing, and short discussions. Effective briefings present information about program expectations and goals. Educating participants about the core principles of effective mentoring is essential to support skill development and good relationships. Make sure to educate participants about their ethical, policy, and legal obligations. Welcoming diversity in the beginning of the program sends an important signal to mentoring participants that all are welcome. Support ongoing mentorship education to improve participants' mentoring skills.

Mentorship education

For many years, mentoring has been viewed as an activity that people automatically know how to do well, like eating or walking. There was an early effort in graduate schools to provide workshops for mentors, which were voluntary. I remember asking several deans of graduate schools (in the United States and in Australia) if 'bad' faculty mentors ever attended. The answer was a resounding no. Mentorship education goes beyond what is included in a briefing.

The point is that mentorship is a skill that can and should be developed. Certainly, there are people who are naturally more skilled in the constellation of behaviors required for effective mentoring – for example, listening, reflecting, encouraging. Much of the focus on mentorship education in the United States has been in science, technology, education, and mathematics (STEM) disciplines (refer to Chapter 14 for STEM mentoring program examples). The following report adds medicine to STEMM for the second M. Increasingly, it is expected that mentors and protégés must improve their mentoring skills: It is no longer seen as a voluntary activity.

The recent National Academies Report titled *The Science of Effective Mentoring in STEMM* calls for greater attention to providing mentorship education (National Academies of Sciences, Engineering, and Medicine 2019). The National Research Mentoring Network (NRMN) is another example of mentorship education provided for the biomedical workforce. While these resources are STEM focused, the content covers topics that may apply to mentorship generally.

Adult learners

The best briefing seminars are interactive and reflect what we know about adult learning. A long seminar with a PowerPoint presentation is the opposite (but usual) of a good practice that facilitates learning. Develop short, five- to ten-minute lectures that might precede or follow discussions or role-playing exercises. Start briefings with questions to the audience and continue to question the audience throughout the briefing to engage them and keep your remarks on track.

Participants new to mentoring may benefit from in-person briefings. However, technology makes high-quality experiences possible online. Judicious use of PowerPoint slides is useful to keep in-person briefings on track. Include minimal text on the slides, never read a slide, and model good learning principles by creating opportunities for interaction and discussion. Your briefing session needs to model how you expect mentoring participants to interact by providing examples and practice opportunities.

Online briefings may be effective for returning mentors or programs with multi-site locations. An online briefing might provide an option for individuals who cannot attend an in-person briefing. Online briefings need to have short, five- to ten-minute modules that are followed by a quiz to allow participants to check their learning. Another option is to video face-to-face training, break it into sections, and have a short survey after each section. (The companies described in Case Study 5.2, Wisdom Share and Xinspire, also provide materials to adapt for briefing content.)

Section summary

Use the principles of adult learning to create interactive, memorable briefing sessions. Sessions can be online or videoed, if there are frequent pauses and opportunities for protégés and mentors to check their learning.

Conclusion

This chapter focuses on practices to consider in recruiting, matching, and briefing mentors and protégés. Effective mentoring programs provide participants some input into the matching process. Use a matching process where there is similarity on a few characteristics only. Finally, briefings are opportunities to ensure participants know about the mentoring program's goals and effective ways to engage in these learning relationships. (See Table 6.2 for an overview of the decisions, questions, and options you can consider related to recruiting, matching, and briefing participants.)

Key terms

- Briefing
- Ethics
- Diversity
- Inclusion
- Matching: similarity versus complementarity
- Mentoring philosophy statement
- Mentorship education
- Recruiting materials and processes

Check your learning

1. What selection criteria do you need to recruit the right participants?
2. What characteristics will you use to match protégés and mentors?
3. How can you make your briefing interactive, interesting, and memorable for participants?

4. What ethical and legal information needs to be included in your briefing session?
5. How will your mentoring program support mentorship education?

Resources

Entering Mentoring: https://cimerproject.org/entering-mentoring/
National Research Mentoring Network: https://nrmnet.net/
Mentorship Education: https://www.nap.edu/resource/25568/interactive/program-development-and-management.html#section1

References

Allen, T. D., L. M. Finkelstein, and M. L. Poteet. 2011. *Designing Workplace Mentoring Programs: An Evidence-Based Approach*. 2nd ed. Hoboken, NJ: John Wiley & Sons.

Bazelon, E. 2015. The Stanford Undergraduate and the Mentor. February 11. Available online at https://www.nytimes.com/2015/02/15/magazine/the-stanford-undergraduate-and-the-mentor.htm (accessed April 16, 2021).

Ensher, E. A., and S. E. Murphy. 1997. "Effects of Race, Gender, Perceived Similarity, and Contact on Mentor Relationships." *Journal of Vocational Behavior* 50(3): 460–481.

Lunsford, L. G. 2011. "Psychology of Mentoring: The Case of Talented College Students." *Journal of Advanced Academics* 22(3): 474–498.

Lunsford, L. G. 2012. "Doctoral Advising or Mentoring: Effects on Student Outcomes." *Mentoring & Tutoring: Partnership in Learning* 20(2): 251–270.

Marable, M. A., and S. L. Raimondi. 2007. "Teachers' Perceptions of What Was Most (and Least) Supportive during Their First Year of Teaching." *Mentoring & Tutoring: Partnership in Learning* 15(1): 25–37.

National Academies of Sciences, Engineering, and Medicine. 2019. *The Science of Effective Mentorship in STEMM*. Washington, DC: The National Academies Press. 10.17226/25568.

Thomas, J. D., L. G. Lunsford, and H. A. Rodrigues. 2015. "Early Career Academic Staff Support: Evaluating Mentoring Networks." *Journal of Higher Education Policy and Management* 37(3): 1–10.

US Department of the Army. 2019. Army Leadership and the Profession. Available online at https://armypubs.army.mil/epubs/DR_pubs/DR_a/ARN20039-ADP_6-22-001-WEB-0.pdf (accessed April 16, 2021).

Wanberg, C. R., E. T. Welsh, and S. A. Hezlett. 2003. "Mentoring Research: A Review and Dynamic Process Model." In *Research in Personnel and Human Resources Management, Vol. 22*, edited by C. R. Wanberg, E. T. Welsh and S. A. Hezlett, 39–124. Bingley, UK: Emerald Group Publishing.

Chapter 7

Step 4: Collect the right data

First get your facts; then you can distort 'em as much as you please.
(Mark Twain in Kipling 1899)

Introduction

You might agree with Mark Twain and believe in your "intuition" more than the "facts." Perhaps you cringe when you hear the words "evaluation" or "assessment," because you believe it involves complicated statistics and confusing surveys. Fear not! You do not need a PhD in evaluation to collect useful information about your mentoring program.

Effective evaluation is important for three reasons. First, collecting data from others may help you overcome your biases and make good decisions about needed programmatic changes. Second, relevant data enables you to improve your program. Third, effective measurement allows you to share program successes with stakeholders and participants. These narratives can be important in securing future resources to operate the program and in recruitment materials to identify mentors and protégés.

Neglecting to collect information about your program's effectiveness is like cooking without a recipe. You might serve a good dish if you are an experienced cook, but it will be difficult for anyone else to make it. You might even be tempted to neglect evaluation (and feel vaguely guilty about it), but avoiding evaluation makes it difficult to share program successes or disseminate what works to others in your organization.

Poorly designed evaluation efforts may be frustrating for you, as you struggle to make sense of information, and for the participants who become annoyed by long surveys. This frustration may create a negative spiral where you avoid evaluation efforts and possibly turn participants off from providing future feedback. Even well-meaning program managers may reuse previous surveys that were tedious to begin with, and do not provide relevant information about the program.

What and how you choose to measure will influence your ability to collect the right evidence to help you make adjustments and improvements

DOI: 10.4324/9781003163862-7

to your mentoring program. The top three questions I am asked about evaluating mentoring programs are:

- "What should I collect to know if my program is effective?"
- "When is the best time to collect information?"
- "How can I get more people to fill out my surveys?"

Evaluation can be an enjoyable and rewarding activity. Why you need to develop a process of data-driven decisions is discussed first. The remainder of the chapter is devoted to answering the what, when, who, and how of measurement. By the end of the chapter, you will have the tools and skills to design an effective measurement strategy for your mentoring program.

Data-driven decisions

Your experience should not be discounted. However, we experience certain biases which can negatively affect our ability to make good decisions (Kahneman et al. 2011). These biases are compounded when we fail to seek information from others. In fact, being aware of these biases does not seem to prevent us from making them (Kahneman, 2011). Three biases you should know about are sunk-cost fallacy, halo effect, and overconfidence.

Sunk-cost fallacy

The sunk-cost fallacy occurs when you are reluctant to make a change because of the time and effort you have invested in a course of action. You may not wish to make a change, even when you should.

We become attached to our ideas, even ones that may need to be discarded or changed. (Case Study 7.1 provides an example of sunk-cost fallacy.) For example, a program manager's reluctance to cancel an orientation dinner for hundreds of protégés to meet their mentors was because she had invested a lot of time and energy into this activity. The sunk-cost fallacy made it difficult for her to accept a change from one large dinner to numerous, smaller receptions.

The halo effect

The halo effect occurs when you draw on prior positive experiences, while neglecting contradictory evidence, to make a decision. Most program managers have had positive mentoring experiences and may be overly positive about what mentoring can do. Or you may have had a terrific mentor last year, who you believe must be terrific this year. For example, a mentor has performed well in the past, so you may be reluctant to reassign their

Case Study 7.1 Measuring mentoring activities

Attendance

At a large university, there was a successful faculty–student mentoring program for low-income students. The program director collected good information about the program activities. She believed that a key component of the mentoring program was a big, formal dinner where mentors and protégés met each other. University leaders attended the event, and a lot of money was spent on renting the room and paying for food for hundreds of people. In addition, considerable time was spent organizing and handling the logistics for such a large dinner: There were always people who could not attend, and she would have to make arrangements to get needed materials to these mentors and protégés. Her boss questioned the expenses related to this event and whether they were necessary to achieve the program outcomes. The program director reluctantly canceled the dinner in favor of working with individual colleges to host smaller, more personal receptions and engage in cost sharing. This change did not affect the program outcomes, which could be demonstrated because effective measurement was in place. In this case, measuring attendance was critical information to make this decision.

Mentoring workshops

A program manager was concerned about the effectiveness of skills-based workshops she organized for mentors and protégés. The same series had been conducted for several years, and while people attended, she was not sure the workshops provided valuable information. I suggested she add a short assessment of each workshop; a look of horror passed across her face at the suggestion. I asked what concerned her about such an assessment. "What if they don't like it?" she asked. I replied: "Wouldn't you prefer to know they do not find it useful so that you may change the workshops?" She agreed that she would prefer to know that but felt that the evaluation might reflect negatively on her, as the organizer. In her case, she worried that the evaluation was about her rather than the mentoring activity. I left the meeting thinking she was unlikely to evaluate the workshops. However, months later she enthusiastically wrote me to say she had used the evaluations, which showed that the participants valued the information. (The evaluation I provided her is in Table 7.1.)

Source: Author's experience.

protégé to someone else, even when the protégé requests a change. You might even say to the protégé a statement along these lines: "Stick it out, she is great, you will see."

If you are quick to dismiss information you receive, then you may be experiencing halo effect. Get another opinion from a trusted colleague. Having another person help you weigh positive or negative information about someone will help you carefully consider if action is required.

The overconfidence bias

Overconfidence bias occurs when we look for evidence and information that confirms our beliefs and discount or ignore information that is at odds with our beliefs. It leads us to extend our assertions further than the evidence we may have to support them. For example, a program manager may assert that everyone is benefitting because of a couple of positive anecdotes.

Developing an effective evaluation plan that you review with others, such as an Advisory Board, will help you to avoid overconfidence bias. Collecting information systematically about your program will help you to review it more objectively.

Section Summary

Be aware of the biases that may influence your decision-making. Three common errors are sunk-cost, halo effect, and overconfidence.

What to measure

Your theory of change (see Chapter 5) guides your measurement strategy. What you measure *must be related to the activities, outputs, and desired outcomes of your mentoring program.* The goal is to collect what you need and nothing more.

Your mentoring program goals and outcomes provide a template for what to measure. If you have not already developed a logic model, now is a good time to do so. A logic model illustrates how program activities align with the theory of change about your mentoring program (see Chapter 5, which provides information on developing a logic model).

Considerable resources are vested in formal mentoring programs in terms of dollars and time (including your time). Collect information to let you know what activities are valuable and warrant future investment and what activities might be eliminated. What else to measure? Measure how much mentoring occurs; which is referred to as the "dosage" of mentoring. There are three categories of items to measure:

- resources,
- people, and
- processes.

Resources

Resources refer to time and money invested by you, your organization, and program participants. Some mentoring programs have a budget associated with them. Other programs may borrow needed materials from other departments, or may receive donations to operate their activities. For example, a mentoring program may be considered part of a human resource activity, and is part of the people development budget. Estimate the amount of money it takes to operate your program. Include the portion of your salary as a program director that is dedicated to running the mentoring program. This information will enable you to calculate a dollar per participant amount that will help you determine what activities warrant this investment. This calculation is referred to as a "return on investment" or "ROI."

Identify a measurement for each output (related to a program activity) and outcome. You might assess outputs by reviewing the event attendance. For example, if you hold a program briefing, then measure attendance to determine if participants were there. You might also develop a short, online quiz about the content of the session and ask participants to take the knowledge quiz to assess how much information they retained.

People

When you measure outcomes you are measuring attitudes or activities in which people engage. Thus, if an expected outcome of your mentoring program is job retention or graduation from college, then you will want to measure if participants do these things. Kirkpatrick (1979) suggests four categories of people outcomes to consider:

1. reaction,
2. learning,
3. behaviors, and
4. results.

Reaction refers to how the mentor and protégé perceive the relationship. Common measures include relationship satisfaction, or measures of psychosocial and career support provided and received. Consider a faculty mentor and his or her graduate student protégé. An end-of-year survey asking each person to report on his or her relationship satisfaction is an example of measuring reactions. At a minimum, use a scale to access satisfaction rather than assuming mentoring has occurred.

Learning refers to information protégés and mentors acquired as a result of their mentoring relationship. Questions about learning should reflect the categories of goals for your mentoring program. You may wish to include a question to collect unanticipated learning outcomes by asking: "Is there anything else you would like to share?" In the case of our graduate student protégé and faculty mentor, protégé learning might be demonstrated by the progress through the degree program. Mentor learning might be demonstrated through a narrative text in his or her annual performance evaluation, which most faculty members are required to submit. A brief evaluation is provided in Table 7.1, which you can adapt to assess briefings or workshops.

Table 7.1 Sample session evaluation form *[name of session] evaluation form*

I learned:	Nothing	| - - - - - | - - - - |	A great deal
This session was:	A waste of time	| - - - - - | - - - - |	Extremely valuable
The content was:	Not relevant	| - - - - - | - - - - |	Relevant
	Not clearly explained	| - - - - - | - - - - |	Clearly explained
	Boring	| - - - - - | - - - - |	Interesting
	Baffling	| - - - - - | - - - - |	I could explain it
The lecturer/ presentation:	No show	| - - - - - | - - - - |	On time
	Thrown together	| - - - - - | - - - - |	Prepared
	Disrespectful/ stifled learning	| - - - - - | - - - - |	Respectful/interested in learning
Of the assigned reading:	Read none	| - - - - - | - - - - |	Read all
The reading was:	Difficult	| - - - - - | - - - - |	Easy
	Too much or too little	| - - - - - | - - - - |	Right amount
	Useless	| - - - - - | - - - - |	Useful
	Not relevant	| - - - - - | - - - - |	Relevant
In the future: Content:	Drop	Alter	Keep
Teaching approach:	Drop	Alter	Keep
Lecturer:	Drop	Alter	Keep

Optional: I liked about this session:
Optional: I disliked about this session:

Behavior change takes longer to measure because attitudes change before behaviors. For example, a graduate student might desire to learn how to write a grant. Learning is involved by reviewing the mentor's previous proposals, and behavior would be demonstrated through his or her effort in writing several drafts of a grant proposal. In a work setting, a behavior change might be demonstrated by a protégé who made more sales calls or delivered a presentation to a client.

An efficient way to measure behavior change on goals is to ask participants about their progress on their goals for the mentoring relationship. Provide three response options – behind, on track, or ahead – and you will have a measure of their behaviors related to goals.

Finally, results refer to the productivity or effort involved. In the graduate student example, the result might be submitting the grant proposal to a funding agency. Or in the case of making more sales presentations (behavior), the result might be closing more business. You could collect this information from organizational records or through a survey asking about these specific behaviors.

Processes

Processes refer to procedures and interactions involved in your mentoring program. For example, if you match protégés and mentors, then you are engaged in a process of matching that differs from the program that allows people to select one another. You might measure the effectiveness of this matching process indirectly through a satisfaction measure or attrition rate. Processes also refer to forms and procedures you implement as part of the mentoring program. Do participants complete your forms and submit them? Track completion and submission rates to help you know if you need to revise the process: for example, in the case of low submission rates.

Dosage

As mentioned previously, dosage refers to the amount of mentoring that takes place. It might seem obvious to assume that mentoring is taking place in a mentoring program, but numerous studies suggest this would be an incorrect assumption (see, for example, Baugh and Fagenson-Eland 2007; Lunsford 2011, 2012). In some cases, the protégé or mentor may have left the organization. In other cases, participants may not be meeting as frequently as you thought or may not be engaged in ways that enable them to achieve individual and program goals. For example, we know that peer mentors are more likely to provide psychosocial support and less instrumental or career advice (Ensher and Murphy 2011; Lunsford 2016). It might be that participants dropped out, for good and bad reasons, and it will be important to know they did not participate (and why). Further, researchers find that even when mentors and protégés are engaged, they rarely report a similar experience. One study even found little agreement in the amount of time mentors and protégés reported they spent together (Ensher and Murphy 1997).

Failure to collect dosage may lead you to believe your mentoring program is not working, when in fact it is working for most participants. However, a small subset of individuals may not be benefiting or involved in the mentorship. Collecting dosage information will enable you to assess how much mentoring your participants engaged in during the mentoring program.

Typical measures of dosage include frequency of meeting, duration of an interaction, and topics discussed during their interactions. The natural calendar of your mentoring program or organization should guide your decision about when it is best to collect information on dosage. Some program managers ask participants to submit a monthly log of meetings, while other program managers ask participants to submit this information at the end of the mentoring program. Remember to collect information from both protégés and mentors.

Memory prompts are helpful in designing survey questions. Always provide a time frame when asking about mentoring. Questions about dosage might be preceded by a statement that asks participants to think about how often they met in the last month or semester (pick the time frame that makes sense for your mentoring program). Sample questions for what to collect are provided in Table 7.2.

Table 7.2 Questions to measure mentoring reactions and dosage

---

Reaction measure – satisfaction
Instructions: Indicate the extent to which you agree with the following statement using the scale provided. [Responses: 1 = "strongly disagree" to 5 = "strongly agree"]
• I am satisfied with my mentoring relationship.
Reaction measure – relationship quality
Instructions: Indicate the extent to which you agree with the following statement using the scale provided. [Responses: 1 = "never," 2 = "rarely," 3 = "sometimes," 4 = "often," 5 = "all the time"]
• I can express my feelings (good or bad) to my mentor/protégé(s).
• I can count on my mentor/protégés even after difficult conversations.
• I think about new ideas as a result of interactions with my mentor/protégé(s).
Dosage measures
Instructions: Think about when you have met with your mentor or protégé(s) in answering the next set of questions.
• In the last month I met face-to-face with my mentor/protégé_____ times: 1, 2, 3, 4, 5, more than 5 times.
• In the last month I interacted with my mentor/protégé using (select all that apply):
Social media (Facebook, Twitter, Instagram, WhatsApp).E-mailVideo conferenceTelephoneTexting.

Section summary

Your theory of change provides a guide about what to measure. Three categories of items to measure are the resources expended, the people involved, and the processes related to mentoring. Collect the dosage of mentoring that participants receive.

When to measure

When is the right time to collect information? How often should you collect information? You do not want to overwhelm participants with too many surveys or questions, but at the same time you need to collect information that will allow you to make needed adjustments to the mentoring program. Consider your organizational calendar in making decisions about when to collect information.

Align with the organizational calendar

The duration of mentoring programs varies and tends to align with your organizational calendar. For example, college mentoring programs usually occur either during summer programs or during an academic term. Youth mentoring programs may follow the school schedule and occur during the academic year, or during breaks such as summer. Corporate programs may align with quarterly goals. Some programs are as short as three months, while others may last for a year.

A survey sent at the end of a financial quarter to bank employees may well be ignored. Think about the natural times that mark beginning, transition, and ending points in your organization when you collect information from stakeholders and participants.

Timing

The timing of data collection relates to demonstrated effectiveness (see Chapter 5). A systematic effort to collect information will help you establish demonstrated effectiveness. Consider having four data collection points:

1. at the beginning of the program (an application or information sheet could include relevant questions);
2. a "check-in" a month into the program to ensure participants are meeting and to identify problem matches;
3. data from an activity or event, for example, photographs, attendance, knowledge quiz; and
4. at the end of the program (focus group, interviews or survey) to capture changes.

A "check-in" will let you identify problems early and rematch participants if needed (see Case Study 6.1 for an example). This check-in will let you know that the participants have connected with one another and if you need to intervene, if the mentoring relationship is not off to a good start.

Some programs require monthly activity reports that provide information about mentoring interactions and outcomes. However, for some organizations monthly reporting would be too burdensome. Consider your organizational culture and norms related to surveys and evaluations when deciding the frequency of administering surveys.

Section summary

Consider the timing of your mentoring program activities and the organizational calendar, to select times when people are not already overburdened or absent. Collect information at the beginning and end of the program to assess change. It is also recommended to have a "check-in" on relationship success and to assess specific activities, such as briefings or workshops.

From whom?

Consider who can provide information about outputs and outcomes. These individuals should include both the mentoring participants (mentors and protégés) and stakeholders such as department heads or funders. Sometimes, program directors are hesitant to ask participants about their experiences. Remember, you are asking people to evaluate the mentoring program, not you! Further, you will never know what to improve unless you ask people about their experiences (Case Study 7.1 illustrates this hesitancy).

Reduce your burden by crafting questions and data collection instruments such that you do not need to reword them for protégés and mentors. Collect information on similar topics for comparison.

Protégés

When data are collected, it is almost always from protégés. Thus, it is likely that you already collect information from these individuals. Consider collecting data anonymously, as it may increase your response rate and reduce survey bias. If you are collecting pre- and post-data, then you may need to know who the person is to connect the records. In this case the data would be confidential but not anonymous.

Mentors

There is growing recognition of the importance of collecting information from mentors. In the United States, there has been an implicit assumption that only protégés learn and develop in mentoring relationships. However, in other countries there is recognition that developmental mentoring engages mentors as well as protégés (David et al. 2013). Thus, collecting information from mentors provides an important perspective on both protégés and mentor experiences. Information collected from mentors, especially about the potential benefits of participation, may inform future mentor recruitment efforts.

Stakeholders

Consider if there are stakeholders from whom it would be helpful to have some information. For example, department heads may be able to provide an assessment about outcomes they see from employees who participate in the formal mentoring program. In addition, collecting information from funders or bosses about their perceptions of the mentoring program might help you anticipate potential problems, or see where you might need to engage in public relations about your program.

Section summary

Attempt to collect information from the participants (mentors and protégés) as well as other stakeholders in your mentoring program. Use your logic model to determine who else provides resources or is influenced by the mentoring program and involve these individuals in your evaluation efforts.

How to measure

You have more "how's" at your disposal than you might realize. It is likely that you use surveys to collect information about your mentoring program. Listed here are methods of collecting data:

- archival analysis,
- focus groups,
- interviews,
- observation,
- photographic evidence, and
- surveys.

All measurement techniques have their pros and cons. (Table 7.3 describes the pros and cons of some measurement techniques.)

Table 7.3 Pros and cons of measurement methods

Method	Pros	Cons
Archival analysis	Records are already available, may save time	Some records may be incomplete or missing
Focus groups	Provides in-depth information, opportunity to ask for clarification	Fewer responses, time-intensive to record and analyze responses
Interviews	Can obtain sensitive information	Time-intensive, response bias
Observation	Easy to collect estimates of participation and engagement	Can be time-intensive if looking for more nuanced behaviors
Photographs	Visual images are powerful ways to convey success	Expense for photographer, poor-quality pictures are not useful
Surveys	Easy to administer and tabulate responses	Response bias, may not ask correct questions

How you collect data may depend on how well developed your program is. For example, closed-ended survey questions work well when you are assessing an established program, or where there are specific items that you wish to know about regarding program activities and outcomes.

Use at least two methods to collect data. Collecting data in multiple ways lets you minimize mistakes and provides better evidence of effectiveness when the information is similar from different methods.

Archival analysis

Archival analysis involves a review of the "records" of the program, and it can be a surprisingly effective way to measure mentoring. For example, you might examine how often mentoring dyads participate in an online program discussion board to assess engagement.

I worked with a researcher to examine the teacher observation forms completed by mentors. We were interested in if mentors encouraged reflective practices in their protégés. Thus, we reviewed only one item on the form: the prompt where mentors were asked to list questions on which their protégés could reflect. To our surprise, more than half of the mentors wrote directive comments rather than reflective questions. This information helped us redesign the briefing and orientation materials for mentors (and we shared our findings with the mentors).

Consider what records you have related to participation, information forms, and so on, which also could be a useful source of information about your mentoring program's effectiveness. (Case Study 7.2 highlights the effective use of archival data that is supplemented by targeted interviews.)

Case Study 7.2   Mentoring metrics in graduate education

The setting

In the rolling hills between the coast and mountains is North Carolina State University, one of the state's two land-grant universities. North Carolina State University is classified as having very high research activity: In 2020, it boasted 60 doctoral programs[1] with 3,370[2] enrolled doctoral students. *Pathway to the Future: North Carolina State's 2011–2020 Strategic Plan* (NC State University n.d.) calls for an increased emphasis on doctoral education, in part by improving the mentoring of doctoral students. Two expected outcomes of this better mentoring are a reduction in time to earn a degree, and an increased completion rate.

In 2014, Maureen Grasso left the University of Georgia to become North Carolina State University's Dean of Graduate School. At the University of Georgia she partnered with the Council of Graduate Schools to contribute to the national PhD Completion Project. She and the associate dean, Mike Carter, knew from experience that there are limits as to what can be accomplished by working on mentoring efforts at the institutional level only. Carter says: "To be more effective we needed to work also at the academic unit and dyad – mentors and their mentees – levels." Grasso adds: "But apart from anecdotes, we had little information about mentoring at those levels."

The pair developed software, Mentoring Metrics, to provide targeted information about mentoring experiences and outcomes. The development process moved forward in stages. It began with an exploration of current data before they identified their guiding questions about mentoring. These questions were used to develop operational definitions, which provided the needed detail for programmers to develop the software.

Exploration and guiding questions

At first, Grasso and Carter were driven by a general curiosity about the state of doctoral mentoring at North Carolina State University. Grasso said:

We offered a smorgasbord of data to graduate programs concerning applications, enrollment, degrees awarded, and time to degree and completion rates. After browsing among those data, we found that they were inadequate to our aim to better understand mentoring on our campus.

To gather information focused on mentoring, they determined what they wanted to know. Four questions guided their mentoring inquiry:

1. How effective were advisors and academic units in contributing to graduate student research?
2. How effective were advisors and academic units in advancing students in a timely manner?
3. How effective were advisors and academic units in enabling students to complete their degrees?
4. How effective were advisors and academic units in contributing to student research in interdisciplinary programs?

These guiding questions were critical to the process of measuring mentoring. They provided not only a structured approach to gathering information about mentoring but also a value framework for inquiry into mentoring. By stating what they valued in mentoring, they supplied implicit criteria for evaluating mentoring. Of course, these questions needed to be well considered because they determined what is important about mentoring and, by implication, what is unimportant.

For example, the first question suggests that good advisors are those who are effective in contributing to graduate student research, and the second suggests that good advisors advance their doctoral students in a timely manner. The last question reflects a strategic emphasis at North Carolina State University on interdisciplinary programs and research.

Operational definitions

It was a challenge to define answers for each guiding question. For example, what does it mean for advisors to contribute effectively to graduate student research? There is no overall correct answer to these questions, but there is a "right" answer if it aligns with achieving the organization's strategic plan. At North Carolina State University, they decided that the first question meant to serve on a sufficiently large number of doctoral committees, especially as chair or co-chair, and to provide a suitable amount of financial support for students doing research. Thus, the operational definitions for the first guiding question were:

1.   How effective are advisors and academic units in contributing to graduate student research?

* number of doctoral committees faculty have chaired or co-chaired;
* number of master's committees faculty have chaired or co-chaired;
* number of committees faculty have served on, other than as chair/co-chair;
* number of research assistants supported.

Querying data

Carter notes, "We discussed the implications of gathering data on an individual level, and decided that because the crucial relationship in mentoring in doctoral education is advisor–advisee, we needed to pursue information that could better illuminate this relationship." This focus on individual faculty was a change in how they analyzed data, and not one they undertook lightly. They also recognized the influence of the "system" on mentoring, which is the department, college, and institutional procedures and practices; therefore, they erred on the side of including a greater number of options, since the guiding questions included both individual faculty members and academic units. Mentoring Metrics allowed searches by college, department, graduate program, all graduate faculty, and individual faculty. All faculty members may be filtered by tenure rank, number of years at the university, gender, and field of study.

Uses for mentoring metrics

Mentoring Metrics provided guidance in performing three tasks that Carter and Grasso believed would better target efforts to improve mentoring and information about the efficacy of their interventions.

Task 1: To identify faculty members and academic units that could serve as exemplars of best mentoring practice.

The software allowed them to view graduate faculty from multiple perspectives, to identify those who are apparently effective mentors. For example, they searched the data to produce a list of faculty members who had advised a large number of students over the past five years, with average times to degrees a full year or less than the university average and six-year completion rates of 80 percent or higher. The obvious question is: What are the practices that these "super mentors/advisors" use that enable them to mentor so many students well? As exemplars, such faculty will bring strong credibility, having supported so many students.

The same strategy may be applied to programs and departments. Carter observed, "We identified six departments that have times to degree at one year or below the university average, and six-year completion rates above 75 percent."

Task 2: To identify faculty or academic units that would benefit from tailored support for developing effective mentoring practices.

One goal was to be more strategic about improving mentoring by targeting faculty and academic units that would benefit most from their assistance. The software identified the kind of interventions that may be most helpful. For example, they used Mentoring Metrics to identify the departments with the largest attrition rates in the university. The next step was to work with these departments specifically on reducing those rates: for example, by investigating admissions practices, records of preliminary examinations, when students leave and why, the structure of the curriculum, and the number of doctoral students per faculty member. The plan was to identify the main contributors to high attrition and target support to those specific areas.

Mentoring Metrics queries data in new ways to identify patterns that were previously invisible, such as when faculty members have too many graduate students to mentor properly. In one such case, they notified the department and set up a meeting with the department head and the director of the graduate program, both of whom were surprised that they had such a disproportionately large number of students. The graduate school collaborated with this department to make a case to the dean for reducing enrollment, to educate faculty members in the department about their disproportionately heavy advising load, and to offer strategies for creating an environment in which they can provide better mentoring.

Task 3: To determine the effectiveness of our mentoring initiatives over time.

Grasso wondered, "How will we know if our work with the faculty members in a department has been effective?" A key to determining the effectiveness of an intervention was to have a baseline against which to measure change over time after that intervention. Mentoring Metrics allows them to take a snapshot of current data at any time, and to use that snapshot as a baseline for later measurements.

Two questions regarding mentoring and metrics

To whom should we give access to mentoring metrics?

Grasso notes, "We are sensitive to the potential negative conse-quences related to identifying data by individual faculty." Their goal was to support, not to evaluate or judge. Yet they recognize that other administrators may have different aims in using this information. Deans, department heads, and/or chairs might wish to use it for ranking faculty in their units by productivity, applying to tenure and promotion cases, or determining merit raises. Perhaps graduate students would like to use it to select their advisors. Grasso observed, "We have misgivings about the data being used for these purposes – and we suspect faculty may have misgivings as well." No tool can be completely neutral, and the issue of access requires careful delib-eration.

To what extent are metrics really an indicator of the quality of mentoring?

Carter says, "It is easy to understand why some people would be suspicious of an attempt to quantify mentoring. After all, mentoring is a complicated relationship." Mentoring is a relationship developed over time that involves two individuals. What metrics can capture the multidimensional aspects of mentoring relationships and outcomes?

Metrics are a proxy for mentoring that serve as indirect indicators. At North Carolina State University, the graduate school is the de facto institutional mentoring coordinator for doctoral students. These administrators took an important and critical step forward in recognizing that mentoring takes place at the individual level and that departmental, college, and institutional policies and procedures influence these relationships. The metrics, then, provide a starting point, not the end point, to help them achieve their three tasks for improving doctoral mentoring at the university, and it helps direct limited resources where they will have the most effect.

North Carolina State University Graduate School: www.ncsu.edu/grad/about-grad/

Source: Interview with Maureen Grasso, Former Dean of Graduate School, and Mike Carter, Associate Dean of Graduate School, at North Carolina State University.

Focus groups

When programs are new or have implemented a major change, it may be more difficult to obtain a full perspective with a closed-ended question. Surveying all of your participants may not be possible; in these cases, focus groups are useful because participants may share relevant information about which you would not have thought to ask.

Focus groups work well when you have between five and seven participants. Fewer than five people may lead to one person taking over the group, or insufficient sharing to build off each other's comments. Further, you want a sufficient number to draw some conclusions. Groups of more than seven people can be difficult to manage in a short time.

Consider having separate focus groups for protégés and mentors. Power dynamics might reduce protégé participation if mentors are present, even if an individual is not the protégé's mentor.

Limit your focus group to 20–30 minutes. It is important to use both your and their time wisely. If possible, audio record and transcribe the responses; if not, have another person present to help you take notes about responses. It's a good idea to decide if you might wish to use any quotes in recruitment or other program materials, as it is easier to ask for permission at the beginning; you can use a permission form for these purposes. Make clear to the participants if responses will be confidential and known only to you (unless they otherwise give you permission), and be sure to let them know that they can stop participating at any time without any negative consequences.

You can ask four to five questions in a 20-minute focus group. Your questions need to relate to information you want to collect. A good practice is to ask your first question, then look around the group to see if anyone wishes to add a response before you move on to the next question. Always ask: "Is there anything else someone wishes to add?" before you close the discussion on a question. Here are listed suggested questions:

- What topics covered in the briefing or mentorship education were most useful to you?
- How did you interact with your mentor/protégé?
- How did you change as a result of this mentoring experience?
- Describe any benefits and costs to you from participating in the mentoring relationship.

Your analysis of the responses would be to determine the themes in the responses for each question. Where possible, count the number of people who echo the theme: for example, you might find that more than half of the participants used information from the briefing in their first mentoring meeting. Identify representative quotes of each theme that you can use in a report, with participants' permission.

Interviews

Interviews are time-intensive and not usually recommended for that reason. However, targeted interviews can be extremely effective in two cases. First, interviews help you understand experiences that deviate from the norm. You may wish to understand better why a small percentage of protégés drop out of your program; or you might wish to understand more about what exceptionally good mentors do to promote their protégés' success. In these cases, interviews are helpful to identify policies, procedures, and practices that warrant change or dissemination to others.

Second, interviews are useful when you start a new program or practice. The opportunity to have a discussion with a knowledgeable mentor may help you learn more about how to position your program to others or develop program activities. Similarly, interviews can help you assess the value of a new mentoring initiative or activity and learn what kinds of questions (and response options) could be included on a survey.

The form of interviews varies from unstructured to completely structured. Semi-structured interviews are recommended for most purposes. It is likely you will have questions about a particular practice or activity, and will want to develop a few questions about these experiences. However, in the course of the conversation you may wish to follow up on some responses to understand them better.

Be respectful of people's time. It is likely you can obtain the needed information in a 20–30-minute interview, which will give you time to ask between four and six questions. Begin the interview by explaining who you are and the purpose of your questions. Then, indicate how you will share the results back with your interviewee. A good practice is to include a final question: "Is there anything else you would like to tell me on the topics we have been discussing?" This question gives your interviewee the opportunity to reflect for a moment and share any other relevant information about which you may not have known to ask.

Audio record the interview if you can (ask for permission before you turn on the recorder) or take detailed notes about the responses. Make sure you let the interviewee know you will be taking notes about the responses, so that he or she does not wonder what you are writing. Identify the relevant themes as you conduct interviews. It is good practice to review your notes or the transcription soon after your interview. Share the identified themes with the people you interviewed to solicit additional feedback, and to ensure that they agree with your interpretation of their comments.

Observation

Naturalistic observation is useful to collect information about attendance estimates without requiring a sign-in sheet, which can be time-intensive if you have a lot of participants. Your observations of how mentors and protégés interact at programmatic events can provide information about their development of rapport and psychosocial support. Do mentors sit with their protégés or do they tend to sit only with other mentors? Are dyads talking with one another or sitting silently? You may wish to develop log sheets to record observations of key events that include attendance, interaction, and engagement. You can even take 10 or 20 second samples of the extent to which dyads take turns talking as a measure of engagement.

Photographs

Photographs can provide visual representations about mentoring experiences. For example, a photograph with protégés and mentors at a briefing session conveys information about who attends and how they interact.

Effective photographs document programmatic activities and the settings of mentoring interactions. They can be photographs that you or the participants take, or you might commission a photographer for certain events. A series of photographs of mentors and protégés interacting in different settings may do more to explain the vitality of the program than words or data ever could. If you choose to use photographs in materials that you will distribute or place online, then consider including a release form for participants to sign at the beginning of the program.

Surveys

A survey is an efficient method to collect information from many people. Surveys, especially online ones, are easy to administer and tabulate if there are no free-response questions. However, participants also may report information inaccurately because they simply do not remember or because they wish to avoid providing critical feedback. Note that there is an over-reliance on survey data in measuring mentoring outcomes (Allen et al. 2008).

Pilot your survey first! Send it to a few people to test if your questions are clear and needed Another benefit of piloting your survey is that you will have fake data to review. Use the fake data to run your planned analysis, and see if the data are collected in a way that allows you to assess program effectiveness. For example, if one goal of your mentoring program is to support female employees, then you may wish to collect the gender of mentoring participants. However, there is no need to collect information about gender if it is not relevant to the goals or processes of your mentoring program. We often count what is easy to count, rather than thinking about what we really need to measure.

Online survey software is freely available. (There are a variety of free, online survey software programs listed in the Resources section at the end of this chapter.) Make sure your survey is visually appealing and simple to use on mobile devices. Group similar questions together in a section. Make sure the font color is easy to read. I remain amazed at how many surveys I receive that are difficult to read.

It is unlikely that you will have a 100 percent response rate on any survey. Response rates under 30 percent may reflect a problem in a burden being placed on protégés to provide information. A response rate between 50 and 80 percent gives you more confidence that the results will be representative of the program experience.

Comparison groups

Another consideration is to determine if you can compare your participants to nonparticipants. There are two ways, with a waitlist or a control group, to make such a comparison, which will help you make a stronger case about the "proven effectiveness" of your mentoring (see Chapter 5 about effectiveness). The waitlist approach requires you to place about half of your interested participants on a wait list, and start their program later. Then you can compare your participants with those who also volunteered but are not participating yet in the program.

A second option is to use a control group. You select a group of nonparticipants who are similar on demographic traits, such as age, gender, ethnicity, and time in the organization (or year in school). Responses or outcomes from nonparticipants can be compared to program participants.

Section summary

Go beyond surveys in collecting information about your mentoring program. Photographs of events, focus groups with participants at the beginning and end of the program, and short narratives from participants at the beginning ("What do you hope to learn?") and the end ("What did you learn?") can provide compelling stories and information about your program. In addition, you may wish to keep records of emails from participants or notes about particular events. These "memo to file" notes can be useful to track changes for next time. Compare participants to non-participants when possible.

Use good instruments

> Everything that can be counted does not necessarily count; everything that counts cannot necessarily be counted. (Albert Einstein)

An instrument refers to any tool you use to collect data. When you can, use or adapt instruments that have been tested and validated. The data you collect need to be guided by the rationale for your mentoring program. The National Academies has provided a list of validated mentoring instruments; the URL is listed under "Resources" at the end of the chapter.

How to ask questions: Top ten practices

There is a science to asking good questions. There are several short books and internet resources that can help you if you are inexperienced in this area. Presented here is a list of top ten practices to help you craft effective questions (Dillman 2011). Consider writing your questions and then reviewing the tips here to revise your questions as needed.

1. *Use memory prompts and time frames in surveys, interviews, and focus groups.* A memory prompt is a statement that encourages a person to think about the topic on which you are getting ready to ask questions. It helps the respondent provide more accurate information. Give a time frame for responding to questions, for example, over the last month or in the last year.
2. *Write short, succinct questions.* Ask one question at a time. Questions that ask two questions are called double-barreled questions, which makes your data hard to interpret. Consider this question: "I felt valued and liked by my mentor." A protégé may have felt liked by their mentor but did not feel valued. You will never know if their response refers to feeling liked, feeling valued, or both.
3. *Go beyond "yes" and "no" questions (categories) and collect continuous data when possible.* You can sort the data later into two categories if necessary. You can always turn continuous data into categories, but you cannot turn categories into continuous data. For example, ask respondents to provide the number of times that they met, rather than responding to categories such as 0, 1–4, 5–9, 10, or more. Similarly, consider this question: "Did your assigned mentor provide mentoring?" (Response: yes/no.) I conducted a study where I asked graduate students to indicate the extent to which they consider their assigned advisor to be a mentor on a 1–5 scale. One-quarter of the 477 respondents were neutral about their advisor being a mentor. You have to wonder if they would have selected "yes" or "no," if only given two response choices (Lunsford 2012).
4. *Place demographic information at the end of surveys.* Some individuals may be put off by being asked to provide personal information at the beginning of a survey. Once participants have started answering questions, they are more willing to provide such information.

5. *Be draconian in selecting what questions to ask, or even what data to collect.* Only ask questions that you will actually use in your assessment of the program's success. If you do not know how you will use a response to a question, then leave the question off the survey. Similarly, if you are unsure what you will do with observation or archival data, do not collect it. Resist the tendency to collect information and decide what to do with it later.

6. *Use online surveys when possible, and minimize the number of free-response questions.* There are several free, online survey services that make it easy to administer an online survey and receive automatic tables of the responses. Google Forms and SurveyMonkey are two such examples (see the Resources section at the end of this chapter). The problem with free response questions is the extra labor to make sense of the responses. Do you really need the question to be free response? Might you have an idea of categories that could be provided as responses along with an "other" option that allows text entry?

7. *Test your questions!* Ask family, friends, or people in your office to answer the questions before you use them. A question might make sense to you (you wrote it!) but not to others. Testing your questions provides you fake data. Are you getting the data in the way that you anticipated?

8. *Word questions so that you can compare the data you collect with information collected in prior years' information, or with data from other programs.* There will be times that you find you need to reword a question. However, make changes only when needed as the ability to compare information across program years can help you to track program improvement.

9. *Ask simple questions that do not require complex calculations.* For example, ask people how often on average they met in the last month, rather than asking them to list each time they met, and for how long. Simple questions reduce the response burden on participants, and make it more likely that they will answer all your questions.

10. *Make surveys that are visually easy to follow.* Put your questions into sections that make sense and label them. Ensure that you have sufficient white space between sections and questions to aid in the readability of your survey.

Section summary

You may need to design questions for your mentoring program to evaluate program activities effectively. There is a science to constructing questions, and this section highlights effective practices.

Protect the data

An important decision that you will need to make is if your information will be anonymous or confidential. Anonymous means that no one, including you, knows who provided each response. Confidential means that you might know who provided a response, but that you will keep that information in confidence and not share it with others. It is important to clarify for participants what will be anonymous, and what will be confidential, as this may influence the honesty of responses.

Where possible, collect anonymous information so that participants feel comfortable sharing negative and positive experiences. Online or paper surveys can be anonymous. Obviously, interviews and focus groups are not anonymous, neither are photographs. A best practice is to replace real names with fake ones. You never know who will have your job after you, and it is important to protect participants from potential harm in sharing information on a survey or in an interview.

Conclusion

Use data-driven information to make decisions about your mentoring program success and future changes. Use the information in this chapter to determine what to collect, when to collect it, from whom, and how. Develop a plan to collect information about your mentoring program activities using different methods, which provides converging data to guide program changes and recruit future participants. Develop a practice of sharing results with your participants and stakeholders, so they can see the value of providing you information.

Key terms

- Anonymous
- Confidential
- Comparison groups or control groups
- Dosage
- Halo effect
- Methods: archival analysis, focus groups, interviews, naturalistic observation, photographic evidence, surveys
- Overconfidence
- Sunk-cost fallacy
- People
- Processes
- Resources

Check your learning

1. How many mentoring activities and outcomes need a measurement?
2. What is the best way to measure mentoring dosage for your program?
3. What methods can you use to collect information regarding your mentoring program activities and outcomes other than surveys?
4. When is the best time to collect information from the participants in your mentoring program?

Resources

The Science of Effective Mentorship in STEMM – Program Assessment & Assessments by Career Stage (scroll to the bottom of the webpage):
https://www.nap.edu/resource/25568/interactive/program-development-and-management.html#section3
Harvard University Program on Survey Research. Tip Sheet:
https://psr.iq.harvard.edu/book/questionnaire-design-tip-sheet
Pew Research Center. Questionnaire Design:
https://www.pewresearch.org/methods/u-s-survey-research/questionnaire-design/
Understanding and Evaluating Survey Research:
https://www.ncbi.nlm.nih.gov/pmc/articles/PMC4601897/
Free Survey Software:
Google Forms: www.google.com/forms/about/
SurveyMonkey: www.surveymonkey.com
Zoomerang: www.zoomerang.com

Notes

1 https://grad.ncsu.edu/programs/
2 https://isa.ncsu.edu/facts-comparisons/fast-facts/

References

Allen, T. D., L. T. Eby, K. E. O'Brien, and E. Lentz. 2008. "The State of Mentoring Research: A Qualitative Review of Current Research Methods and Future Research Implications." *Journal of Vocational Behavior* 73(3): 343–357.

Baugh, S. G., and E. A. Fagenson-Eland. 2007. "Formal Mentoring Programs." In *The Handbook of Mentoring at Work: Theory, Research, and Practice*, edited by B. R. Ragins and K. E. Kram, 249–271. Los Angeles, CA: Sage Publications.

David, M. S., D. Clutterbuck, and M. D. Megginson. 2013. *Beyond Goals: Effective Strategies for Coaching and Mentoring*. Farnham, UK: Gower.

Dillman, D. A. 2011. *Mail and Internet Surveys: The Tailored Design Method*. New York: John Wiley & Sons.

Ensher, E. A., and S. E. Murphy. 1997. "Effects of Race, Gender, Perceived Similarity, and Contact on Mentor Relationships." *Journal of Vocational Behavior* 50(3): 460–481.

Ensher, E. A., and S. E. Murphy. 2011. "The Mentoring Relationship Challenges Scale: The Impact of Mentoring Stage, Type, and Gender." *Journal of Vocational Behavior* 79(1): 253–266.

Kahneman, D. 2011. *Thinking, Fast and Slow.* New York: Macmillan.

Kahneman, D., D. Lovallo, and O. Sibony. 2011. "Before You Make that Big Decision." *Harvard Business Review* 89(6): 50–60.

Kipling, R. 1899. From Sea to Sea and Other Sketches, Letters of Travel. Project Gutenburg. https://www.gutenberg.org/files/32977/32977-h/32977-h.htm.

Kirkpatrick, D. L. 1979. "Techniques for Evaluating Training." *Training & Development Journal* 33(6): 78–92.

Lunsford, L. G. 2011. "Psychology of Mentoring: The Case of Talented College Students." *Journal of Advanced Academics* 22(3): 474–498.

Lunsford, L. G. 2012. "Doctoral Advising or Mentoring: Effects on Student Outcomes." *Mentoring & Tutoring: Partnership in Learning* 20(2): 251–270.

Lunsford, L. G. 2016. "Mentors as Friends." In *Psychology of Friendship,* edited by M. Hojjat and A. Moyer. New York: Oxford University Press.

NC State University. n.d. The Pathway to the Future: NC State's 2011–2020 Strategic Plan. https://strategicplan.ncsu.edu/archive/pathway-to-the-future/index.html (accessed August 16, 2021).

Chapter 8

Step 5: Create your success story

Change before you have to. (Jack Welch in Belasen et al. 2016, 292)

Learning is not compulsory... Neither is survival. (Edwards Deming in Voehl 1995, 125)

Introduction

The final step to creating an effective mentoring program is to share the successes and make incremental improvements. Your mentoring program is more likely to thrive and be sustainable if others know of its success. Sharing about the program's success will help you to recruit future participants, rally others to be an ambassador for your program, and secure future funding for the program.

You worked hard to collect the right data (see Chapter 7). Now you can put that data to work for you to decide which activities need to be eliminated or improved. Not so long ago, organizational and managerial practice was guided by the saying "If it ain't broke, don't fix it." The current thinking is that you had better break it before your competitors do. As noted earlier, CEO and chairman of General Electric, Jack Welch, and renowned strategy guru Edwards Deming assert that change is required to keep up with your competitors. The quickening pace of change and the globalization of business and education also contribute to a need for change. Or as Senge (2006) writes in the *Fifth Discipline*, a learning organization is "an organization that is continually expanding its capacity to create its future... it is not enough merely to survive" (14).

It might be easy to understand that businesses need to maintain their competitive advantage. Yet so too nonprofit organizations and academic institutions need to maintain a competitive advantage. These organizations may not be focused on a profit margin but are expected to work better, and more efficiently, if they hope to attract students, donors, and volunteers to their cause. The COVID-19 pandemic has quickened the pace of tightening budgets. In addition, governments all over the world seek to limit budgets,

DOI: 10.4324/9781003163862-8

which influences the competitive advantage of governmental and not-for-profit organizations.

Mentoring programs exist as part of an organizational strategy to achieve organizational goals. Thus, mentoring programs are one way that organizations promote organizational learning to facilitate individual and organizational change. As a program manager you have a responsibility to share the successes and make improvements to your mentoring program to be responsive to these organizational realities.

The aim of this chapter is to identify what is successful (and to change what is not) so that you can share your success story with your stakeholders. It discusses answers to questions such as:

- Why do I need a success story?
- How do I create a success story?
- What and how do I improve (and it is not everything!)?
- How can I sustain support for improvement efforts?
- How can my mentoring program promote a culture of mentoring in my organization?

Why do I need a success story?

The work involved in mentoring programs is often invisible to others. Thus, such work may be taken for granted. You need to tell others about the success of the mentoring program efforts to increase engagement, demonstrate a good return on investment, and increase the program visibility. Funders might expect a report to learn if the mentoring program was successful in achieving the desired objectives.

Stories provide a memorable and compelling way to communicate about your mentoring program to stakeholders. Long, tedious reports are rarely read and are time-intensive to produce. Programs funded by grants may need to provide such detailed reports; however, it will still benefit you to create the "fast facts" of your program's success. Use your theory of change and data collection efforts to tell the story of transformation for participants and the organization. Part of developing your success story is identifying areas for improvement.

Usually, improvement is warranted for one of three reasons. First, it might be the case that the needs of the participants have changed. An effective mentoring program started in 2010 may not be effective now because of advances in technology, new experiences, or generational expectations.

Second, the organization's goals may have changed, thus necessitating a change in the mentoring program's goals. Perhaps your organization has achieved its early goals and has set new ones that suggest different needs for mentoring. Alternatively, it might be that the organizational climate has changed in some way that warrants a refocus of the mentoring program efforts. For example, a division may have received permission to hire a significant number of new employees. An existing mentoring program might be refocused to help orient these new employees successfully into the division.

Third, your program may need to change certain activities to use resources better or to achieve the program's goals. It might be that your program is new, and you are slowly adding to it over time, or your evaluation suggests that certain activities or processes are no longer effective.

Section summary

Tell your stakeholders about the success of your mentoring program by crafting a story about the transformation the program has supported. Sharing your success story will increase program engagement and secure resources for its continued operation. Mentoring programs need to change to be responsive to individual and organizational needs and goals. Improvement efforts will help you to be a good steward of program resources.

Create a success story

Collecting the right data (see Chapter 7) will enable you to create a compelling success story. Some funders or organizations may require a more detailed written report. I recommend you develop a one-page infographic or executive summary with visuals to share your program successes.

Refer back to your logic model (developed in Chapter 5). Select evidence that supports the elements in your logic model. Create a one-page summary that presents the following information:

- A one-paragraph description of the mentoring program that covers:
  - Dates and length of the program
  - Outcomes and goals of the program
  - Who participated and type of mentoring (1:1, peer, group)
  - Activities
- Photograph(s) of participants at events or activities
- Quote from mentor or mentee that highlights an outcome
- Tables or charts (two) to illustrate survey data on outcomes or impact
- Organizational brand or logo and mentoring program name

I often ask program coordinators to imagine the success story at the beginning of the program. What photos, quotes, and tables might demonstrate success? Envisioning your success story at the beginning of the program can guide your data collection efforts.

You can design your success story using word processing software. Or consider freely available design software like Canva to create a template you can reuse. Is there a graphic designer in the communications department of your organization who can create a template for you?

A word about little evidence for success. Is every mentoring program a success that needs to be shared? Research suggests that are many ineffective programs or programs that have small effects on participants. However, if you have followed the steps in this handbook, you are more likely to create transformations for people and for the organization. If you find little evidence for success, then you may have missed a step in the design phase related to your theory of change. Or it could be the case that activities were not fully implemented. Creating a success story may involve identifying the change needed to realize desired outcomes. The logic model you created along with the data you collected will pinpoint the problem area(s).

What and how to improve?

Improvement efforts often focus on what is not working well, or what some scholars call "closing the deficit gap," or taking a "deficit-based approach" (Cameron and Lavine 2006, 28). This section first returns to the importance of the mentoring ecosystem (refer to Chapter 2) to make improvement decisions. Second, two perspectives from psychology may support effective program improvement: the abundance perspective and small wins strategy.

The mentoring ecosystem

Chapter 2 presented the idea of a mentoring ecosystem (see Figure 2.1). Formal mentoring programs are embedded in organizations with contexts and are enacted through individuals who are part of these contexts. Improvement efforts often focus on the micro activities in a mentoring program: that is, the activities that relate to what is happening in the mentoring dyad. The mentoring ecosystem highlights the importance of improving your program at both the micro and macro levels (Shadish 2004, 95).

A micro-level focus will examine the discrete mentoring program activities or aspects of mentoring participants' experiences (e.g., satisfaction, skills). A macro-level focus places attention on the overall mentoring program outcomes and how they align with, and are supported by, the organization. A focus on both levels is needed for program improvement. This perspective acknowledges that individual experiences may be influenced by organizational contexts and vice versa. The mentoring ecosystem highlights how improvement efforts can consider individual experiences, as well as the alignment of mentoring program outcomes and organizational goals.

Review the goals for your mentoring program. You should be able to align these goals with one or more of your organizational goals. Creating that alignment will situate your program in the organization's strategic initiatives to achieve overarching goals. Such alignment will help you to make the case for resources and make improvements if there is misalignment.

Examine the processes and procedures in your department or organizations. Do they fully support your mentoring efforts? When I consult with organizations, I review their employee or student handbooks. I find mentoring rarely mentioned in such documents. A systematic study I conducted with colleagues confirmed my anecdotal experience. We reviewed 100 tenure and promotion documents for faculty members in universities that had paid to join the Council on Undergraduate Research (CUR). Only 14 of these institutions, which purported to value undergraduate research, mentioned undergraduate research in their faculty members' evaluation criteria (Baker et al. 2017). Your efforts are misaligned with the organizational goals when mentoring is not documented in your organizational processes.

There is a cautionary note about improving your mentoring program. Examining the structures in the mentoring ecosystem that support mentoring may help you to avoid maintaining an undesired status quo through mentorship. As described in Chapter 11, mentoring programs may perpetuate an unacceptable organizational status quo that limits participation in mentoring to certain groups of people. Monitor improvement efforts to be sure that a change will benefit all participants or at least that it will not favor some participants over others. Before you enact a change, consider if the change will increase access to mentoring for diverse groups, rather than limit it. Will the proposed change make the mentoring program easier for protégés and mentors to engage?

The abundance approach

A focus on exemplars is useful in directing our attention on what to change. A deficit-based model, where you seek to identify and fix problems, will only move your mentoring program to an average, steady state. Cameron and Lavine (2006) documented compelling examples of exemplars, which they refer to as an "abundance approach," to drive improvement efforts. This approach focuses on what is working exceptionally well to identify the elements of success that can be shared with others.

The abundance approach suggests that assessment and evaluation need to be designed to identify the exemplars, or what is working extraordinarily well in your mentoring program. For example, can you answer these questions?

- Are there mentoring dyads that appeared to benefit greatly from participation?
- Did certain program activities go better than expected?

Your goal might be to talk with these extraordinary participants to identify what made their relationship so successful. As you learn about their experiences, you can decide what to share about their practices with future participants. Relatedly, you might examine what made a program activity so successful and attempt to duplicate those key elements in other program activities.

This approach highlights the areas of your mentoring program that might warrant sharing with other units in your organization. This dissemination, or sharing, of best practice can support the development of a mentoring culture (as described in Chapter 3) in your organization.

Leverage small wins

Having the time to implement changes can feel overwhelming or time-consuming. Using the strategy of "small wins" will help you focus on making small, incremental changes that are not overwhelming.

Make small, incremental changes

A classic article in the social change literature is about small wins (Weick 1984). The idea is that small changes are less stressful, so small changes may increase the performance of the individuals who experience these changes. Weick defines a small win as "a concrete, complete, implemented outcome of moderate importance" (43). One such change may seem unimportant, but the power is in the pattern of cumulative small wins, which attract little attention yet add up to meaningful change. Small changes are like small experiments where you can determine if a new activity or process works or not.

Small changes are effective for two reasons. First, we are limited in how much information we can process and handle at one time. A small change enables people to understand and operationalize the change. In contrast, a big change can be frustrating when protégés or mentors try to master a new way of interacting or participating in a mentoring program. People are more likely to comply with small changes and experience these more positively. Second, this approach allows you to "fail small." Even if a small change is not positive, it will not be as memorable as a big change that fails. We feel good when we experience success and bad when we experience failure. Small failures will not derail your work.

Thus, one of the best strategies for improving your mentoring program is to make small, frequent changes rather than one large change (Case Study 8.1 is an example of the effectiveness of this approach: Elmhurst University has an effective monthly mentoring activity report, yet it was refined over many years, using a small-win strategy responsive to participants' feedback).

Case Study 8.1 Getting to gold at Elmhurst University

Gold certified

Even a cursory conversation with Larry Carroll, Executive Director of the Center for Professional Excellence, or Julie Gonzales, former Assistant Director of Education Enrichment Programs, leaves you wanting to know more about mentoring. Their program gives you an appreciation of what a great mentoring program can do, for both its participants and an institution. The mentoring initiative focuses on developing individuals into better professionals who will make a difference in the world. It is an academic year mentoring program for undergraduates and working professionals.

Elmhurst University's mentoring program was the first to be accredited as a high-quality program (Gold Accreditation) by the International Mentoring Association (IMA). The Center for Professional Excellence (CPE) is the home department for the successful mentoring program.

An elementary start

Carroll started the program in 1997, with what he claims were "elementary forms" developed after he attended an IMA conference. As he tells it, "We wanted students to recognize this was a learning experience, and that they were partners in their development." This goal has driven the program development and assessment. The mentor and protégé activity forms are examples of an effective, multipurpose tool that continue to be developed.

Continuous improvement

Initially, only the protégés completed an activity report, which was designed to encourage a protégé to reflect about their self. Soon after implementation of this form, the mentors said that they were learning as much as the student. Thus, mentors and protégés now submit an activity report. As Gonzales noted: "There may be communication between the mentor and protégé during school breaks, and we want to know if they are still communicating."

The activity report lets the program coordinator know if relationships get off track or become dysfunctional. Gonzales used the forms to encourage individuals to reflect and provide her insight into the relationship. "We gather this data to see changes, and we will contact them if the relationship is rated lower." Gonzales noted, "I read the reports thoroughly and address any concerns quickly." For example, she observed discrepancies when a mentor reports that everything is fine, while the protégé does not. She then would reach out to the protégé to coach him or her on how to talk with their mentor.

The report also guides mentoring participants on topics to discuss and action plans. The end of the activity report asks mentoring participants to indicate the date of the next meeting. This simple technique ensures that a subsequent meeting is planned. Failure to set the next meeting is one way student mentoring programs can quickly get off track.

A skills assessment exercise and SMART goal development worksheet with an action plan were added to the activity forms, because mentors wanted to better support protégés but were not sure what to discuss. Skills assessments help protégés report skills they might focus on or how these skills match up with desired careers. The SMART goal worksheet with an action plan helps to keep them focused and measure goal success.

Will they go platinum?

Carroll thinks often about how to improve the mentoring program. Carroll said:

> Let me give you a dream. We are committed to having our students participate in international studies. When recruiting mentors, we seek professionals who understand the importance of international learning opportunities in preparing students for the world of work and work with them to see how global experiences can be part of their professional development.

The IMA may need to develop a platinum-level accreditation for this program in the future. Carroll's institutional knowledge and lengthy tenure have provided an important foundation for this program. Elmhurst's mentoring program illustrates three lessons for program coordinators:

1   great programs continue to evolve;
2   data-driven programs allow for the tailoring of mentoring; and
3   collection of the right data can dramatically improve a program.

Mentoring Forms:
https://www.elmhurst.edu/academics/career-education/mentoring-
and-shadowing/
IMA accreditation:
https://mentoringassociation.org/program-accreditation/
Source: Interview with Larry Carroll, Professor Business
Administration and former Executive Director of the Center for
Professional Excellence, and Julie Gonzales, former Assistant Director
of Education Enrichment Programs, Elmhurst University.

Improvement is iterative

Iterative improvement builds on the idea of a small win. It means that you make small changes as you regularly review your mentoring program. You do not need to wait until the end of a mentoring program cycle to make a small change; instead, you engage in process improvement as you receive feedback about the program activities and outcomes. For example, consider an early mentoring check-in, which reveals that 10 percent of your protégés are reporting neglectful experiences. Iterative improvement means that you intervene with these dyads before the program ends, check in with them again in a month, and create a process to reduce this frequency of dysfunction in the next program cycle. You might also review evaluations on the program activities on a regular schedule to assess where improvements need to occur.

You may think of a mentoring program as a fixed activity that has a cycle with a beginning and an end – and be tempted to wait until the next cycle to make a change. However, consider when it also might be appropriate to make a change or adjustment during the cycle. View your mentoring program as an experiment, and you will be more comfortable making small changes. For example, you might dedicate 30 minutes each month to think about the mentoring program and reflect on questions such as:

*   What about this program works well and for whom?
*   What kinds of support seem more effective and at what time?

Your answers might point to areas where a change is warranted in the current cycle of your mentoring program.

Section summary

The mentoring ecosystem highlights the importance of examining micro and macro influences on your mentoring program. Ensure that proposed changes increase access to mentoring and that they do not support an organizational status quo that might limit access to mentoring. The abundance perspective requires you to focus on the exemplars, which provide models for what to improve. Improve your mentoring program with a small wins strategy to make small, frequent changes. Avoid a complete overhaul of your mentoring program all at one time, as such changes may frustrate or confuse program participants and other stakeholders.

Sustain improvement

Sustaining effective mentoring programs takes effort and more than a program coordinator. If your program is dependent on your presence, then it is unlikely to be sustained. Create the infrastructure to support the mentoring initiative and to ensure the knowledge about the mentoring program is shared by others. Establishing institutional policies to support mentoring and creating a group of engaged stakeholders are the best two actions to create sustainability. Further, such sustainability efforts will create a wider audience with whom to share your success story and further embed the mentoring program in the organizational culture.

Institutional policies

Institutional policies refer to the processes and rules people follow in your organization. Consider how your mentoring program is reflected or aligned with such policies. There are two approaches you can consider to embed your mentoring program in supportive institutional policies.

First, review existing policies and documents to determine where you can align your mentoring program to them. For example, what items in your organization's strategic plan might be supported by formal mentorship? I usually first search for the term "mentor" on the institution's website and in targeted documents listed here. If I find nothing, I will scan the materials for phrases that might align with mentoring, even if the term is not used. For example, one of my university's strategic aims is to "develop faculty to become better teachers and scholars." This aim can easily be connected with a mentorship initiative. Such a review should take an hour or two and will be an investment that helps you align your program in a way that may connect it to needed resources.

There may also be policies and procedures for promotion or employee development. Examine such policies to see where mentorship might be aligned. For example, do some positions have an expectation of coaching or mentorship? If so, you might consider how to align your mentorship efforts to prepare those individuals to mentor others well. A list of common documents or policies to examine are as follows:

1. mission statement;
2. strategic plan; and
3. human resource employee handbooks, promotion policies, and key job descriptions.

Second, you may discover that your institution does not yet mention or appear to value mentorship in existing documents. Such a discovery means there is misalignment between your efforts and your organization's stated aspirations and deployment of resources. It is critical to advocate for the inclusion of mentorship in your institution's policies and plans if you wish the program to have stability and sustainability. I have worked with programs that lacked such institutionalization, and they disappear after the person who championed the program leaves the position or organization.

Share your success story with the individuals who have an interest in the organization achieving its strategic aims or supporting key policies. For example, send your success story to the head of your human resources department. Ask your boss to share the success story with the organizational leader. Is there a way to share your success story through an organizational newsletter to show how the mentorship efforts align with the organizational goals?

Advisory boards

Creating a group of ambassadors will help you to sustain your mentoring program and have advocates who will be glad to share your success story. An advisory board (or advisory committee) is one effective way to develop such ambassadors and to have a group of friendly critics. Sometimes, I hear groans from workshop participants when I mention "advisory board." Not everyone has had good experiences working with board members who may seek to micromanage or misunderstand their roles. You may view an advisory board as too much work for more unwanted oversight.

Advocate for a working board that will support you and mentorship without micromanaging. You may already have an advisory board or committee and may recognize its value in providing an outside perspective, being a friendly critic, and serving as great ambassadors. Or, it may be the case that you are in a department with an advisory board that could be "borrowed" to work with you as part of their purview. Consider establishing an advisory group for two reasons:

1. create sustainability for the mentoring effort; and
2. provide support for you.

A mentoring ecosystem highlights a need to establish the organizational infrastructure, to sustain program improvement efforts. The program manager's role is important, but what about when an experienced program manager leaves their position? You can institutionalize improvement efforts so that they continue even after you move on to your next opportunity. Establishing an advisory committee is one method to sustain effective mentoring programs.

There are also times that unpopular decisions need to be made. Having an advisory board as a sounding board, which can also back you up, will help you make those decisions. The rest of this section reviews the benefits of establishing an advisory board and tips for setting up and working with one.

Benefits

Some program managers fear that an advisory board will dictate or micromanage their work: that is not the kind of board being advocated for here. Your advisory board can be established such that it will support and sustain your mentoring program effectively. The board is advisory – as in they will provide advice, not dictates.

There are multiple benefits of an advisory board. First, engaging with a board once or twice a year will provide important reflection time for you. Meeting with such a board may help you step back from day-to-day operations and think broadly about mentoring program activities, participants, and alignment with organizational or institutional goals.

Second, an advisory board can help you identify your sphere of influence and perhaps even extend it. A board may provide an outside view of what you can reasonably expect to accomplish or improve. Further, board members may provide assistance in accessing resources for your mentoring program – they might be aware of institutional resources unknown to you.

Third, an advisory board can serve as spokespersons for your mentoring program. For example, they might help you educate stakeholders about the reasons for changes, especially if your program has been around for a while. They could be great ambassadors for your program, sharing successes and promoting formal and informal mentoring opportunities.

Fourth, an advisory board can provide protection for you if a change does not go as well as anticipated. Its members may attest that any proposed change was well considered and was in the organization's interest, even if it did not go well.

Establishing an advisory board

There are three steps to consider in setting up a board. The first step is to identify its purpose. Note that a board does not have to be solely dedicated to your mentoring program; there already may be a board or committee that handles similar tasks for your unit or department, and you might ask that group to provide advice to you on the mentoring program. In this case, you might request that their purpose be enlarged to provide advice about your mentoring program. For example, in a university there may be a graduate council that provides advice about a mentoring program for graduate students.

Three steps to establishing an advisory board

1. Identify the purpose.
2. Decide the categories and length of membership.
3. Recruit members.

Advisory boards usually handle tasks such as providing:

*   guidance about policies and practices in your mentoring program – for example, matching strategies;
*   connections to additional resources – for example, people or funding; and
*   advice about the program's expenses and outcomes.

An example of a board's purpose is listed in the following box. Note that this board is asked to set the requirements for mentors but otherwise provides recommendations and advice.

Example of purpose statement
As AACE puts it: "The Mentoring Success Advisory Committee (MAC) was created to provide oversight of the AACE International Mentoring Program and to promote participation [in] and support of the mentoring concept within the Association." The Mentoring Success Advisory Committee sets the requirements for mentors and makes recommendations regarding the administration and promotion of the mentoring program.
AACE International: www.aacei.org/career/mentor/committee.shtml

---

The second step is to decide the membership: who should serve and for how long. Identify categories of stakeholders who may be appropriate for membership. For example, a workplace mentoring program might include people from these categories:

- mentor,
- protégé,
- department head or director,
- human resource personnel, and
- a person outside your immediate organization or unit who has expertise in mentoring.

The board should be small enough that everyone feels they can make a contribution but large enough to provide a wide perspective. A group of 8–12 members is a good size.

Establish terms for members: two- to three-year terms will provide time for individuals to become familiar with your program. Consider rotating terms so that everyone does not rotate off at the same time. Decide if you will allow members to serve a consecutive term: it might be the case that you have a valuable member whom you do not wish to lose. However, there is also a benefit to involving different individuals to enlarge the program's circle of friends.

Third, recruit your members. You may ask stakeholders or department heads for recommendations of people in your target categories of membership. Prior mentoring participants might be good candidates, or they might provide recommendations of other individuals for membership. After your advisory board is established, you can rely on the members to provide nominations for membership. Write a letter of invitation that outlines the purpose of the advisory board, as well as their responsibilities to attend meetings and provide input.

Working with your advisory board

You can greatly influence the helpfulness of your advisory board through preparation and good communication. If you are clear in your communications about meetings and responsibilities, and use their time well to gain their input, then you will benefit from an advisory board.

Most boards need to meet only two or three times a year. State the meeting dates in the letter of appointment and keep your meetings short, one to two hours. Ask one of the board members to serve as the chair: He or she can consult with you about the agenda items for the meeting and will run it. All the best practices of running a meeting apply to your advisory board:

- provide an agenda and informational items a week in advance of the meeting – your agenda should note the requested discussion or action items;

- provide a summary of the recommendations soon after the meeting, along with the proposed actions you plan;
- make sure your meetings have time for discussion among members – if you spend most of the time talking, then you have wasted both their time and yours.

The value of the advisory board is to provide feedback on the mentoring program – not to hear exclusively about program successes.

Share successes

Improving mentoring also refers to contributing to a culture of mentoring in your organization. Sharing the successes of your mentoring program may provide role models, examples, and incentives for others to engage in mentoring interactions both formally and informally. Identify the core elements of your program that may be successful for other departments or units in your organization and promote this information to others in your organization.

You might use your success story to create a more detailed annual report that might be sent to "higher ups," your advisory board, and mentoring participants. Your goal is to use your success story to create a narrative that will contribute to an organizational culture that values mentoring. Remember that the story is about the participants' experiences and how they support individual and organizational goals. Thus, a newsletter might have photos of participants rather than a photo of the program manager.

Section summary

You are investing considerable time and resources to mentoring – help it to succeed in the future. Examine institutional aims, policies, and procedures that might align with mentorship efforts. Work with an advisory board, whose members may broaden your perspective on the mentoring program's activities and future.

Sharing successes requires you to recognize and collect compelling narratives of positive outcomes, learning, and successes. It is the story that emerges that is important. Visual information and quotes help you tell the story about your mentoring program to stakeholders and potential future participants.

Conclusion

This chapter is about how to create a success story that is the foundation of a narrative that can be shared with others. Success also means improving the practice of mentoring. Be a friendly critic of mentoring as you view your mentoring program as undergoing constant revision. Look for transformative experiences for participants that contribute to a positive culture of organizational learning. Consider how to leverage your mentorship success to align the program with institutional goals and to recruit a board of advisors who will be champions and supporters. Your creation of a success story makes it easy to share mentorship successes with others and sustain mentoring excellence.

Key terms

- Abundance approach
- Advisory board
- Incremental change
- Iterative change
- Small wins

Check your learning

1. Why is it important to create a success story for your mentoring program?
2. How might you go about making improvements in your mentoring program?
3. How does an abundance approach focus your attention on what to improve in your mentoring program?
4. How can a board of advisors help you create and tell your success story?

References

Baker, V. L., J. Greer, L. G. Lunsford, M. Pifer, D. A. Ihas. 2017. "Documenting the Aspiration Gap in Institutional Language about Undergraduate Research, Scholarship, and Creative Work." *Innovations in Higher Education* 42: 127–143. 10.1007/s10755-016-9372-9

Belasen, A. T., B. Eisenberg, and J. Huppertz. 2016. *Mastering Leadership: A Vital Resource for Healthcare Managers*. Burlington, MA: Jones & Bartlett Learning.

Cameron, K. S., and M. Lavine. 2006. *Making the Impossible Possible: Leading Extraordinary Performance: The Rocky Flats Story*. San Francisco, CA: Berrett-Koehler Publishers.

Senge, P. M. 2006. *The Fifth Discipline: The Art and Practice of the Learning Organization*. New York: Doubleday/Currency.

Shadish, W. R. Jr. 2004. "Program Micro- and Macro-Theories: A Guide for Social Change." *New Directions for Program Evaluation* 1987(33): 93–109.

Voehl, F. 1995. *Deming: The Way We Knew Him*. Boca Raton, FL: St Lucie Press.

Weick, K. E. 1984. "Small Wins: Redefining the Scale of Social Problems." *American Psychologist* 39(1): 40–49.

Part III

Enriching and strengthening the processes

Chapter 9

Support the beginning, middle, and end

Maybe a little disinterested in the kind of mentoring I had to offer.

Seemed responsive initially, but rarely followed through with plans we made.

He has never contacted me, although I tried to reach him several times. (Mentor responses on a post-mentoring program evaluation survey)

Introduction

Why were the experienced mentors quoted here unable to connect with their protégés at the early stages of their relationship? These comments are from a program evaluation of a year-long academic mentoring program. Unfortunately, comments such as the ones here are not uncommon. Why is it that mentors and protégés fail to connect initially? Why might a relationship fail to progress after a first meeting? How can you support mentors and protégés effectively from the beginning to the end of their mentoring relationship?

A mentoring relationship is like other relationships in that it develops over time. Scholars propose that this relationship development takes places over predictable, ordered stages. Individuals get to know one another, then they engage in activities together. Ultimately, all relationships will end, and this period can be a positive or negative experience for mentoring participants.

Researchers have found that program and relationship quality, rather than if mentoring is part of a formal program or not, predicts relationship outcomes and success (Eby et al. 2013). Thus, it is important that relational partners be equipped with the skills to engage successfully in the relationship. These skills change over the course of the relationship, as it moves from the beginning to the ending stage.

First, this chapter provides an overview of psychosocial developmental stage theory as a foundation to understand relationship stages. Next, the needs and related activities for the beginning, middle, and end of the

DOI: 10.4324/9781003163862-9

mentoring relationship are described. Finally, information about communication styles is provided.

Stage theory

Erik Erikson's (1968) theory of psychosocial development describes how healthy adult development proceeds through successful resolution of challenges over eight life stages. An understanding of stage theories in general, and Erikson's theory specifically, is useful for two reasons. First, mentoring scholars have drawn on this perspective, notably Kathy Kram (1985) in her seminal work on mentoring functions and stages of mentoring relationships. Thus, knowing about Erikson's theory of psychosocial development may help you understand stage theories for mentoring relationship development. Second, stage theories highlight why individuals might be motivated to participate in a mentoring relationship. This information may help you to support mentoring participants to address the key tasks in each stage of their relationship.

Erikson's psychosocial theory of development

According to Erikson's theory, individuals face a unique challenge that must be resolved at each of eight stages for healthy psychological development to occur (Erikson 1963). A person develops psychological strengths, such as love or wisdom, after successfully resolving each challenge. The stages occur in a predictable, cumulative order from childhood through late adulthood and are thought to be universal: that is, they apply to people in any culture (Erikson 1968). Progress in each stage relies on successful resolution of the challenge in the stage before it. The first four stages pertain to childhood up to adolescence. The last four stages relate to adolescence through late adulthood, which are described next in detail to highlight potential motivations for individuals who participate in mentoring. The four stages of *adult* development are:

Stage V   identity versus identity confusion;
Stage VI   intimacy versus isolation;
Stage VII   generativity versus stagnation; and
Stage VIII   integrity versus despair.

Stage V: Identity

Individuals may benefit most from a mentor during the period of identity development (Erikson 1968). Individuals must have a need which can be met by a more experienced person before they will seek a mentor (Levinson 1978; Vaillant 1977). This perspective highlights the protégé as an active participant who engages a mentor based on their identity needs. For example, individuals who are sure about their values and career choice (high identity commitment) may benefit from career support from a mentor, while someone with low identity commitment may not. A young adult who is unsure of his or her degree major may be reluctant to seek the advice of a faculty mentor, even if he or she is in an assigned program. The young person may be concerned that investing in mentoring would be a waste of time.

Stage VI: Intimacy

Women are more likely than men to develop their identity through their relationships with others (Josselson 1987). Women have been found to anchor their identity in their family of origin, new family (partner/spouse/children), career, or friends. You may wish to consider the extent to which intimacy needs are addressed in the mentoring program. For example, a discussion about work–life balance may be an important and needed topic of conversation for some individuals, depending on organizational support for families and on the life stage of the protégé.

Stage VII: Generativity

Generativity refers to the desire to leave a legacy. In mentoring relationships, this legacy may be achieved by investing in protégés. As mentioned previously, individuals often participate as mentors because of a desire to leave a legacy or give back to their community or profession; therefore, an understanding of generativity needs might help program managers recruit and retain mentors. For example, senior people benefit from feeling that they serve an important role in sharing knowledge with a younger generation.

Stage VIII: Integrity

Finally, integrity needs may be relevant in recruiting and retaining mentors. Integrity refers to the need to reflect on the whole of your life and career with a sense of satisfaction and accomplishment. Individuals are also quite active, even in retirement from their careers. There may be an opportunity to appeal to the integrity needs of older individuals, even those who have retired, to serve as mentors in your program.

Section summary

Individuals continue to develop as adults. Their life stages focus on predictable challenges, which can shed light on mentoring needs and motivations.

Stages of mentoring relationships

Just as individuals develop throughout their life, so do mentoring relationships evolve over time. Two well-known models of mentoring relationship stages by Kram and Clutterbuck are described here. These models are similar in that the stages follow the predictable order marking the beginning, middle, and end stages of mentoring relationships. A successful mentoring program supports participants at each stage. Table 9.1 summarizes the timing of stages and the key task and activities.

Kram's four-stage model

Kram (1985) first identified stages of mentoring relationships in her qualitative study of 18 mentoring dyads in a large utility company. She found that mentoring partners moved through four stages (Kram 1985) in their mentoring relationship:

1. initiation – development of interpersonal bonds; protégé looks for support and guidance while mentor looks for possible developmental opportunities;
2. cultivation – mentors provide challenging work, coaching, protection, and visibility while protégés develop increased competence;
3. separation – structural and psychological separation from mentoring partners; and
4. redefinition – informal interactions, possibly friendship evolves.

The stages proceed in order but may overlap. For example, individuals may

Table 9.1 Relationship stages, tasks, and activities

Timing	Stages	Tasks	Activities
Beginning	Initiation and goal setting	Develop rapport	Share background experiences, values, and learning preferences. Identify relationship purpose or goals.
Middle	Cultivation or progress making	Learn to collaborate	Select a topic or activity on which to collaborate.
End	Separation and redefinition or winding up and moving on	Reflect and learn	Reflect on lessons learned, identify future professional development needs. Transition to relationship that is collegial, friendship, or ad hoc. Check in occasionally to maintain the connection.

be still getting to know one another as they start the work together in the cultivation stage. In her original study, Kram reported that these naturally occurring relationships lasted between three and five years, which affects the timing of these stages. More recently, researchers have found these stages to occur in formal mentoring programs with shorter durations (Weinberg and Lankau 2011).

Clutterbuck's five-stage model

At about the same time, Clutterbuck identified five stages of mentoring relationships (his book is now in its fifth edition; Clutterbuck 2014):

1. initiation – where rapport and trust are established;
2. goal setting – the purpose or goals of the relationship are established;
3. progress making – which is marked by interchange and learning;
4. winding up – the dyads review what they have achieved and their plans to move forward, either independently or together;
5. moving on – from the mentoring relationship; how mentors and protégés decide to interact together in the future, if at all.

Section summary

Mentoring relationships progress through stages. They are marked by a beginning, middle, and end. Mentors and protégés will benefit from understanding that different tasks are required in each stage.

Beginning: Initiation and goal setting

Initiation

Program managers tend to devote much of their attention to activities that precede relationship formation – perhaps this allocation of effort is related to a desire to get the program going. For example, you might focus on developing recruitment materials to identify the right participants who will benefit from the mentoring program. I have witnessed program managers expend considerable effort on matching potential mentors and protégés (there is software for that!).

You might provide a guide to facilitate the first meeting, perhaps with suggestions about what to discuss. This support is especially important for new or less skilled mentors and protégés who may not know what to discuss and, as a result, fail to develop the rapport needed to move the relationship forward.

In both Kram's and Clutterbuck's stage models, the period of initiation refers to the start of the relationship, when mentors and protégés meet and get to know one another. Rapport is the key task during initiation. Development of trust and psychological safety create rapport. It is through early conversations that rapport is established. Mentors and protégés need to discover their shared values; trust is cultivated through conversations about their personal or work history, background experiences, and personal preferences. Such trust provides a foundation for individuals to share and receive critical feedback, and for learning to take place in the later stages.

Kram (1985) reported that the period of initiation might last 6–12 months; yet in modern mentoring programs, 12 months might be the duration of the entire program. Some organizations have shortened the time even further by having six-week (Lunsford, 2016) or three-month formal mentoring programs (Wanberg et al. 2003). Thus, support is important during the initiation stage to facilitate individuals getting to know one another quickly, especially in formal mentoring programs of shorter durations.

Initiation may begin during a matching period if protégés and mentors have an opportunity to select one another through a pre-mentoring meeting, a reception, or online information. You can make a difference in the success of mentoring relationships by encouraging mentors and protégés to be intentional in how they begin their relationship. When trust is lacking in either the mentor or protégé, then there may be disinterest in meeting or investing in the relationship.

Provide appropriate resources to individuals directly. For example, new mentors in a formal, organizational mentoring program might be more interested in developing their communication skills than experienced senior faculty at a university. Mentors and protégés may have different levels of skills. You can help mentors and protégés ask the right questions. Suggested prompts for a first meeting are:

1. "What I wish you knew about me is that..." or "What do you wish your [mentor/protégé] knew about you?" (adapted from Strauss 2015);
2. "My top three items in each category of 'must have' and 'can't stand' are...";
3. "I tend to... [be on time, procrastinate] and prefer [face-to-face meetings, communicating through e-mail]";
4. "My motivation for participating in this mentoring program is...."

Goal setting

Goal setting is a separate stage in the Clutterbuck (2014) model. Goal setting refers to an emphasis on moving the relationship forward, from getting to know one another to establishing a shared purpose or goals. In other words, a relationship needs its own identity or purpose, if both relational partners believe their time together will be a worthwhile investment. Effective relationships are marked by a goal or purpose that aligns with the aspirations, needs, and competencies of the mentor and protégé.

For example, a mentor may desire to give back to a younger professional. Their protégé might have more instrumental or concrete goals that relate to producing learning a new skill to be considered for a promotion. What is important is that both relational partners reflect on and recognize the purpose of their relationship in a formal mentoring program.

Practitioners and researchers have developed models to set, manage, and track goal-setting activities in an organizational context. The GROW and SMART models are perhaps the best-known tools used in coaching and mentoring relationships. The GROW model was developed by Whitmore (2002) in the United Kingdom and presents a sequence of questions. The model for a SMART goal was developed in the United States and refers to characteristics against which goals can be assessed (David et al. 2013, 23).

GROW model

The GROW model stands for:

Goal setting
Reality checking
Options and alternatives
What is to be done, when, and who will do it (David et al. 2013, 22).

The model provides a framework to develop questions related to goal setting. It may be difficult to disentangle the difference between the goals for the relationship and the goals of the individuals. The GROW model focuses on individual goals, but it may be useful to consider the goals for the relationship and how they match up against the GROW standards. Individual goals need to align with, and support, the achievement of the relationship goals.

For example, a shared goal might be for a mentor and protégé to publish a paper or develop a project proposal together. In this case, a good relationship goal will help the mentor and protégé accomplish their individual aspirations. A mentor might wish to demonstrate his or her ability to mentor a novice, while a protégé might desire to learn how to prepare a manuscript for publication.

Using the GROW model, the mentor and protégé may devote a meeting to brainstorming the best possible outcomes from their work together. Identifying the ideal outcome can be a motivating and inspiring experience. Both short and long-term goals would be part of this discussion, along with developing a timeline designating when mentors and protégés can check in on their progress. They may then run a reality check to ascertain if they have the resources or skills to accomplish this project together. Perhaps the protégé will need to take a workshop or course, or learn a new skill.

Options might be examined by determining if writing a paper together is the best way to achieve their individual and relational goals. They might find that a shorter technical paper or a presentation would be better to accomplish the goals and use their resources.

Finally, goal setting involves critique of, and reflection on, the "Ws" of what is to be done, when, who will do it, and the motivation for the work to be accomplished. Again, establishing a timeline is helpful to assess progress.

SMART goals

The SMART model refers to goals that are:

Specific
Measurable
Attainable
Realistic
Time-bound.

Specific goals include details. Measurable means that the goal is sufficiently specific to allow for it to be measured or assessed. Attainable means that the goal is possible to achieve in the time frame specified. Realistic goals are ones that can be accomplished with current resources (e.g., materials or people). Time-bound refers to a deadline, often with milestones to achieve the goal.

Consider a protégé who wishes to learn from his or her mentor how to select and supervise a team for an upcoming software project. A SMART goal might be that he or she wishes to learn how to select and motivate her team. This goal will need to be broken into two components: selection and motivation. A more specific goal would be for him or her to work with human resources to come up with a recruitment and interview process to select five team members in the next month.

The downside of goals

You have an essential role in helping mentors and protégés determine what kind of goals are needed and when it is best to set them. However, there is a concern that goals can be too specific or limiting (David et al. 2013, 25) – there are times when goals need to be changed, and adherence to outdated or irrelevant goals may be counterproductive in these cases. It is possible to become so focused on the specifics of the goal and measuring progress that the overarching learning goals become neglected.

There are also times when the value of a mentoring relationship is the space that it provides for reflection or time to think about what is important. Having flexibility to engage in thinking, rather than reporting on goals, may be important in supporting mentoring participants to achieve the mentoring program goals. The benefit of some mentoring relationships is that they help a protégé explore possible futures or develop a career vision. In these cases, setting goals too early may result in a rigid adherence to inappropriate goals, which might be counterproductive; or the relationship purpose might be best served by having time for goals to emerge.

Supporting appropriate goals

This section is about providing communication resources for your participants, such as guiding questions or conversation starters. There are specific ways that you can support mentors and protégés in the initiation stage of relationships.

1. Provide questions to identify experiences, learning preferences, and shared values. Provide suggested questions or conversation topics for the first and second meetings that focus on sharing their values, background experiences, and learning preferences. These questions reflect organizational goals for the mentoring program. Questions about work history might be more appropriate in a formal mentoring program for a corporation, while educational experiences might be appropriate to share in a college or university setting.
2. Provide suggested questions or conversation topics to discuss the purpose of their relationship and goal setting.
   a. "At the end of our relationship, I hope we have..."
   b. "In two years, I hope to look back on this relationship and be grateful that..."
   c. "What I most need help with is..."
   d. "The way I expect to be different after meeting with you is..."
3. Encourage mentors and protégés to discuss their relationship progress at the end of their second meeting. Establish an early check-in and support relational partners to determine if the relationship should go forward or if they should have a "no-fault divorce" (Ragins et al. 2012, 9).
4. Encourage participants to ask themselves "how often are you talking when you interact in your mentoring relationship?" (Watch out for one person dominating the conversation.)

Managing difficult starts

Even the best mentoring programs will not have a 100 percent success rate. There are times when unexpected life events may make a mentor or protégé unavailable, and have less time than he or she thought. At other times, there may be a mismatch in protégé and mentor needs and competencies. Your role as a program manager is important when relationships do not get off to a great start. A program manager can turn what seems like a failure into both a learning opportunity and a success (as illustrated in Case Study 3.1 in Chapter 3).

The best strategies involve being proactive in preparing for inevitable relationship challenges. Many challenges may be avoided by selecting the right mentors and protégés, and by briefing them fully on the program expectations (see Chapter 6 for more details on these points). Identify problems early by establishing regular times to check-in on relationship progress. In addition, develop an established process by which mentoring participants can leave the program gracefully before it is over, including a provision for reassignment if possible. You can check in with both mentors and protégés within the first month of the formal mentoring program: It can be done informally through a telephone call or e-mail. Some programs use an activity log or tracking report submitted by mentors and protégés that indicates their meeting frequency and conversation topic. Such a report can be submitted efficiently online, through e-mail, or on paper.

There may be times where you must react and handle a poor mentoring match. In these cases, it is best to help the protégé or mentor make a change quickly to another mentoring relationship, and to avoid placing blame on either individual.

Section summary

Building rapport and arriving at a common understanding of goals and expectations are the key tasks in the beginning stage of any mentoring relationship. You can provide mentoring participants with goal setting models such as SMART or GROW frameworks. Goals may also need to be adjusted. Put in place program processes to prevent or manage relationship difficulties.

Middle stage

Program managers often provide less support to mentors and protégés on how to cultivate their relationship through the middle stage. Yet most of the work of the relationship is done after protégés and mentors come to know one another. This period of the relationship is when engagement can transform participants and may be the productive one. High-quality relationships can be characterized by engagement and collaboration.

Successful progress in the middle stage depends crucially on the goals for the relationship established in the beginning. As mentioned previously, Kram (1983) notes that the stage of cultivation is when the work of the relationship takes place, while Clutterbuck (2014) refers to this time as "progress making." Mentors and protégés now have a shared sense of purpose for their meetings, which take place as needed to achieve relational goals. It is a time when learning takes place and helpful feedback is shared. Conversations reflect more of an interchange, rather than a directive from mentor to protégé.

The career functions of mentoring help individuals interact and come to know each other, which also may promote development of the psychosocial functions of mentoring. Remember that individuals need to have a certain amount of trust to engage in the relationship. The psychosocial value of the relationship may emerge fully after productive interactions with one another. Researchers have found collaboration on projects or goals to be an important behavior that propels the relationship forward (Lunsford 2014).

During the middle stage it may be appropriate for mentors and protégés to revisit and even revise the goals for their relationship. It might be the case that a goal was too ambitious and needs to be adjusted. Mentors or protégés may take on new roles in their organization, which requires an adjustment in the mentoring relationship activities. In an academic setting a student protégé may change their major, which might suggest that a different mentor is needed. You can support this process by informally or formally checking in to ask if the relationship is on track, or asking protégés and mentors to report on their products and progress to date. Table 9.2

Table 9.2 Check-in questions during the middle stage

Questions	Possible responses options
Describe the most beneficial aspect of your mentoring relationship to date.	Open-ended question *or select one:* Career advice/Learning a new skill/Confidence building/Encouragement/Other [list]
Describe the least beneficial aspect of your mentoring relationship to date.	Open-ended question *or select one:* Useless advice/Infrequency of meetings/Conversations go on too long/Other [list]
In what areas would you like more support from mentorship?	Specific skills, such as… [list]Networking with others/Specific advice on… [list]
My progress on the goals for the mentoring relationship are _____ of schedule.	*Select one:* Behind, On Track, Ahead
Describe the professional goals you discussed during the past month.	Open-ended question
Indicate the number of times you communicated with your mentor/protégé in the past month (face to face, email, text, etc.).	Numerical list from 0 to 20

presents sample questions that might be appropriate for checking in during the middle stage of a mentoring relationship (Thomas et al. 2015).

If your program is new, you might want to use open-ended responses when you check in with mentoring participants. This approach will identify possible categories for a short survey with fixed responses in future years. You can develop drop-down lists on relevant goals for your mentoring program for some of the questions, when possible. A check-in can be an informal way for you to monitor relationship progress; you can use this information as well to assess program success (see Chapter 8 for more information about assessing program success). For example, you might ask participants if they have had an initial meeting (yes, no, planned in the next week) and if they have set up their next meeting (yes, no). To check-in on relationship progress you might ask mentees if they are "behind," "on-track," or "ahead" of their planned schedule for achieving their goals.

During this time, mentors and protégés should intentionally think about what opportunities might be growth experiences for both individuals. For example, a mentor might support a protégé to present his or her ideas to the leaders in their department or to other scholars at a conference. A growth experience for the mentor might involve working for the first time with a junior person to co-author a paper, co-direct a project together, or engage in group or peer mentoring.

Section summary

The work of the relationship is completed during the middle stage. Collaboration is an important behavior if products are produced. The mentoring functions of psychosocial and career support are fully realized during this time of the relationship. You can promote progress during the middle stages by checking in and asking relevant questions about frequency of interaction, topics discussed, and progress made on goals.

Ending stages

A formal program usually marks endings of relationships, if they have the resources, with an event that recognizes its participants and celebrates their work together. There is an opportunity for program managers to support mentoring participants on how to bring their relationship successfully to an end, or transition to friendship.

Kram (1985) refers to "separation" and "redefinition" as two stages that mark the end of mentoring relationships. Similarly, Clutterbuck (2014) refers to "winding up" and "moving on" as the stages that denote the conclusion of a mentoring relationship. In formal mentoring programs, a structural separation occurs when the program ends. However, note that separation refers to structural and psychological separation. Mentors and protégés who discuss their plans to end the relationship report more positive mentoring experiences (Lancer, Megginson and Clutterbuck 2016). These individuals shared what they learned in the relationship and their future personal development goals. More negative mentoring experiences are characterized by protégés and mentors who simply drifted away from one another (Johnson and Nelson 1999, 206).

The end of formal mentoring means there is a structural separation where the protégés and mentor are no longer expected to meet. The time of separation may lead to anxiety, and even a sense of loss, at the end of the relationship. Mentors have been known to block the progress of their protégés in an attempt to avoid separation. For example, in doctoral education, advisors who are loath to separate may state that their protégé is not ready to defend their dissertation. In organizational settings, mentors with protégés in their departments may block promotion or moves to other areas of the organization. It is also natural to feel sadness or even grief at the separation of a mentoring relationship, and individuals may be unprepared for these feelings (Lunsford et al. 2013, 10).

Redefinition is a time when the relationship develops into another kind of relationship, or it ends altogether – this stage has an indefinite time period. Many individuals become friends with their mentor or protégé, and there may be an initial, awkward period of adjustment to their becoming peers. In other cases, there is little to no contact between individuals. Similarly, moving on refers to the transition of the relationship into a more informal, ad hoc relationship. In Case Study 9.1 we see how Robin Milne redefined her mentoring relationship with her protégé, who went on to take Robin's top job at Phoenix Suns Charities. (The case study is an example of how mentors may intentionally navigate the stages of a mentoring relationship.)

Case Study 9.1   Points or assist? A mentoring playbook

Robin Milne, former Executive Director of Phoenix Suns Charities, wrote the playbook when it comes to intentional mentoring at each stage of the relationship. The Suns Charities was started in 1988 as the philanthropic arm of the National Basketball Association's Phoenix Suns team. Milne came on board in 2012 and soon found herself mentoring Sarah Krahenbuhl, director of the Phoenix Suns Charities. After a three-year mentorship, Milne had mentored Krahenbuhl such that she was ready (and selected) to take on the position of executive director when Milne stepped down in 2015.

Developing the playbook

How did Milne learn to support such a successful transition? First, she had two really good mentors she could emulate. These mentors engaged in conversations that encouraged her to think: If she had their job, what would she do? These mentors helped Milne think about the next job she would have as she developed her professional skillset. In fact, Milne reflects that they mentored her as if she would become their successor. She never took their jobs, but she used these experiences to develop her mentoring playbook.

Second, Milne notes that the work environment has changed such that it is easier to look at mentoring as part of talent development and succession planning:

> The workforce is much more fluid than it used to be. It is not perceived as negative to move around to other jobs in the same industry. In fact, it makes you more valuable to have experience in different companies.

The mentoring playbook

Milne's mentoring playbook is full of basketball analogies that might help others have successful mentoring relationships. She says: "The mentor is like a point guard in basketball. A point guard runs the offense and figures out how to score points for the team to win the game." She explains how a mentor "wins the game" by achieving results for their organization and their protégé. Point guards set up the plays, just like mentors may guide protégés to the right situation to achieve success for the organization.

Her mentoring playbook highlights the flexibility of the mentor's role. Milne notes:

> You may be the player making the point or, just as importantly but not as noticeable, you may be the player providing the assist that enables another player to make the basket and earn the points for the team.

There are times that a point guard will score the points, just as a mentor may serve as a role model for a protégé to watch and emulate. At other times a point guard provides an "assist" and throws the ball to another player to make the basket. A mentor also supports his or her protégé to score after the mentor has set up the play.

Milne views mentoring as a team activity. Just like point guards help other teammates develop their ball-handling skills, mentors put their protégés in appropriately challenging situations with others to develop their skills.

Purposeful beginning

When Milne stepped into her new role as leader of the philanthropic organization, she knew that an important first step was to find "a better expression of the Suns brand through philanthropy." She created a new position at Phoenix Suns Charities from administrative positions. Milne then "looked purposefully for a person who understood brand management, and found Sarah." Krahenbuhl understood the marketplace but needed mentoring to understand the deeper organizational strategy. Milne's aim was to develop Krahenbuhl's raw talent. She recognized the different skill levels that her protégé had and knew that she could not put her out front to "make the baskets" in the beginning. Krahenbuhl says about Milne: "She had a level of respect for the experience I brought to the organization." Mentoring was a mutual back-and-forth relationship and not a one-way flow of information: "It was much more powerful because it was a shared experience."

At first, Milne needed a talented person to "be a surrogate and address the community with a similar voice." The mentoring relationship started as alignment mentoring, where Milne helped Krahenbuhl develop a consistent voice and message for the Phoenix Suns Charities. Milne reflects that she had yet to develop her personal goals for how long she might serve as executive director, and she certainly did not think she was hiring her replacement.

Intentional ending

Given Milne's understanding of mentorship and openness to change, she realized that her protégé was reflective and observant. "I saw her watching me or me giving her an 'assist.' It really started shaping up and I looked at her as being my replacement at some point. But this didn't happen until about a year into the mentoring."

Milne tested what she was seeing in her protégé in the second year of the relationship. As they approached their third year, Milne focused on making sure that her protégé also understood the "playbook" for the organization. Milne told her protégé that she would lead by getting out of her way.

About her mentoring experience, Milne said:

I am feeling even more success. The bottom line is on the deliverables on the job you are getting paid to do. What I know is that the best thing for the charity is for my protégé to come and take it over.

Krahenbuhl reports: "At the root of our relationship we have become friends because of the mutual respect we have for one another."
Phoenix Suns Charities: www.nba.com/suns/suns-charities
Source: Interview with Sarah Krahenbuhl, Executive Director of the Suns Charities, and Robin Milne, former Executive Director.

Some mentoring programs will award a certificate of completion or hold a celebratory event to mark the end of the program. However, most participants are unsure about how to end a formal mentoring relationship or how to redefine their relationship. In organizational settings, participants may benefit from a discussion about how they might like to keep in touch, or what kind of communication might be welcomed or appropriate. Similarly, in educational settings, students may need assistance understanding how to keep a mentor in their developmental network. It is likely the student will need letters of recommendation or advice in the future. However, protégés are often unsure how to maintain appropriate connections with former mentors. Encouraging protégés to send a short update on a regular basis, or once a year, is one way that they can stay in touch and share their progress. In peer mentoring programs it may be useful to have a discussion about whether the peer mentors may like to stay engaged (or not) to extend their developmental networks.

Section summary

Endings are marked by transitioning to a different relationship. Mentors and protégés may become peers, colleagues, or trusted advisors. In some cases, the individuals may decide the relationship is over and it is time to invest elsewhere. There are costs associated with ending relationships, especially if they have become close mentorships. You can celebrate these transitions with an official event or "thank you."

Communication preferences

There are differences in how individuals respond to one another. Some mentoring scholars suggest that reflective, non-directive conversational styles promote more learning in mentoring relationships (Crasborn et al.

2011). You can think of communication responses as falling into one of four categories:

1. deflecting;
2. probing;
3. advising; and
4. reflecting.

Deflecting responses dismiss a concern or indicate that the topic is not important. Probing responses involve asking follow-up questions to understand fully the point being communicated by the other person. An advising response is more directive and provides guidance about what the other person should do. Reflection responses involve making comments or asking questions that help the other person reflect on possible solutions and their best response.

Protégés often desire an immediate answer to the challenges they face. However, effective learning relationships (which is the focus of this handbook) are characterized by conversations that encourage reflection and probing more than deflecting and advising. Here are two scenarios that can be used to raise awareness about the differences in communication styles, and what protégés and mentors prefer. Engaging mentor–protégé dyads in a role-playing exercise is useful to help individuals both identify their preferences and increase their awareness of the importance of, and difficulty in, reflective conversations.

Role-playing exercises: Communicating supportively

Divide the mentors and protégés into pairs and have them read the scenario. Ask the mentors to select the best response, and protégés the response they would prefer. Then ask the mentors and protégés to look at the communication style matching their selection (at the bottom) and discuss their responses.

Role play 1: Communication

Protégé: I've been in this job now for six months, and I hardly know anyone at all. I just can't seem to make friends or to be accepted by other people. Most people are extremely busy and don't take time to socialize. I feel isolated from what is going on.

Response options*

A. Don't be concerned about not making friends as soon. Things will get better the longer you are here, you'll see.

B. When you first meet people, what do you say? Are you the one to be friendly first?

C. Because teachers are so busy, probably no one had time to get close socially. You shouldn't expect too much.

D. So you're feeling that people haven't accepted you?

E. It's not as serious as you may feel. When I first started teaching, it took me more than six months to get adjusted. I still don't know some of the people in several departments.

Role play 2: Communication

Protégé: I can't stand my boss. She is the most autocratic, demanding person you can imagine! I've never worked around anyone who cared less for students and employees than she does. Her complete insensitivity and lack of humanity have made this a miserable place to work.

Response options**

A. You sound as if you're having difficulty dealing with the rigid control and authority.

B. I know how you feel, because last year we had a man in our department who would drive anybody crazy. He was the ultimate domineering boss.

C. You're going to have problems unless you work this out. I think you should go to her and tell her how you feel.

D. You really are having a hard time adjusting to your boss, aren't you?

E. Why is it you feel so strongly about her?

*Role play 1: Response styles

A. Deflecting
B. Probing
C. Advising
D. Reflecting

**Role play 2: Response styles

A. Reflecting
B. Deflecting
C. Advising
D. Probing

Conclusion

Relationships develop in stages. Mentoring relationships can be characterized by stages that mark the beginning, middle, and end of the relationship. Each stage has specific tasks and activities. Support mentoring participants by providing resources for each relationship stage. Developing rapport and setting relational goals are the critical challenges at the beginning stages of the mentoring relationship. Collaborating on shared projects or goals and adjusting goals as needed are a hallmark of the middle stage of formal mentoring relationships. Formal mentoring relationships come to an end, and you can help participants be intentional about how they redefine their relationship. Educating mentors and protégés about communication styles may enhance learning conversations.

Key terms

- Adult development: identity, intimacy, generativity, integrity
- Collaboration
- Communication styles: advising, deflecting, probing, reflecting
- GROW: goals, realistic, options, what/when/who
- Relationship stages: beginning, middle, end
- Rapport
- Reflective/non-directive
- SMART: specific, measurable, attainable, realistic, timely

Check your learning

1. How can you support development of rapport during the initiation stage?
2. How can you support goal setting in appropriate ways for mentors and protégés?
3. What questions would be best to assess progress in the mentoring relationship during the middle stages?
4. What activities or process can you put in place to support mentors and protégés to end their formal mentoring relationship successfully?

Resources

Beyond goals: Effective strategies for coaching and mentoring. (David et al. 2013) – an excellent book on goal-setting strategies in coaching and mentoring.

References

Clutterbuck, D. 2014. *Everyone Needs a Mentor*. 5th ed. London: CIPD Press.

Crasborn, F., Hennissen, P., Brouwer, N. Korthagen, F. & Bergen, T.2011. "Exploring a Two-dimensional Model of Mentor Teacher Roles in Mentoring Dialogues." *Teaching and Teacher Education*, 27(2):320–331. 10.1016/j.tate.2 010.08.014.

David, M. S., D. Clutterbuck, and M. D. Megginson. 2013. *Beyond Goals: Effective Strategies for Coaching and Mentoring*. Farnham, UK: Gower.

Eby, L. T., T. D. Allen, B. J. Hoffman, L. E. Baranik, J. B. Sauer, S. Baldwin, M.A. Morrison, K. M. Kinkade, C. P. Maher, and S. Curtis. 2013. "An Interdisciplinary Meta-Analysis of the Potential Antecedents, Correlates, and Consequences of Protégé Perceptions of Mentoring." *Psychological Bulletin* 139(2): 1–36.

Erikson, E. 1963. *Childhood and Society*. New York: Norton and Company.

Erikson, E. 1968. *Identity: Youth and Crisis*. New York: Norton and Company.

Johnson, W. B., & Nelson, N. 1999. Mentor-Protégé Relationships in Graduate Training: Some Ethical Concerns. Ethics & Behavior, 9(3): 189–210. 10.1207/ s15327019eb0903_1.

Josselson, R. 1987. *Finding Herself: Pathways to Identity Development in Women*. San Francisco, CA: Jossey-Bass.

Kram, K. E. 1985. *Mentoring at Work: Developmental Relationships in Organizational Life*. Glenview, IL: Scott, Foresman, and Company.

Lancer, N., Clutterbuck, D., & Megginson, D. 2016. Techniques for Coaching and Mentoring. London: Routledge. 10.4324/9781315691251

Levinson, D. 1978. *The Seasons of a Man's Life*. New York: Knopf.

Lunsford, L. G., Baker, V. Griffin, K. A. & Johnson, W. B. 2013. Mentoring: A Typology of Costs for Higher Education Faculty. Mentoring & Tutoring: Partnership in Learning, 21(2):126–149. 10.1080/13611267.2013.813725.

Lunsford, L. G. 2014. "Mentors, Tormentors, and No Mentors: Mentoring Scientists." *International Journal of Mentoring and Coaching in Education*, 3:4–17. 10.1108/ijmce-02-2013-0007.

Lunsford, L. G. 2016. "Mentors as Friends." In *Psychology of Friendship*, edited by M. Hojjat and A. Moyer. New York: Oxford University Press.

Ragins, B. R., Clutterbuck, D., & Matthewman, L. 2012. *Mentoring and Diversity*. London: Routledge. 10.4324/9780080496559

Strauss, V., 2015. *Washington Post*, April 17. Available online at www.washingtonpost.com/blogs/answer-sheet/wp/2015/04/17/i-wish-my-teacher-knew-poignant-notes-from-students/ (accessed April 23, 2021)."I Wish My Teacher Knew": Poignant Notes from Students

Thomas, J. D., Lunsford, L. G., & Rodrigues, H. A. 2015. "Early Career Academic Staff Support: Evaluating Mentoring Networks." Journal of Higher Education Policy and Management, 37320–329. 10.1080/1360080x.2015.1034426.

Vaillant, G. E. 1977. *Adaptation to Life*. Boston, MA: Little, Brown.

Wanberg, C. R., E. T. Welsh, and S. A. Hezlett. 2003. "Mentoring Research: A Review and Dynamic Process Model." In *Research in Personnel and Human*

Resources Management, Vol. 22, edited by C. R. Wanberg, E. T. Welsh and S. A. Hezlett, 39–124. Bingley, UK: Emerald Group Publishing.

Weinberg, F. J., and M. J. Lankau. 2011. "Formal Mentoring Programs: A Mentor-Centric and Longitudinal Analysis." *Journal of Management* 37(6): 1527–1557.

Whitmore, J. 2002. *Coaching for Performance: GROWing People, Performance, and Purpose*. London: Nicholas Brealey.

Chapter 10

Promote learning conversations

We're looking for things that come in a minute. It just doesn't happen. You have to go understand that life and baseball is littered with all kinds of obstacles and problems along the way. You have to learn how to overcome them to be successful in life. (Dave Winfield, inductee to National Baseball Hall of Fame, in Cotton et al. 2011)

Introduction

Mentoring could be added to "life and baseball" in the epigraph here. Mentoring relationships are learning relationships, and as such they too must handle the obstacles and problems encountered by mentors and protégés.

Cotton et al. (2011) studied the developmental networks of major league baseball players inducted into the Baseball Hall of Fame. The researchers examined player's acceptance speeches to identify what kind of mentoring support mattered most to elite performers. These players benefited from the traditional psychosocial and career support provided in mentoring relationships. However, these elite performers also identified the importance of "inspiration and motivation" (27), and those who received it were more likely to be inducted earlier into the Baseball Hall of Fame. This type of psychosocial support gave the players a good feeling that motivated them to perform, and translated motivation into action.

Daniel Levinson would not have been surprised about the importance of inspiration. Nearly four decades ago, he studied the development of men over their life course. Mentors provided important, even critical, roles for men early in their careers. Levinson (1978) noted the important roles of teaching, sponsorship, and advice and also observed: "The mentor has another function, and this is developmentally the most crucial one: to support and facilitate the *realization of the Dream*" (98; emphasis in original).

Levinson's work on adult development provided the foundation for later mentoring scholars such as Kathy Kram, yet the "realization of the dream" is understudied by scholars and neglected by practitioners. Work in the area

DOI: 10.4324/9781003163862-10

of human flourishing and thriving highlights the importance of striving to be our best self. Conversations that help mentors and protégés realize their dreams will promote learning, flourishing, and developing the psychological capital that benefits individuals and organizations.

Effective formal mentoring programs support participants to provide valued feedback to one another; however, mentors and protégés are unsure sometimes about how to have conversations that promote learning through feedback. Rarely do people receive assistance on how to support and sustain successful learning relationships. In fact, talented individuals may have little experience with critical feedback and may be challenged to provide or receive it (Argyris 1991).

Psychologists have found that how we talk to ourselves and to others influences our motivation to learn, overcome challenges, and flourish (Fredrickson and Losada 2005; Seligman and Csikszentmihalyi 2000). This chapter is about techniques that will enhance learning conversations between mentors and protégés. Mindset is covered first, to provide a framework for engaging in learning conversations. Then three techniques will be described that promote learning conversations: reflection, redirection, and realization.

Mindset

How people view challenges influences their motivation to learn. Carol Dweck (2006) is well known for scholarship on our learning beliefs: She refers to them as "fixed" and "growth" mindsets. Consider the following questions:

1. When you were in school, did you focus on the grade you would receive?
2. Did you feel bad if you earned a poor grade on a quiz?
3. Did you ever take a course or workshop because it sounded interesting, even though you might earn a lower grade because it was outside your major or discipline?
4. If you attend professional conferences, have you ever attended a session outside your interest or expertise?

Fixed mindset

If you answered "yes" to the first two questions here, you may have a fixed mindset. People who focus on their performance feel good when they earn an "A" or the highest mark for an event. A performance learning orientation may work well until you encounter failure. However, a focus *only* on performance may demoralize and demotivate when you encounter failure.

People who have a fixed mindset believe that their intelligence is fixed. These individuals make statements such as: "I'm not very good at math." They also may hold such beliefs for others. Thus, when someone performs poorly, a person with a fixed mindset will likely attribute their poor performance to lack of ability or intelligence, rather than lack of experience or learning. If you explain your (or someone else's) performance in this manner, then it is unlikely any learning conversation will be helpful because you do not believe that effort will make a difference.

Growth mindset

If you answered "yes" to the last two questions, you may have a growth mindset. You may expect poor performance when learning new skills or tasks. In fact, you may view failure as a challenge to be overcome through practice. A growth mindset is the belief that, with time and effort, you can change certain aspects of yourself.

Our mindset is learned. Fortunately, it also can be relearned. Mentors and protégés will benefit from understanding the difference between fixed and growth mindsets, and engaging in conversations that promote growth mindsets. One way to de-emphasize performance and emphasize growth is to share examples of people who have failed (there are many YouTube videos that feature "famous failures"). You can promote an explicit emphasis on effort in your mentoring program by asking mentors and protégés to develop mentoring plans or milestones that emphasize effort.

Another approach is to ask participants to complete the learning inventory in Table 10.1 (developed by Button et al. 1996). Provide the inventory online or in paper form. Place the scoring instructions at the end of an online survey or on the reverse side of the paper, so as to not influence their responses. People may score their results and bring them to a briefing session as an introduction to learning about a growth mindset.

Mindset is an easy concept to grasp intellectually but often difficult to implement. Traditionally, Western culture – especially schooling – has emphasized performance, although this is beginning to change through the work of Dweck and others. Case Study 10.1 provides an example of how the growth mindset was used in a new mentoring network for student teachers. It took several years for experienced mentors to use a growth mindset in their mentoring relationships. The faculty invited a trainer from the Heroic Imagination Project to run a 90-minute workshop for mentors and protégés on how to develop a growth mindset. Mentors were trained on running future workshops. This approach transformed the practice of the program manager, as well as many of the mentors and protégés.

Table 10.1 Learning orientation inventory

Instructions: Use this scale to select the best response for each question.
1: strongly disagree, 2: somewhat disagree, 3: disagree, 4: mixed, 5: somewhat agree, 6: agree, 7: strongly agree.

Items

1. I prefer to do things that I can do well, rather than things that I do poorly.
2. The opportunity to do challenging work is important to me.
3. The things I enjoy most are the things I do best.
4. When I fail to complete a difficult task, I plan to try harder the next time I work on it.
5. I'm happiest at work when I perform tasks of which I know that I won't make any errors.
6. I prefer to work on tasks that force me to learn new things.
7. The opinions that others have about how well I can do certain things are important to me.
8. The opportunity to learn new things is important to me.
9. I feel smart when I do something without making any mistakes.
10. I do my best when I'm working on a fairly difficult task.
11. I like to be fairly confident that I can perform a task successfully before I attempt it.
12. I try hard to improve on my past performance.
13. I like to work on tasks that I have done well on in the past.
14. The opportunity to extend the range of my abilities is important to me.
15. I feel smart when I can do something better than most other people.
16. When I have difficulty solving a problem, I enjoy trying different approaches to see which one will work.

Scoring:
Add up your responses to the even items and divide by 8. ___ (Growth Mindset Score)
Add up your responses to the odd items and divide by 8. ___ (Fixed Mindset Score).

Source: Adapted from Button et al. 1996.

Section summary

Learning conversations are useful when participants have a growth mindset. A growth mindset also builds resiliency and motivation (Dweck 2006) and enhances mentoring relationships.

Reflection

Reflection is effortful but necessary. Support mentoring participants to understand how their brains operate when they engage in reflection. Prepare participants to recognize types of dialogue that support reflective conversations. Teach mentors and protégés specific techniques frameworks and techniques, such as approach, action, reflection; the feedforward exercise; or after action reviews (AARs) (described next).

Case Study 10.1   Mentoring mindset for student teachers

Time for a change

When asked to provide a "thought question" for their protégés, more than half of the mentors in a teacher mentoring program wrote directive, and sometimes negative, statements. These mentors modeled the training manual, which was more a list of "dos and don'ts" rather than a resource for improving mentoring practice. Etta Kralovec applied for, and received, a multimillion-dollar grant to prepare new math and science teachers for positions in high-need schools along the Arizona border with Mexico. She recruited a team to improve mentorship of student teachers (protégés).

Change is possible

One team member was Catherine Parker, an experienced math teacher. She thinks back on her first-year mentoring in this program:

> I was doing it all wrong. I was evaluating. Once that seed was planted, it was like a weed. It was really difficult to cultivate a positive relationship. I had strong teachers who were colleagues and was lucky to have strong principals, but I didn't have an official, formal mentor – and certainly not one who would fit the model I've been using now.

Just as Parker has evolved, so too has the teacher mentoring program. Parker notes that the new mentoring observation tools in the first two years of the grant "were too evaluative, and mentors were rating protégés." She observes that mentoring is about the right kinds of communication. Capacity-building coaching provides communication tools that build the protégé's capacity to be self-reliant and to grow as a professional. "Evaluating, consulting or helping conversations end up with protégés being threatened or over-reliant," she says.

The protégés responded well to the new mentoring approach. Parker says the protégés were put in charge of deciding what they worked on and where they wanted to see growth. It helped steer them around from the mentors who might otherwise say: "Here is what I did, here is the answer, the trick, the solution."

Developing a mentoring mindset

Parker modeled the new mentoring techniques when teaching them to the mentors and protégés. The coaching approach focuses on reflection. She says: "It is compatible with a growth mindset because it is not evaluative and consulting. It promotes a growth mindset." Parker had a two-hour session where she modeled a classroom setting and role-played being the mentor and the protégé with an experienced mentor. She notes: "We didn't script it but would work through the guiding questions before I did my lesson, and then would model the reflective piece." The mentors and protégés liked the session because it helped to give them a model of good mentorship. "I would ask them, 'Did you see where I struggled when I was trying to ask a question as a mentor?' You can get stuck asking 'yes/no' questions."

Structured interactions

Using a capacity-building coaching model, Parker provided a template for three meetings in a "mentoring episode" along with guiding questions. She said: "The skill is learning to ask open questions, rather than closed-ended ones."

First, there is a planning meeting. Mentors engage protégés in a conversation with guiding questions such as:

- What is your goal?
- What strategies do you have to meet that goal?
- Ideally, what would it look like if you did it perfectly?
- What do you want me to observe as your mentor?
- What qualitative or quantitative data can I collect for you during a classroom observation?

Second, the mentor visits the protégé's classroom and collects the desired data. Parker notes:

> I find that the observation is the hardest part, to just focus on collecting the data the protégé wants. You see so many other things you want to collect feedback about, or there may be areas of concern and you have to work not to be directive or evaluative. Hard to stay true to the coaching.

Third, the mentor and protégé meet to reflect on how the class went. The mentor shares the data that he or she collected, and they discuss if this information aligns with the protégé's expectations. Mentors ask questions such as: "What went well?" and "What might you hope to do differently next time?" The overarching goal is to support protégés to engage in reflective conversation and consider how this experience, as Parker puts it, "fits into the larger picture of their goals as they develop their teaching practice."

Challenges

Challenges remain. Parker said that "it was challenging for mentors to focus on observable data." Sometimes mentors collected too much information or would write a critique rather than collect data that the protégés requested. The protégés, she observed, "did a better job of narrowing down a focus for growth, but their goal and desired data didn't always match up." However, she said they "want praise and direction on what they need to work on. It is hard not to give into that."

Parker reflects:

> This approach can be challenging for "people who have a fixed mindset about their students." She relates that it was hard to explain to protégés that using these strategies would make it easier, not harder, to "catch up" their students on material. Yet some protégés could only "focus on deficit thinking – 'This won't work for my students' – They wouldn't even try it."

Successes

Parker reflects:

> This approach works well when protégés lean toward being growth minded; they liked thinking about this perspective. It was a relief to protégés to realize that classroom management can't be your goal. It was a comfort to know they wouldn't have a long checklist that was evaluative.

This approach is about mentors guiding protégés to figure out how to improve. These conversations are more relaxed. When protégés ask, "What do you think?" or "What should I do?", mentors learn to redirect and ask another question. The anxiety drops from the protégé. He or she relates his or her own experience using this approach: "The nervousness of the protégé I'm observing does not seem to be as intense. I'm sure it is because they know I am not judging them." They are learning together.

Source: Interview with Catherine Parker, Curriculum Instruction and Assessment, Patagonia Schools, and Etta Kralovec, Professor Emeritus of Teacher Education, University of Arizona South.

Brain systems

We have two systems in our brains: an efficient but lazy system, and an inefficient but deliberate system (Kahneman 2011). Kahneman refers to the first system as System 1, which helps us handle many of the automatic tasks that we encounter each day, such as driving to work, navigating routine activities, and reading a person's facial expression. System 1 works well for us most of the time.

Reflection requires the use of System 2. System 2 uses a lot of energy (glucose), so we cannot operate it for long. Most of his book *Thinking, Fast and Slow* (2011) is about the predictable errors we make in using System 1, when we need to engage System 2.

Routine parts of mentoring conversations might be well served by using System 1. However, learning requires System 2 to engage. System 2 is effortful, deliberate, and reflective. There are three implications from this work for mentoring conversations. First, conversations need to be structured such that System 2 engages to ensure learning occurs. Second, recognize that such learning is effortful and hard. Third, it will be difficult for mentors or protégés to use System 2 for long – so adjust expectations accordingly.

Types of dialogue

Mentoring conversations can be categorized along two dimensions: directive/reflective and reactive/active (Crasborn et al. 2011, 322). Directive statements involve telling rather than asking. For example, a protégé might ask for help deciding between two new opportunities at work. A mentor who says to take option A because it will provide more visibility would be engaged in directive conversation. In contrast, a mentor who asks the protégé to describe the pros and cons of the two opportunities would be engaging in reflective conversation.

Help mentors and protégés be on guard from engaging in too many mentoring episodes that are directive, so as not to encourage protégés to rely overly on their mentor without developing their professional sense of autonomy or confidence. Mentors or protégés may need to engage in directive conversation. At times, mentors may share good advice with their protégés based on their prior experiences, and there might be occasions when it is appropriate to tell a protégé exactly what to do. However, if the mentor's conversation style is usually directive, then it is unlikely to support independent learning and development.

How active or reactive mentors and protégés are with one another is a second dimension of the mentoring dialogue. Active conversations refer to the extent to which one individual introduces topics of conversation. A reactive conversational style involves responding to the ideas presented by the other person. In co-mentoring, peer mentoring, or developmental mentoring, protégés and mentors might engage in both active and reactive dialogue. Supervisory mentoring might involve more active dialogues. This dimension is helpful in thinking about the kind of mentoring relationships that your program supports, and the extent to which each relational partner will introduce topics for discussion.

Developmental mentoring relationships focus more on learning rather than using the power or status of a mentor to provide unilateral benefits to a protégé. Prepare your mentoring participants to emphasize reflection and reaction. At the first meeting, both individuals might share a hope to learn over the course of their relationship and exchange thoughts on how best to meet their learning goals.

Approach, action, and reflection framework

Some scholars suggest that reflective conversations promote learning agility (DeRue et al. 2012a, 265). One technique involves three steps: approach, action, and reflection. Mentors and protégés can identify their learning goals and reflect on previously identified learning goals as part of the conversation.

Approach involves working from a framework that promotes learning. The idea is that learning is a concept to be embraced and approached, rather than feared. The development of a shared mentoring philosophy is helpful for mentoring participants. For example, a mentor might use the idea of a growth mindset and craft their questions to focus on effort rather than performance.

Action involves actively seeking feedback. During this part of the conversation, mentors and protégés might share their responses to prompts such as: "What new things will you try?" or "What experiments might you do?" They might also use a feedforward (rather than feedback) exercise (Ashford 2015), where the protégé states his or her goal to the mentor. The mentor responds with "My suggestion is…" (to meet the goal). The protégé then thanks his or her mentor and moves on. The last step is important, as it prevents the protégé from reacting defensively and helps him or her learn to accept the guidance graciously.

> **Feedforward Exercise**
>
> Protégé: My goal is...
> Mentor: My suggestion for you is...
> Protégé: Thank you!

The reflection stage involves the protégé and mentor reflecting on any experiments or new activities tried since they last met. A discussion might focus on what was learned that will inform future actions.

After action review

The focus of an AAR conversation is on how to make changes to improve future efforts. AARs (DeRue et al. 2012b; Morrison and Meliza 1999) were developed by the US army. Scholars report these reviews increase individual and team performance by 20–25 percent (Tannenbaum and Cerasoli 2013).

Team AARs may last about 30 minutes and may work well in peer mentoring programs; AARs may be less than 30 minutes in a one-on-one conversation. Three questions guide the reflection:

1. What happened in the learning attempt?
2. Why did it happen?
3. What can be done to improve in the future?

Encourage participants to focus on what went well and how to make changes to improve for the future.

Section summary

Reflection makes greater demands on our brains. Mentoring conversations can be categorized as reflective versus directive, and as active versus re-active. Think about the kind of conversations that will best promote your mentoring program's goals. Use exercises such as feedforward and AARs to support mentors and protégés in engaging in reflective practices to promote learning.

Redirection

Redirection can help protégés and mentors to restructure conversations about overcoming challenges. There is a belief that focusing on what did not go well or what was particularly upsetting might provide an emotional release. Unfortunately, this line of thought may lead mentors and protégés to believe they need to listen to all conversations with an equal amount of attention when in fact some topics do not deserve much attention.

An important role of a mentor is to redirect or reframe conversations about challenges and obstacles in ways that move the relationship forward and help protégés to learn. Similarly, protégés need to be aware of the importance of redirecting conversations both for themselves and to ensure that they do not get caught in a negative conversation spiral with a mentor.

Conversations that help people reframe their experiences have been found to build resiliency and optimism (Seligman 2016). Seligman (2016) described this technique as "thought catching," or the ABCDE model (shown in the pull-out box). These techniques come more naturally to some people than to others; however, most individuals report being able to engage naturally in this kind of conversation with minimal practice. Use role-playing exercises for protégés and mentors to learn how to engage in this reframing dialogue.

Redirection Prompts

A. describe Adverse event.
B. describe Belief as a result of the adverse event.
C. describe the Consequences of holding this belief.
D. Dispute the belief by identifying other explanations.
E. discuss the Energy one has, if an alternative explanation is used.

The first step is to identify clearly the adverse event which has precipitated the challenge or made an obstacle visible. It is important to clarify the specific challenge. For example, a protégé may share that he or she is concerned about an upcoming presentation. Probe the concern to determine what the specific source of anxiety is. It might be that he or she is worried about the quality of his or her materials, lack of time to properly prepare, or speaking in front of others. Be sure to identify the concern, rather than making an assumption about what it is.

The second step is to discuss the belief that emanates from this adverse event. Does the protégé believe he or she will be viewed as unintelligent or unmotivated? Identify what the protégé believes will happen in the worst-case scenario, should those fears come true.

The third step is to identify the consequences of this belief. Will the protégé's colleagues wish to distance themselves from the protégé? Or perhaps the supervisor will be present at the meeting, and the protégé is concerned that he or she will miss out on a future plum assignment? The goal is to clarify the possible consequences of holding the particular belief.

The fourth step is to dispute the belief. The goal is to identify other possible explanations that could be equally true. In our fictional scenario, the protégé might observe that his or her boss realizes that a short time has been given to prepare for the presentation, and as long as the main points are covered, it is okay if the content is short on details. Another explanation might be that the protégé has given presentations before, but not to such an important group, and colleagues might expect some nervousness. The idea is to generate as many other possible explanations about what people might believe. It is fine to list fictional possibilities, because such an activity sometimes helps protégés then identify realistic ones.

The final step is to reflect on the protégé's energy, if one of the other scenarios were to be true. How does the protégé feel if he or she realizes that his or her manager may be making accommodations for the short presentation time? This part of the conversation enables the protégé to realize that how he or she thinks about the adverse event can be demotivating or energizing.

It is possible to move through these first three steps quickly with practice. You may need more practice on the fourth step as most people struggle with learning to dispute a belief.

Section summary

Redirection is an important conversational skill for mentors and protégés. Learn how to redirect conversations in ways that emphasize an ability to bounce back from challenging events. The ABCDE model is a tool to help relationship partners redirect their conversations, rather than ruminate on negative experiences.

Realization

David Cooperrider (2015) believes that we "live in worlds our questions create." Indeed, conversations that promote realization involve specific ways of asking the right questions. He developed a technique called "appreciative inquiry," which has been used to create positive change in many organizations around the world (Cooperrider and Whitney, 2001). Appreciative inquiry focuses on identifying questions that recognize individuals' strengths while adopting a noncritical attitude of curiosity to chart an action plan to achieve stated aspirations for individuals and organizations.

Realization draws on appreciative inquiry techniques for mentoring conversations. Two examples will be described here: one that may be used during an initial meeting and another that may help protégés and mentors collaborate.

Initiation: Realization conversations

Conversations that focus on realization may benefit protégés and mentors at the start of their relationship, in the initiation stage (see Chapter 9 for the specific stages). The task during the initiation stage of the relationship is to become familiar with each person's preferences, experiences, and goals. However, some individuals can feel that this initial conversation is forced or awkward. This technique may support individuals to engage in genuine interactions that propel the relationship forward.

This type of conversation engages relational partners in a dialogue about their best scenario of how they might be different at the conclusion of the formal mentoring program, as a result of participating in it. These conversations have four overarching themes:

1. identify through inquiry a best experience;
2. relational partners answer questions that describe lessons from this experience;
3. the experience is used to create a template to achieve a similar success;
4. questions focus on reflecting and anticipating next steps.

Guiding questions for such a conversation are presented next.

Exercise: Initiation

Best experience

1. Describe your most successful experience of learning from another person. This might have been as a mentor protégé or simply working as a team member. What made this experience so successful and rewarding? What was it that you did? How did the other person contribute to this experience?
2. How did you contribute to this experience? What did you learn from it? How do you feel now, discussing it?

Share realizations

Each person shares his or her responses to these questions, listens respectfully, and identifies common or contrasting themes.

3. What are the commonalities of these experiences? How are these experiences different? What do these experiences tell you about how you might work together?

Develop a template

4. Think about what your relationship might be like at the end of the formal mentoring program. What do you learn from one another? Do you look forward to interacting? What might you create as a result of your relationship?

5. What strategies and timelines might be important to establish in your work together?

Anticipate

6. What do you hope to accomplish by or at your next meeting?

7. How will you reflect on your progress together?

Source: Adapted from Stratton-Berkessel 2010.

Cultivation: Realization conversations

In mentoring programs of longer duration, protégés and mentors may experience a lull in the relationship. The protégé might achieve his or her goals early in skill development or professional development. Alternatively, mentors might believe that protégés are ready to take on more responsibility and co-create or collaborate on a project. These conversations may occur during the cultivation stage of the relationship (see Chapter 9 for more on the relationship stages).

Exercise: Cultivation

Best experience

1. Describe a time when you successfully collaborated with someone to produce an event, product, or new knowledge. What did you produce? Describe the details of the event, product, or how you shared new knowledge. What was the scope of the project?
2. How did you decide on the project? How did you decide who would handle different tasks? What feedback did you receive that made you believe the project to be successful?
3. What did you learn from it? How do you feel now discussing it?

Share realizations

Each person shares their responses to these questions, listens respectfully, and identifies common or contrasting themes.

4. What were the shared strategies on determining responsibilities or the scope of the project? How do these experiences inform how you might work together?

Develop a template

5. What is an ideal project that would benefit us both? Are other people needed to complete the project?

6. How will you work together to develop a timeline and to complete the work?

Anticipate

7. What will you accomplish by or at your next meeting? How will you engage others, if needed?

8. How will you chart your progress? What milestones will be important?

Source: Adapted from Stratton-Berkessel 2010.

Another tool that supports appreciative inquiry conversations is Dialogi, which supports participants to use questions to achieve results. It was developed for coaching conversations, which are part of mentoring relationships. Dialogi takes participants quickly through a framework that allows questions to be empowering, motivating, and revealing.

Section summary

Mentoring relationships that support participants to realize their dream both empower individuals and motivate them to achieve individual and organizational goals. Appreciative inquiry is a useful approach in designing questions that engage participants in powerful learning conversations. Exercises are provided of how to realize the best possible scenarios, both at the start of the relationship and during the cultivation stage of the relationship. A practical tool, Dialogi, may support more effective questions that achieve positive results.

Conclusion

Formal mentoring programs connect individuals to develop their skills and knowledge. Learning is at the heart of these relationships. However, many individuals may not have developed the skills to use questions that promote learning. This chapter highlighted how mentors and protégés can engage with one another in ways that promote reflection through development of a learning mindset, redirection of negative experiences, and realization of ideal outcomes.

Key terms

- Active versus reactive dialogue
- After action review
- Appreciative inquiry
- Dialogi
- Directive versus reflective dialogue
- Feedforward
- Mindset: fixed, growth
- Reflection: ABCDE model, thought catching, reframing
- Redirection
- Realization

Check your learning

1. How can you promote a growth mindset among participants in your formal mentoring program?
2. To what extent do you expect participants in your formal mentoring program to engage in directive versus reflective dialogue?
3. To what extent do you expect participants in your formal mentoring program to engage in active versus reactive conversations?
4. When might redirection or realization techniques be useful for mentors and protégés?

Resources

Appreciative Inquiry Commons and resources: https://appreciative inquiry.case.edu

Appreciative Inquiry for Collaborative Solutions: www.pfeiffer.com/go/appreciativeinquiry

Dialogi: a practical tool to help mentoring participants work through a reflective conversation: https://dialogi.co.uk/

Heroic Imagination Project: https://www.heroicimagination.org/
Minset: Dweck's book and additional resources: https://www.mindset
works.com/

References

Argyris, C. 1991. "Teaching Smart People How to Learn." *Harvard Business Review*. May–June. Available online at https://hbr.org/1991/05/teaching-smart-people-how-to-learn (accessed April 23, 2021).

Ashford, S. 2015. "Mindful Engagement: A Practical and Positive Tool for Leadership Development." Workshop Presented at the Fourth World Congress on Positive Psychology, Lake Buena Vista, FL, June 25–28.

Button, S. B., J. E. Mathieu, and D. M. Zajac. 1996. "Goal Orientation in Organizational Research: A Conceptual and Empirical Foundation." *Organizational Behavior and Human Decision Processes* 67(1): 26–48.

Cooperrider, D. 2015. "Mirror Flourishing: Appreciative Inquiry and the Designing of Positive Institutions." Plenary Lecture at the International Positive Psychology Association Convention, Lake Buena Vista, FL, June.

Cooperrider, D. L., and D. Whitney. 2001. "A Positive Revolution in Change: Appreciative Inquiry." *Public Administration and Public Policy* 87: 611–630.

Cotton, R. D., Y. Shen, and R. Livne-Tarandach. 2011. "On Becoming Extraordinary: The Content and Structure of the Developmental Networks of Major League Baseball Hall of Famers." *Academy of Management Journal* 54(1): 15–46.

Crasborn, F., P. Hennisnen, N. Brouwer, F. Korthagen, and T. Bergen. 2011. "Exploring a Two-Dimensional Model of Mentor Teacher Roles in Mentoring Dialogues." *Teaching and Teacher Education* 27(2): 320–331.

DeRue, D. S., S. J. Ashford, and C. G. Myers. 2012a. "Learning Agility: In Search of Conceptual Clarity and Theoretical Grounding." *Industrial and Organizational Psychology* 5(3): 258–279.

DeRue, D. S., J. D. Nahrgang, J. R. Hollenbeck, and K. Workman. 2012 b. "A Quasi-Experimental Study of After-Event Reviews and Leadership Development." *Journal of Applied Psychology* 97(5): 997–1015.

Dweck, C. 2006. *Mindset: The New Psychology of Success*. New York: Random House.

Fredrickson, B. L., and M. R. Losada. 2005. "Positive Affect and the Complex Dynamics of Human Flourishing." *American Psychologist* 60(7): 678–686.

Kahneman, D. 2011. *Thinking, Fast and Slow*. New York: Macmillan.

Levinson, D. 1978. *The Seasons of a Man's Life*. New York: Knopf.

Morrison, J. E., and L. L. Meliza. 1999. *Foundations of the After Action Review Process* (No. IDA/HQ-D2332). Alexandria, VA: Institute for Defense Analyses.

Seligman, M. E. P., and M. Csikszentmihalyi. 2000. "Positive Psychology." *American Psychologist* 55(1): 5–14.

Seligman, M. 2016. *Learned Optimism: How to Change Your Mind and Your Life.* New York: Vintage Books.

Stratton-Berkessel, R. 2010. *Appreciative Inquiry for Collaborative Solutions: 21 Strength-Based Workshops.* San Francisco, CA: Pfeiffer.

Tannenbaum, S. I., and C. P. Cerasoli. 2013. "Do Team and Individual Debriefs Enhance Performance? A Meta-Analysis." *Human Factors* 55(1): 231–245.

Chapter 11

Welcome diversity and inclusion

> Diversity is the child of context and complexity and the "right" answers sometimes become "wrong" in specific circumstances. (Clutterbuck and Ragins 2002, x)

Introduction

Do people from underrepresented groups benefit from a mentor who shares their group membership? For example, is it better if women have female mentors, or if black youth have black mentors? Will you have a less rich experience if you do not have a mentor who is similar to your demographic characteristics, or will you benefit? What if there is not anyone who "looks like you" to serve as a mentor or role model?

This challenge faced Michelle Howard. She decided on a career in the navy after watching a documentary about military academies as a child (NPR, 2014). Howard won a coveted spot at the US Naval Academy and went on to become the first African American woman to command a ship in the navy, or to earn three stars. Howard was the first woman to earn a four-star admiral position. Her accomplishments are legendary, and her rescue of Captain Phillips from Somali pirates was later made into a movie, *Captain Phillips* (2013). She says:

> I don't believe mentors have to look like you to be good mentors or your protégé must look like you. The folks who work for me and work with me my whole career have not looked like me, and as a leader I'm obligated to help them be successful. At some point, you come to the realization that it's about people who have the same purpose and motivations in life. What is it you want to accomplish, what attributes are you trying to gain in yourself, what do you see as the paragon of success in your field or in character? Go find the person who has those attributes.[1]

DOI: 10.4324/9781003163862-11

For her, that person was Rear Admiral Gene Kendall, who became the twelfth African American in the history of the US Navy to achieve the rank of rear admiral (Fenn 2015).

This chapter draws on research to support Howard's mentoring advice. An understanding of diversity and inclusion can strengthen your mentoring program. A framework for defining diversity and inclusion in your mentoring program is provided. Then, how diversity influences three process of mentoring are highlighted:

1. matching protégés and mentors,
2. the beginning of the relationship, and
3. the types of mentoring support provided.

Finally, the "sink or swim" mentoring philosophy is explained so that you can make mentoring participants aware of how to avoid it. The aim of this chapter is to increase your understanding of diversity, inclusion, and mentoring, so as to create learning spaces for mentoring conversations to flourish. Some scholars have found that mentoring programs that include participants from diverse backgrounds also may support organizational diversity goals. In other words, such mentoring programs may provide "stealth" diversity training, as majority members report learning more about underrepresented groups (Reddick et al. 2012).

What is diversity?

Diversity refers to the composition of groups as identified by traits or characteristics of its group members (Roberson 2006). I find that people have one of three responses when we discuss diversity and mentoring. A few people feel passionate about their definition and believe in targeted mentoring efforts for certain groups or that mentoring excludes some people. Other well-intentioned individuals avoid talking about diversity for fear of offending others or utter safe platitudes from an organizational mantra such as "We value diversity" or "We are diverse and inclusive." However, most people truly want to understand how to think about diversity in their mentoring programs but often are not sure what to ask or how to begin.

Some researchers write about demographic characteristics as *surface* characteristics, suggesting that we can see these characteristics, or that they exist on the outside. Surface characteristics are usually visible characteristics such as "race", gender, disability, age or even part-time workers (Eby et al. 1998, 270). In contrast, there are *deep* characteristics, which refer to cognitive or personal traits such as values, morals, or work preferences. Our emphasis tends to be on what we can see – the surface characteristics. In fact, gender, ethnicity, and "race" are among the most researched characteristics in terms of mentoring relationships, matching, and outcomes (e.g., O'Neill 2002).

Yet even surface characteristics may not be visible, which adds more complexity to understanding diversity. In the United States, the number of multiracial individuals is increasing (United States Census Bureau 2018). England and Wales (Office for National Statistics 2015) (and many other countries) have become more ethnically diverse. The transition of famed Olympian Bruce Jenner from male to female shines a spotlight on the invisibility of transgender individuals (CBS, 2016 CBS News 2016). Other surface characteristics such as religion, sexuality, or social class may not be visible but may influence mentoring relationships.

Diversity and power

The diverse characteristics mentioned here refer to an aspect of group membership that places a person in a minority group, which has unequal access to organizational or cultural opportunities and benefits. Power refers to the formal and informal networks or processes in an organization that enable you to advance your ideas and projects, or to accomplish tasks. Power is an essential part of diversity as it relates to mentoring relationships. Ragins (2002) defines diversity as "relationships comprising mentors and protégés who differ on the basis of race, ethnicity, gender, sexual orientation, class, religion, disability or other group memberships associated with power in organizations" (24).

Mentoring relationships are about connecting individuals for personal and professional growth. In the United States, mentoring is often associated with sponsorship or connection to social networks that provide career access and power. Even in developmental mentoring or co-learning relationships, people may participate based on their perceived status or power. Thus, any group membership that may limit participation in mentoring warrants attention to ensure that your mentoring program is not perpetuating inequities.

Who defines diversity?

Who defines diversity in a formal mentoring program? Will the mentoring participant, you as the program manager, or organizational leaders define which diverse characteristics are important? Diversity seems to matter more for the protégé, who is typically the less powerful person in the relationship. Yet protégés may value different parts of their social identity at different times. Case Study 11.1 illustrates how gender mattered for some mentoring relationships, but not for others. Some women resent being labeled a "female engineer," while other women see their gender as part of their professional identity. Men and women are unsure how to handle cross-gender relationships out of a concern of sexual innuendos cast at either participant (Hurley 1996; Johnson and Smith 2016).

Case Study 11.1   Navigating gender and ethnicity

Michele Tam, an Asian American, was an outstanding student and earned a full-ride, four-year merit scholarship to attend North Carolina State University. In her little spare time she co-founded the Park Scholarships symposium, which brought distinguished speakers to campus, and served as student chief justice. Even then, she was aware of the stereotypes of Asian American females as being quiet and submissive. She remains sensitive to how she might be perceived because of her appearance while navigating her career. At times, she has worked actively to counter the stereotype. Tam reflects that she thought she would "gravitate more towards a mentor who looks like me." She continued on a successful trajectory, most recently demonstrated by her ability to navigate one of corporate America's most notoriously difficult interview processes (Miners 2013). She landed a position at McKinsey & Company after stints at Procter & Gamble (P&G) and PepsiCo. After college, Tam began work in finance, a field where women have long been underrepresented. Her first job was at P&G, a company that increased the percentage of women employees to 30 percent in their finance division. P&G has a strong commitment to diversity and inclusion (Procter and Gamble 2014), including mentoring initiatives. She observes that formal mentoring programs provided most of her mentoring opportunities.

Importance of demographic similarities

Tam participated in several formal mentoring initiatives at P&G. A mentor program early in her career paired people of the same gender who were working at the same location. Tam was matched with a female manager in finance, one level above her position. The program encouraged mentors and protégés to connect initially in a one-on-one meeting, or over lunch. Their relationship lasted more than four years. However, as Tam noted, this was a unique opportunity as there were few senior women at the company.

Tam noted the value of a woman's perspective. Her mentor helped her handle challenges unique to women. For example, they discussed how to navigate career aspirations in parallel with personal interests, such as starting a family and pregnancy. Tam is assertive, but her mentor helped find her voice when she needed to be more vocal about her positions on some teams. Tam notes that it was useful "to have someone who I could bounce career questions off of and have another perspective... I always knew I could reach out to her." Tam maintained this relationship even after moving to a position in Baltimore, Maryland. She would meet with her mentor about twice a year when she returned to the company headquarters in Cincinnati, Ohio. This and other mentoring experiences provided Tam with "a template for what a mentoring relationship could look like."

Tam also felt that the presence of female mentors helps protégés (and others) manage unconscious bias. For example, she had a female mentor at PepsiCo who was not in her own management line, but was in the room when performance ratings were discussed. Her mentor's presence gave Tam confidence that "these discussions remained focused on data-based results rather than softer factors."

Value of demographic differences

Tam recounts that "it was a bit surprising" how she gravitated to an informal mentoring relationship with an African American, male senior executive. She had a prior relationship with this mentor when he was a senior vice-president in her chain of management in her early career at P&G. Tam believes that he valued her work, after seeing good results from her efforts as a financial analyst. She felt comfortable seeking his advice on work-related matters. When she accepted a new position in a division at another site, he encouraged her to stay in touch. Other former managers made a similar offer but Tam took him up on his offer, perhaps because she sensed the genuineness of it. For example, he called her new managers to check on her progress. Tam's initial connection with her mentor was because he was in finance and they had attended college in the same state.

This mentor did what great mentors do: He pushed her in appropriate, although sometimes uncomfortable, ways and opened up her thinking to new possibilities. Tam observed that there were times when she might take notes into a meeting with him to guide their discussion. Her mentor would ask her to put them away in favor of a conversation. During one mentoring check-in, he asked Tam some sensitive questions about her personal and professional goals. When she replied, "I am not comfortable pursuing this line of questioning," he countered by asking her why these questions made her uncomfortable. Tam recognized the value of conversations such as these. In the immediate sense these questions were uncomfortable. She recounts: "I appreciated the questions and get more value when people ask me to be reflective. I needed someone to encourage me to take risks and get out of my comfort zone."

Her mentor was at a senior level in the company, and could provide Tam a bigger view across the organization. He both gave her a broader perspective and acted as a sponsor for her, mentioning opportunities to her that she had not considered. In fact, he made the case that a new opportunity in his area would provide her the chance to build new skills. Ultimately, Tam felt comfortable making career choices without consulting him, and decided on her own to leave P&G.

Her greater sense of power and autonomy meant a change in the relationship. However, she reflects that having formal mentors helped her to be open to informal mentors, and that she valued her relationship with this mentor *because* he was different and could provide a diverse perspective.

Source: Interview with Michele Tam, expert consultant, McKinsey & Company.

As a program manager, you might believe that certain diverse characteristics may be relevant to mentorship. Organizational leaders may desire to support people with certain characteristics or backgrounds whom they feel could be overlooked. For example, many universities in the United States have summer research programs to prepare underrepresented students for graduate programs. In these cases both federal agencies, which provide funding for such programs, and university administrators determine what surface characteristics are considered (Case Study 11.2 is one such example of a program). Yet this case study highlights the challenges in oversimplifying diversity. Cindy thinks of herself as of mixed ethnic heritage, even though both of her parents would be considered Hispanic. Further, her status as a first-generation student may have influenced her mentoring experience more than her ethnicity.

Similarly, organizational environments have been found to influence when "race" matters in mentoring (Ragins 2002). On the one hand, being a member of an underrepresented ethnicity may not matter in a multinational corporation with heterogeneous employees. On the other hand, being African American in a company where most of the employees are European American might make "race" an important factor in a mentoring relationship.

Identify the role of diversity in your organization and give mentoring participants an opportunity to identify when diversity matters to them. How can you determine if a particular group membership is important to a mentor or protégé? The simple answer is to ask them. In terms of matching, best practice is to allow participants to indicate what characteristics are important to them, relative to a mentor or a protégé (Ragins 2002). In

Case Study 11.2   When diversity matters: Undergraduate research mentoring

Many universities in the United States offer summer mentoring programs to prepare underrepresented students for graduate programs. The Undergraduate Research Opportunities Consortium (UROC-PREP) is one such program offered at the University of Arizona for 15–20 undergraduates each year. UROC-PREP pairs undergraduates with a faculty mentor for a ten-week research experience. The program coordinator matches students to mentors based on student request, or by their discipline.

To what extent does diversity matter in these short-term, formal mentoring relationships? Ivan Aispuro and Cindy Chavarria participated as protégés in the 2014 program. Their experiences highlight the complexity of diversity. Aispuro was a Mexican American student who was matched by the program coordinator, based on his research interest, with an Anglo female faculty member. Chavarria considers herself to be of mixed Hispanic background from Nicaragua on her father's side, and Guatemala on her mother's side. She was the first in her family to attend college. She requested to be matched with a Hispanic male faculty member.

Initiation and scaffolding

Aispuro experienced mixed feelings when he first met his faculty mentor. "I was pretty excited, I was nervous," he stated. However, he notes that his mentor "was so open... she was not distant or strict." His mentor gave him a tour around the laboratory and provided background about her research. Aispuro pointed out that being in such an environment was new to him: "It was the first time in a lab setting, and I needed to be comfortable." His mentor spent 20–30 minutes talking with Aispuro about what she expected, and asked what his interests where. The tour and initial talk about her and Aispuro's needs set the groundwork for a positive learning atmosphere. Aispuro felt welcomed, rather than an outsider. At the same time, his mentor also was assessing Aispuro's skills and knowledge. This initial experience was positive, and Aispuro noted: "She made me feel very comfortable."

Chavarria had met her mentor previously but had not worked with him in a laboratory. She was nervous about the initial formal meeting. "I was so scared, and at some point in time I wanted to turn around and leave – but meeting my mentor changed my attitude." Her mentor asked if she was familiar with his research, and assessed her knowledge about research. She recalls her mentor "asking if I knew how to do references in APA [American Psychological Association]... he saw my anxious face and told me to use Google Scholar. 'Everyone uses Google scholar,' he said."

This first meeting was not about ethnicity or other demographic characteristics. Their initial conversations focused on the mentor assessing their protégé's knowledge and orienting their protégé to research – a goal of the mentoring program. It is likely that the mentors were unaware of how nervous their protégés were. Showing interest in them as people created a positive learning environment for the protégés.

When diversity matters

Aispuro considered if his diverse characteristics influenced his mentoring experience and decided it was not an issue. However, he observed that there was diversity among the other students in the laboratory:

> One of the guys was Arabic, from Iraq, I was brown, and the other guy was Asian. She [the mentor] had three male students that were from different ethnicities, and we were all treated equally – there was so much support in a group and individually.

In his case, the presence of other diverse students may have provided role models for him, so that his mentor did not need to be explicit about diversity. His mentor "was helpful to all the students." Diversity was valued in the learning environment and as such did not come up as a topic of conversation for Aispuro and his mentor.

Diversity may have mattered most for Chavarria during a time of crisis. On one occasion, her anxiety levels rose and she began to doubt her competence. She explains:

> There was a time when I thought that I could not do what my mentor was asking of me. He is a statistics wizard, and I only had a basic idea of statistics. I thought that I could not do it, I was not smart enough.

Her mentor recognized her concerns and gave her needed feedback. She recalls that he said:

> Cindy, whatever idea you have in your head that you cannot do it – let it be your anxiety, your culture, or your sex – you are wrong.

I have mentored many Hispanic students and many female students, and they could do it, you can. I have observed you, and I know that you are smart enough to do this.

She notes that she cried, and while her mentor was awkward with the tears, she gave him a hug and went home. She observed that she completed what she needed to do and that afterwards their relationship turned out even better. "We became closer and I trusted him a lot more."

Both students achieved the goal of the formal mentoring program and completed their graduate studies. Their mentors were inclusive by assessing their protégés' knowledge and creating learning environments where they were expected to succeed. In Aispuro's case, he was reassured of fair treatment by observing other students of diverse backgrounds in the laboratory. In Chavarria's case, her mentor addressed her insecurities, which may have been rooted in her gender or cultural identity, by acknowledging her identities and assuring her that she had the ability to succeed if she tried.

UROC-PREP: https://grad.arizona.edu/uroc/uroc

Source: Biographical narrative of Cindy Chavarria, and interview with Ivan Aispuro.

addition, consider your organizational context and program goals as you determine if there are certain characteristics that matter in your program.

Myths

A belief remains that women and ethnic or racial minorities may not have the same access to mentoring relationships; however, researchers find little evidence to support this belief (Kammeyer-Mueller and Judge 2008; Wanberg et al. 2003). In fact, it appears that women and underrepresented people engage in mentoring at the same rate as do men and majority individuals. This finding suggests that formal mentoring programs have been successful in promoting access to mentoring (O'Neill 2002).

Having a mentor of the same ethnicity or gender does not appear to influence mentoring outcomes. Several studies have found that having the same "race" or gender mentor did not influence outcomes such as student grade-point average (Blake-Beard et al. 2011), relationship quality, or workplace learning (Allen and Eby 2003). Of course, it might be argued that if relational partners cannot embrace their differences sufficiently to stay in a mentoring relationship then they would not be included in such studies.

Unknown factors

We still do not know very much about other diverse characteristics such as sexuality or disabilities, and their influence on mentoring. However, what does influence relationship outcomes is shared values and attitudes, and mentors who can meet the needs of their protégés (Blake-Beard et al. 2011). Demographic similarity may be important initially, but it seems that values are what matter as the relationship progresses.

Section summary

Diversity goes beyond what you can see and is more than ethnicity, "race," or gender. Diversity in mentoring relationships refers to access to power. If a group membership influences a person's status or power, then that characteristic might influence the mentoring relationship. Ask participants about how they self-identify and consider organizational goals and contexts in developing a mentoring program that is welcoming and inclusive. Demographic similarity may not be important in matching mentors and protégés.

When does inclusion matter?

The real question is: When do program managers need to be concerned about diversity in a mentoring program? Many formal organizational mentoring programs in the United States were begun in the mid-1980s as a response to lawsuits on discrimination. The idea was that mentoring programs might help female and minority employees advance in the organization.

Inclusion refers to how people are accepted and welcomed (Roberson 2006). Thus, it is not enough to support people of diverse backgrounds in a mentoring program; it is critical to consider how accepted they may feel to engage in formal mentoring relationships. There are three areas to consider when examining if your mentoring program is inclusive:

- access;
- at the initiation of the relationship; and
- the type of support provided.

Access to power and social capital

As the example of Admiral Howard demonstrates, sometimes there simply are not sufficient mentors who share demographic characteristics with protégés. Women and people of certain ethnic groups remain under-represented in many industries and in higher education. Even if demographic similarity is desired, it might not be available. An effective mentoring program is inclusive by welcoming differences, and supporting mentoring participants to identify their shared values as they work to achieve their personal and professional goals. Johnson and Smith (2016) advocate, as one example, that men can learn to mentor women effectively.

Formal mentoring programs usually exist to connect protégés to mentors they might otherwise not meet. Do people of diverse backgrounds have access to formal mentoring opportunities in your organization? Further, if people perceive that your mentoring program is not meant for them, based on demographic characteristics, then your program is not inclusive.

Mentoring programs often provide access to power and social capital. If a group in an organization has less access to power or social capital, then it is also likely that this group is underrepresented in executive or influential positions. For example, Admiral Howard could not locate many African American mentors, much less women. If protégés from underrepresented groups desire the same racial or gendered mentor, they may automatically have less access to power, influence, and social capital. Such access may be less important in European countries, where mentoring is less about sponsorship and more about developmental mentoring. However, even in these contexts, it may be important if the mentor has less knowledge about the organization (Clutterbuck 2002).

During initiation

Diversity appears to matter most at the beginning, or initiation stage, of the relationship. "Longer relationships may reach a level of 'diversity saturation' in which group or individual differences that were salient in the beginning of the relationship become less noticeable or important with time" (Ragins 2002, 31). Apparent differences in background or culture may need to be embraced to develop a relationship. For example, in the United States a Native American protégé may believe it is disrespectful to look directly at their mentor. However, a mentor who is unaware of this cultural difference may perceive lack of eye contact as disinterest.

Of course, characteristics such as "race" and gender are proxies for differences in backgrounds. Relationships might not move past the initiation stage if a protégé or mentor does not feel valued or understood because of these differences. Scholars have suggested three ground rules for formal mentoring programs that may be ones you wish to promote in your mentoring program. These rules should (and will) vary from relationship to relationship.

Suggested diversity ground rules

1. Identify and celebrate our differences.
2. Differences are not good or bad, they are just different.
3. Just because an experience is unbelievable, does not mean that it should not be believed.

Ragins 2002 suggests three diversity ground rules, as shown in the box. The first ground rule supports mentors and protégés sharing about their differences rather than ignoring or neglecting them. This ground rule might support conversations about how to avoid perceptions of assimilation, or that the minority person needs to be more like the majority. The second ground rule may help mentoring participants to explore differences in ways that help each person embrace and acknowledge them. The third ground rule values people's experiences. People from the majority culture may have difficulty believing the stories that their minority relational partners relate, either because they do not have those experiences, or have not witnessed them. It can be difficult for mentoring participants to learn about discrimination in their organization, especially against someone they have come to know as a protégé or mentor.

Type of mentoring support

Gender and "race" seem less of a factor in access to mentoring (Wanberg et al. 2003). Women have mentors at the same rate as men, and there do not appear to be racial or ethnic differences in who participates in mentoring. However, gender and "race" may influence the type of mentoring that protégés receive.

In general, female protégés receive more psychosocial support than do male protégés, regardless of their mentor's gender. However, female mentors provide more psychosocial support to their protégés, while male mentors provide more career mentoring (Allen and Eby 2004; Ensher and Murphy 1997). It may be that women are receiving less sponsorship mentoring, and this equates to having less career success than male protégés (Ibarra et al. 2010). Both functions of mentoring are important, and you can help your mentoring participants, especially women, be aware that career support is important to both give and receive.

People sometimes prefer the same racial or gendered mentors, but this preference does not influence the outcomes of mentoring. Minority undergraduate and graduate students in science, technology, engineering, and mathematics (STEM) subjects reported a slight preference for mentors of the same ethnicity or gender (Blake-Beard et al. 2011). Protégé–mentor dyads of the same "race" liked each other more (Blake-Beard et al. 2011). Yet this preference did not affect the outcomes of the mentoring relationships – which were the same, regardless of ethnicity or gender.

Section summary

There are three ways that diversity and inclusion influence your mentoring efforts: accessing mentoring, at the initiation of the relationship, and the type of support provided. Diversity does not appear to influence access to mentoring. In many cases, diversity does not influence mentoring outcomes, but it does appear that differences in career support by and for women may reduce the positive benefits of mentoring. We still know little about other kinds of diversity and how these characteristics influence mentoring relationships or mentoring program outcomes.

Challenges to diverse and inclusive relationships

A lack of awareness about diversity and inclusion can influence the inner workings of mentoring relationships in subtle, negative ways. You can raise awareness of possible biases by learning about them and educating mentors and protégés. A "sink-or-swim" attitude (outlined here) about mentoring may place protégés from diverse backgrounds at a disadvantage. Fundamental attribution error and confirmation bias contribute to a sink-or-swim mentoring philosophy. We have unconscious beliefs that influence the decisions we make daily (Kahneman 2011). These beliefs provide useful short-cuts for us much of the time. There are also predictable ways some short-cuts introduce wrong information in our decision-making. Such decision-making is often referred to as a bias. Mentors may also support an inappropriate status quo, which is at odds with why the mentoring program was established. The goal is to create learning spaces for mentoring relationships to flourish.

Watch out for the following:

- A "sink-or-swim" mentoring philosophy – the protégé is responsible for their success or failure.
- Fundamental attribution error – when an individual overestimates the contribution of personality to a behavior, while underestimating contributions from the setting or context.
- Confirmation bias – when an individual interprets ambiguous information as supporting their opinion, while disregarding possible contradictory evidence.
- Mentoring practices that support an undesired status quo.

"Sink or swim" mentoring

We adopt mentoring philosophies from those around us. "Sink or swim" is one such philosophy that is harmful for protégés and bad for the organization. Sink or swim mentoring practices place the responsibility for the relationship on the protégé. It implies that capable protégés will ask for help when they need it, and that those who belong in your organization are those who are successful. The implication is that if protégés are not successful, then it is due to their personal traits or abilities, rather than the context or a lack of mentoring provided to them. Sink or swim mentoring comes from mistakes in thinking, such as fundamental attribution error and confirmation bias (outlined here). This attitude has been documented among academic faculty in higher education (Morzinski et al. 1994, 267; Rockquemore 2011) and in teacher and principal preparation in schools (Johnson and Kardos 2002).

Fundamental attribution error

The fundamental attribution error occurs when you attribute a person's behavior to their personal traits and underestimate the contribution of the situation (Heider 1944). Consider the example of a mentor who has an opportunity for their protégé. She calls the protégé and leaves a message about the opportunity with a request that the protégé return the call as soon as possible. A day goes by, and the call is not returned. The mentor is likely to wonder why their protégé has not been responsive to the phone message. A mentor who explains this lack of a response because of protégé laziness (personal trait) may be committing a fundamental attribution error. What if the protégé in this scenario is a woman? A mentor might believe that that recent diversity initiative to hire women is responsible for such low-quality employees who do not bother to return a call. Yet, the employee might have had an emergency that made it impossible for her to return the call. The reason is unknown, and this situation is when fundamental attribution errors are likely to occur. Help your mentoring participants seek information about situations before drawing their conclusion about protégé interest or motivation.

Confirmation bias

Confirmation bias occurs when you interpret ambiguous information in ways that confirm your beliefs (Kahneman 2011). In this case, we tend to search for confirming information and to ignore information that contradicts our preconceptions. For example, a mentor may believe that their protégé is quite capable and ready for greater responsibility and a promotion. The mentor fails to seek information about their protégé's areas of needed development. In this case, the mentor only solicits feedback about the protégé from employees who like their protégé. Further, the mentor may only pay attention to positive information about the protégé, even when negative information is provided.

When left unexamined, these biases contribute to a sink or swim mentoring philosophy, which attributes protégé lack of success to the protégé, rather than to organizational or structural obstacles. Mentors with these beliefs may explain protégé attrition as good attrition. They believe that if the protégé really belonged or wanted to be in the organization, then he or she would have been successful. The problem is that that protégés also adopt this belief and use it to explain their own successes or failures. Sink or swim mentoring is similar to benign neglect. Mentors who hold these beliefs think that protégés will know when to contact them for assistance; yet protégés are novices and feel that asking questions may reveal a lack of competence on their part (Thomas et al. 2015).

Status quo

Mentors (and mentoring programs) unintentionally can reinforce an undesired status quo. For example, a mentor may suggest that a protégé needs to conform to majority standards of dress, speech, or behaviors. Yet these strategies may backfire. For example, a male mentor who tells a female protégé that she needs to be more assertive, may be unaware that assertive women are perceived more negatively than are assertive men. Similarly, a protégé may feel that he or she must change an aspect which reflects a valued part of their cultural background to have success. The mentor in Case Study 11.2 (presented subsequently) could have easily perpetuated a status quo about female performance in math. Instead, this case illustrates how a male mentor of a similar minority background, with a female protégé, was not sure if her difficulties were due to her ethnicity, gender, or some other reason. He was unable to identify the source of her concerns, but was able to build her confidence so that she could be successful rather than drop out when she encountered difficulty.

Mentors support inequities unintentionally by reinforcing protégé beliefs in a status quo that limits their performance. For example, scholars of teacher mentoring programs have found that mentors may reinforce (rather than contradict) protégés' beliefs that ethnically underrepresented students cannot learn (Achinstein and Athanases 2005). A mentor may wish to reassure a protégé about a poor classroom experience by noting that their students face challenges at home, and so it is unreasonable to expect students to increase their poor performance or to respond to such a challenging lesson plan. The mentor unintentionally reinforces a status quo of low achievement for ethnically underrepresented students that is at odds with efforts to prepare student teachers to teach students of diverse backgrounds.

Section summary

Be aware of how biases such as fundamental attribution error and confirmation bias can promote sink or swim mentoring attitudes in your organization. Educate mentors so that they do not perpetuate inequities. Be intentional in supporting mentoring participants to check their assumptions, by asking their relational partner about challenges before assuming the cause. Help mentors recognize that they need to participate actively in the mentoring relationship, rather than rely on protégés to determine when to interact, or what to discuss. The goal is to support meaningful mentoring conversations.

Cultural competence

There is increasing attention to cultural competence in mentorship education. Practice has outpaced the literature and it is unclear if more culturally competent mentors and protégés leads to better mentoring program outcomes. Some individuals believe cultural competence is a required skill for effective mentorship while other individuals believe it is the latest fad. Scholars theorize that cultural competence works by recognizing person's external realities and making him or her feel understood and empowered (Chu et al. 2016). There is evidence that mentors in the biomedical fields report an increase in skills related to cultural awareness in training focused on cultural competence (Byars-Winston et al. 2018). Such training finds self-report evidence for activities like a "culture box" to increase cultural competence.

Conclusion

The workforce is becoming more diverse, as globalization has contributed to the mobility of people across borders. Your mentoring program needs to ensure that participants from all backgrounds can develop a professional identity by participating in your program. Diversity and inclusion are important to consider when people have group memberships that may limit their power or access to resources. Inclusion is most important at the beginning of the relationship, when protégés and mentors seek to identify shared values and develop rapport. Encourage women to intentionally provide and ask for career support in addition to psychosocial support. Confirm that your mentoring program reduces organizational inequities, rather than fosters them through mentoring. One way to do this is to educate yourself and mentoring participants about biases that may lead to a sink or swim mentoring philosophy.

Key terms

- Confirmation bias
- Cultural competence
- Deep versus surface characteristics
- Diversity
- Fundamental attribution error
- Inclusion
- "Sink or swim" mentoring philosophy
- Status quo

Check your learning

1. Who defines diversity in your mentoring program?
2. What diverse characteristics may be important in your organization?
3. How do mentors perpetuate inequities in mentoring, and how can your mentoring program reduce this from occurring?
4. Describe any sink or swim mentoring philosophies that you have witnessed, and how you might reduce them.

Resources

Unconscious Bias Course: https://my.nrmnet.net/program/p/UnconsciousBiasCourse

Online training for cultural competence: https://nationalmentoringresourcecenter.org/index.php/14-practices/234-mentor-training-for-cultural-competence.html

Cross-Cultural Inventory: https://www.evidencebasedmentoring.org/wp-content/uploads/2014/11/Cross-CulturalInventoryRevised-Mentors.pdf

References

Achinstein, B., and Athanases, S. Z. 2005. "Focusing new teachers on diversity and equity: Toward a knowledge base for mentors." Teaching and Teacher Education, 21(7):843–862. 10.1016/j.tate.2005.05.017.

Allen, T. D., and Eby, L. T. 2003. "Relationship Effectiveness for Mentors: Factors Associated with Learning and Quality." *Journal of Management*, 29(4): 469–486. 10.1016/s0149-2063_03_00021-7.

Allen, T. D., and L. T. Eby. 2004. "Factors Related to Mentor Reports of Mentoring Functions Provided: Gender and Relational Characteristics." *Sex Roles* 50(1–2): 129–139.

Blake-Beard, S., M. L. Bayne, F. J. Crosby, and C. B. Muller. 2011. "Matching by Race and Gender in Mentoring Relationships: Keeping Our Eyes on the Prize." *Journal of Social Issues* 67(3): 622–643.

Byars-Winston, A., V. Y. Womack, A. R. Butz, R. McGee, S. C. Quinn, E. Utzerath, C. L. Saetermoe, and S. B. Thomas. 2018. "Pilot Study of an Intervention to Increase Cultural Awareness in Research Mentoring: Implications for Diversifying the Scientific Workforce." *Journal of Clinical and Translational Science* 2(2): 86–94.

Captain Phillips. 2013. Directed by Paul Greengrass. [feature film]. Culver City, CA: Sony Productions.

CBS News. 2016. Caitlyn Jenner's Transformation. Available online at http://www.cbsnews.com/pictures/bruce-jenner-over-the-years/ (accessed April 21, 2021).

Chu, J., A. Leino, S. Pflum, and S. Sue. 2016. "A Model for the Theoretical Basis of Cultural Competency to Guide Psychotherapy." *Professional Psychology: Research and Practice* 47(1): 18.

Clutterbuck, D. 2002. "Establishing and Maintaining a Formal Mentoring Programme for Working with Diversified Groups." In *Mentoring and Diversity: An International Perspective*, edited by D. Clutterbuck and B. R. Ragins, 87–113. Oxford: Butterworth-Heinemann.

Clutterbuck, D., and B. R. Ragins. 2002. *Mentoring and Diversity: An International Perspective.* Oxford: Butterworth-Heinemann.

Eby, L. T., C. D. Johnson, and J. E.A. Russell. 1998. "A Psychometric Review of Career Assessment Tools for Use with Diverse Individuals." *Journal of Career Assessment* 6(3): 269–310.

Ensher, E. A., and S. E. Murphy. 1997. "Effects of Race, Gender, Perceived Similarity, and Contact on Mentor Relationships." *Journal of Vocational Behavior* 50(3): 460–481.

Fenn, D. 2015. "5 Tough Leadership Lessons from the Navy's Top Female Commander." *Fortune*, May 25. Available online at http://fortune.com/2015/05/25/5-tough-leadership-lessons-from-the-navys-top-female-commander/ (accessed April 21, 2021).

Heider, F. 1944. Social perception and phenomenal causality. Psychological Review, 51(6):358–374. 10.1037/h0055425.

Hurley, A. E. 1996. "Challenges in Cross-Gender Mentoring Relationships: Psychological Intimacy, Myths, Rumours, Innuendoes and Sexual Harassment." *Leadership & Organization Development Journal* 17(3): 42–49.

Ibarra, H., N. M. Carter, and C. Silva. 2010. "Why Men Still Get More Promotions than Women." *Harvard Business Review* 88(9): 80–85.

Johnson, S. M. and S. M. Kardos. 2002. "Keeping New Teachers in Mind." *Educational Leadership* 59(6): 12–16.

Johnson, W. B., and D. Smith, 2016. *Athena Rising: How and Why Men Should Mentor Women.* Routledge.

Kahneman, D. 2011. *Thinking, Fast and Slow.* New York: Macmillan.

Kammeyer-Mueller, J. D., and T. A. Judge. 2008. "A Quantitative Review of Mentoring Research: Test of a Model." *Journal of Vocational Behavior* 72(3): 269–283.

Miners, Z. 2013. Survey: Consulting Firm McKinsey Boasts Toughest Job Interviews. August 9. Available online at www.pcworld.com/article/2046289/mckinsey-beats-google-facebook-for-having-the-toughest-interviews.html (accessed April 23, 2021).

Morzinski, J A, Simpson, D E, Bower, D J, & Diehr, S. 1994. Faculty Development Through Formal Mentoring. Academic Medicine, 69(4): 267–9. 10.1097/00001 888-199404000-00003.

NPR. 2014. A Phone Call Helped Navy's First Four Star Admiral Embrace Her Path. October 10. Available online at www.npr.org/2014/10/10/353565847/a-phone-call-helped-navys-first-four-star-woman-embrace-her-path (accessed April 21, 2021).

Office for National Statistics. 2015. 2011 Census Analysis: Ethnicity and Religion of the Non-UK Born Population in England and Wales. June 18. Available online at www.ons.gov.uk/ons/dcp171776_407038.pdf (accessed April 21, 2021).

O'Neill, R. 2002. "Gender and Race in Mentoring Relationships: A Review of the Literature." In *Mentoring and Diversity: An International Perspective*, edited by D. Clutterbuck and B. R. Ragins, 1–22. Oxford: Butterworth-Heinemann.

Procter & Gamble. 2014. Winning Moments of Truth: 2013–2014 Diversity & Inclusion Annual Report. Available online at www.annualreport.pg.com/en_US/downloads/company/purpose_people/PG_DiversityInclusion_AR_2012.pdf (accessed April 23, 2021).

Ragins, B. R. 2002. "Understanding Diversified Mentoring Relationships: Definitions, Challenges, and Strategies." In *Mentoring and Diversity: An International Perspective*, edited by D. Clutterbuck, and B. R. Ragins, 23–53. Oxford: Butterworth-Heinemann.

Reddick, R., K. Griffin, R. Cherwitz, A. Cérda-Pražák, and N. Bunch. 2012. "What You Get When You Give: How Graduate Students Benefit from Serving as Mentors." *Journal of Faculty Development* 26(1): 37–49.

Roberson, Q. M. 2006. "Disentangling the Meanings of Diversity and Inclusion in Organizations." *Group & Organization Management* 31(2): 212–236.

Rockquemore, K. A. 2011. "Sink or Swim." *Inside Higher Ed*, October 17. Available online at https://www.insidehighered.com/advice/2011/10/17/sink-or-swim (accessed April 23, 2021).

Thomas, J. D., Lunsford, L. G. & Rodrigues, H. A. 2015. Early career academic staff support: evaluating mentoring networks. *Journal of Higher Education Policy and Management*, 37(3): 320–329. 10.1080/1360080x.2015.1034426.

United States Census Bureau. 2018. U.S. Classroom Diversity on the Rise. December 11. Available online at https://www.census.gov/library/visualizations/2 018/comm/classroom-diversity.html (accessed April 21, 2021).

Wanberg, C. R., E. T. Welsh, and S. A. Hezlett. 2003. "Mentoring Research: A Review and Dynamic Process Model." In *Research in Personnel and Human Resources Management, Vol. 22*, edited by C. R. Wanberg, E. T. Welsh and S. A. Hezlett, 39–124. Bingley, UK: Emerald Group Publishing.

Part IV

Vignettes and trends

Chapter 12

Student-alumni–industry mentoring programs

Introduction

This chapter responds to the interest of colleges and universities as well as professional societies, nonprofit organizations, and corporate leadership programs in alumni and industry mentoring programs. These programs are workplace mentoring programs. Alumni mentoring programs are unique in their requirement that the mentor has graduated from the organization or program in which the mentee is enrolled or is interested in attending. For example, alumni of leadership initiatives may be asked to mentor emerging leaders in such initiatives. In the case of new initiatives, colleges, or degree programs, there are no alumni to serve as mentors. Thus, universities may reach beyond their alumni pool to include community and industry leaders in mentoring schemes. Industry mentoring programs connect industry experts with junior people to help them develop a career identity and direction.

Alumni and industry mentoring programs benefit protégés and mentors. The mentor is viewed as a knowledgeable professional who has inside knowledge that might benefit the protégé. However, mentors benefit from giving back to others, which is explained by the legacy needs mentioned in Chapter 9.

In *university* alumni programs, the organizational benefits may result from more engaged alumni and friends who support the institution with their financial resources or contacts, for example, to hire new graduates. Research on university alumni mentoring programs in Australia reported that mentored students felt more prepared for the workforce, enjoyed their university experience more, and were more likely to become an alumni mentor than were non-mentored students (Dollinger et al. 2019).

Effective programs from two universities are described next based on interviews with the program directors. Their responses were organized to illustrate the five-step framework described in Chapters 4–8.

The Peter Lougheed Leadership College (PLLC) at the University of Alberta, Canada, was founded in 2015, launching a mentoring program that kicked off with its inaugural class and aimed to connect those students

DOI: 10.4324/9781003163862-12

with leaders in the community. The program was redesigned during the 2018–2019 academic year to include more specific outcomes. It is hoped that as PLLC graduates more students, the mentor team will consist of more alumni. The University of Georgia (UGA) in the United States started a university-wide alumni mentoring program in 2019.

Step 1: Identify the why

The PLLC Mentorship Coordinator, Kelly Hobson (personal pronoun = they), worked with stakeholders to develop a rationale for why mentoring was essential to the college's goals. Hobson says the idea was to "connect the leaders of tomorrow with the leaders of today." Hobson realized the program needed specific goals to support that vision.

Hobson crafted and redrafted language to share at several advisory board meetings: "People were relieved and it catalyzed conversations that started to reveal areas of misalignment about what we were trying to do. Once you drill down past the beautiful tagline, what does it mean in practice?" When Hobson took over the portfolio, there was no data about how many students were participating in the mentorship program. Further, it was unclear what constituted engagement.

The UGA Mentor Program launched a pilot program in the spring of 2019 after a year of discussion at the leadership level. A working group was convened that led to the hiring of a program manager, Jeremy Daniel (personal pronoun = he). The program's vision reflects the UGA culture: Every Bulldog has a mentor in their corner prior to going beyond the Arch. (The Bulldog is their mascot and refers to students. The Arch is a reminder of the university's ties to Georgia as the birthplace of public higher education in America and its commitment as a land-grant and sea-grant university to serve the people of Georgia.) The mentoring program is part of the Mentor Lab, located in the UGA Career Center, whose mission is to foster a culture of mentoring across the university community. UGA enrolls about 37,000 students. "Every Bulldog" entails a lot of mentoring.

Step 2: Map your theory of change

The theory of change reflects the assumptions and beliefs about how mentoring will result in changes for participants and for the organization (refer to Chapter 5 for more information).

The PLLC mentoring program describes three cornerstones of the mentor's role, adapted from *The Mentor's Guide: Vision, Challenge, and Support* (Zachary 2011). The program website provides details for participants about these cornerstones. For example, under "Vision," mentors are asked to help mentees see the bigger picture by modeling professional behavior and encouraging new perspectives. Thus, the PLLC mentoring program believes that if students have a mentor who demonstrates professional behaviors and connects students to need ideas, then it is more likely the program goals will be met. "Mentor" is viewed as a *gift word*. Hobson says: "it must be bestowed upon you by a mentee. *Mentor Team members* can't call themselves a mentor. We always use the language Mentor Team or Mentor Team members."

When Hobson took over the program, it was unclear how students were participating in the program or what engagement meant. They said: "was it enough if a student emailed me to inquire about participating? If they came to one of our mentorship events?" By spring 2019, mentees were considered "engaged" if they completed an intake session with the Mentorship Coordinator, attended a mentorship event, or met with a Mentor Team member. Students were "interested" if they reached out to inquire about mentorship but didn't follow through. In 2020, the intake session was replaced by structured mentee training. The training reviewed roles and expectations, clarified the purpose of the program, and involved mentees clarifying their own goals for their mentorship journey – a requirement to be considered an engaged mentee.

"When we described what engagement looked like we started to see a clear purpose. It made our value proposition very clear," says Hobson. Being an engaged mentee in the program means taking the initiative to participate and to sustain mentoring relationships. While that expectation may be atypical of most mentorship programs, it is a belief at PLLC that supports mentees to develop transferrable skills that will allow them to seek mentorship at any time, regardless of whether they have access to a formal program.

PLLC program goals and outcomes

To develop goals and outcomes for the mentorship program, the Mentorship Coordinator consulted PLLC's Mentor Team Board of Advisors, which is comprised of Mentor Team members, first-year and second-year scholar representatives, and PLLC staff. The team used information from this handbook to refine the goals proposed by the Board of Advisors. Dr. Lunsford was also consulted via email (see Case Study 4.2 for more details).

A survey sent to the Board asked the following questions:

- What is the goal for PLLC's mentorship program?
- Why is this goal important to you?
- How should PLLC's mentorship program achieve the goal you described?
- How will PLLC know whether the mentorship program was successful?
- How do you expect participants to be different after engaging with PLLC's mentorship program?

Table 12.1 PLLC mentoring goals, outcomes, and evaluation

Goal	Outcome	Evaluation tools
Challenge PLLC scholars to develop their self-awareness, so they know who they are and can identify what they need.	Career & Motivational	Describe an increase in their self-awareness about personal preferences and areas to develop.
Help PLLC scholars cultivate the self-confidence required to turn their ambitions into realities.	Behavioural & Motivational	Identify 3 to 5 personal and professional goals to achieve in the next year.
Engage external leaders through the Mentor Team, which will enhance PLLC's reputation of excellence in the community.	Attitudinal & Reputational	Information gathered colloquially by Mentor Team members and PLLC staff.
Offer Mentor Team members an opportunity to hone their leadership practice through coaching and collaboration.	Career	Report that the program honed their leadership practice through coaching and collaboration.

Using the survey results and discussions with Lois Harder, PLLC Principal, and Dr. Lunsford, the Mentorship Coordinator developed the goals and outcomes for the mentorship program (see Table 12.1). These goals guide the summative evaluation and are subject to the approval of the Mentor Team Board of Advisors. It is also important to ask:

- Can something else achieve these goals?
- Why is it that mentorship must be used?

The UGA Mentor Program reflects the belief that mentoring needs are student-driven and that all students should have access to mentoring when they are ready. Of the mentoring program, Daniel said it was "critical to build awareness and to design a program that was inclusive for all students." Daniel explained that their theory of change is that students will move through the stages of mentoring relationships (see Chapter 2 for more information about stages) and the program is set up to support them to do so, as described later. The hallmarks of a mentoring culture (see Chapter 3) are used to guide if the Mentor Lab is advancing their mission of fostering a culture of mentoring at UGA. As one example, the Mentor Lab created a university-wide community of practice, the UGA Mentorship Meetup, which consists of about 30 faculty and staff members who meet quarterly. The mission of the group is to foster a culture of mentoring across the University and to ensure that every student, faculty, and staff has access to meaningful mentoring relationships.

Once Daniel clarified how the mentoring program would be expected to result in participant changes, he found it easier to make the design decisions about program expectations, length, and activities. The program is a 16-week e-mentoring program with a strong web presence. There is a rolling intake. Potential mentees are provided three suggested mentors based on the criteria the program manager established in the mentoring platform. Students can also search up to 20 criteria to generate a list of potential mentors from which they can request a mentor. The mentors have the option of accepting or declining the request.

UGA program goals

The program goals are listed here.

1. Support students in developing their personal and professional networks with UGA alumni and friends.
2. Provide an avenue for students to explore professional goals, career interests, and workplace preferences.
3. Help students to gain an appreciation for mentoring as a personal and professional development tool.
4. Provide a meaningful opportunity for alumni and friends to connect with UGA students around life, career, and professional experiences.
5. Inspire alumni and friends to strengthen their relationship with and support of the University.

Step 3: Recruiting and preparing the right participants

The PLLC mentoring program has an intake process that reflects a belief that mentoring is reciprocal and should be available when students need it. Thus, students can join the PLLC mentoring program at any time. Prospective mentees originally met with Hobson in an intake meeting to determine the best fit for a mentor and mentoring model. Students were coached on how to articulate their goals and challenges. After the intake session, mentees can opt to engage with Mentor Team members one-on-one, attend an event with facilitated activities, or participate in moderated group mentorship. An unanticipated benefit of the group mentorship sessions was that peer mentoring emerged as an effective part of the experience. After the program redesign, the mentee training session offered at the start of the fall and winter semesters became a prerequisite to connecting with Mentor Team members or attending mentorship events.

The Mentor Team members are required to renew their term annually by signing an agreement that codifies expectations about their role, conduct, and minimum volunteer requirements. PLLC requires Mentor Team members to attend an intensive, eight-hour coaching training session, facilitated by an organization called Roy Group, which focuses on how to empower others and position them for success.

In the UGA mentoring program, there is a mandatory, 30-minute formal orientation for students prior to them being eligible to request a mentor. Each week a student ambassador shares their mentoring testimonial to inspire their peers to connect with an alumni mentor. Moreover, there is a five- to ten-minute mentor overview video that orients alumni on the goals of the program and their expectations as a mentor. The Mentor Lab launched the "UGA Mentor Skills" program in April 2020 to provide their alumni mentors with bi-monthly programs to develop their mentoring competencies. The UGA student-alumni mentoring relationships are guided through an optional curriculum to support the relationship development. There are three milestones suggested each month.

Having a consistent brand was key to the program success, for example, they developed a style guide to deliver a consistent message to their constituents. Campus partners are also provided consistent branding related to communications about the mentor program.

Step 4: Collect the right data

Hobson collected data using surveys. Hobson reports: "When you are looking at what really moves the needle, it lets you shed the work that isn't contributing... and drill down to what is important and how to prioritize." Using data, Hobson can create responsive and flexible approaches to mentoring. As a result, PLLC piloted a coaching program for students who desired a more structured experience. Mentors and mentees have four, hour-long meetings over ten weeks.

Hobson observed that knowing that the process is iterative takes the pressure off getting it exactly right the first time. The right data also provides confidence the program is working. Hobson noted: "Pandemic aside, we are confident that the tools and elements of our program contribute to the outcomes we are looking for." PLLC is now aligning the mentoring program to a leadership competency framework being implemented to evaluate the impact of each element of PLLC programming. The program is supported with software from Graduaway, which provides an interactive virtual space for the participants. Hobson says: "One of the primary desires to implement the software was to collect more robust data about connections and engagement." The next step for PLLC is figuring out how the program aligns with the strategic goals of their organization and the whole university.

The UGA Mentor Program collects data through the Xinspire mentoring software. They can track how many matches occurred, how often they are interacting, and the outcomes of these relationships. This data has enabled the program manager to make data-driven decisions to fine-tune the Mentor Lab's systems and structures.

Daniel's initial benchmarking revealed no student-alumni mentoring programs with an assessment plan. They had to start from scratch. Now, they consult with their Career Center internal mentoring committee, a Division-wide working group, a Diversity Equity Inclusion Working Group, and other partners to continue scaling an inclusive, mentoring program. Daniel emphasizes the "importance of knowing the why and goals for the program at the beginning. We return to the five overarching goals of the program when considering new opportunities."

Step 5: Success story

Hobson drafted a vision of their success story in our workshop together. This activity helped Hobson think about the data that needed to be collected from the beginning. With photos, quotes, and statistics that identified the mentoring program's successes, Hobson created a success story in a two-page spread in the 2019–2020 PLLC Annual Report.

The PLLC mentoring program had 47 mentors, referred to as Mentor Team members, in 2019–2020. The program is face-to-face, but because of the good design it was able to transition to virtual meetings when the COVID-19 pandemic made in-person meetings impossible. Hobson noted that "moving people around is easier online. [There was] more uptake by the students in the online program and it broadened the number of mentors." However, there were challenges working across time zones, and participants have expressed that they miss the energy of being in a room together.

The UGA Mentor Program started with 116 dyads in a 90-day pilot program. Piloting a new program is beneficial for three reasons, as it:

- sets participant expectations that they are in a new program;
- engages participants in helping to create and improve the mentoring experience; and
- allows you to fail "small" if there are problems.

Daniel can pull reports from the mentoring platform about successful matches and satisfaction with the program. The data collected suggests that the program has been successful to date. The mentoring program expanded to support 1,336 mentoring relationships in 2019–2020. The success story is shared with participants and all university alumni. A visually appealing presentation of data, quotes, and photographs makes it easy for stakeholders and potential participants to know the program is well-run and worth their investment (Table 12.2).

Daniel also provides a bimonthly update on the program to keep all the stakeholders informed, engaged, and inspired. He shares data, along with a quote from a mentor–mentee pair.

Table 12.2 Excerpt from UGA success story

MENTEE GOAL ACHIEVEMENT	
After participating in the UGA Mentor Program…	
96%	of mentees reported that they felt the University supported them in developing their personal and professional network with UGA alumni and friends
97%	of mentees reported gaining an appreciation for mentoring as a personal and professional development tool.
94%	of mentees reported that the University provided them with an avenue to explore career interests and professional goals.

The UGA Mentor Program was only slightly affected by the pandemic as it was designed to be virtual. Mentoring program software is required for their program to manage the larger numbers. It is an e-mentoring program that successfully connects thousands of participants each year.

Both programs have quickly scaled to meet the needs of students and alumni. The programs also have a strong foundation to continue to innovate and evolve.

Source: Interviews with Jeremy Daniel, Director, UGA Mentor Program and with Kelly Hobson, PLLC Mentorship Coordinator.

Key terms

- Alumni mentoring
- Industry mentoring

Check your learning

1. What goals and outcomes do alumni or industry mentoring programs have?
2. How are participants prepared to participate in alumni and industry mentoring programs?
3. How can the success of alumni and industry mentoring programs be determined?

Resources

http://52.39.66.81/lougheed-leadership-college/undergraduate-program/mentorship/
https://issuu.com/pllc_uab/docs/pllc_annualreport2019_issu_final
https://issuu.com/pllc_uab/docs/pllc-annual-report-2020–011020-digital_lr
https://mentor.uga.edu/
https://www.linkedin.com/company/uga-mentor-program

https://realtalkump.buzzsprout.com/
https://www.instagram.com/ump_ambassadors/

References

Dollinger, M., Arkoudis, S., & Marangell, S. (2019). University alumni mentoring programs: a win-win? Journal of Higher Education Policy and Management, 41, 375–389 10.1080/1360080x.2019.1617657.

Zachary, L. J. 2011. *The Mentor's Guide: Facilitating Effective Learning Relationships.* Hoboken, NJ: John Wiley & Sons.

Chapter 13

First-generation student mentoring programs

Introduction

Like alumni/industry mentoring programs described in Chapter 12 there is great interest in first-generation (FG) mentoring programs. Support for FG students is not new, although it may be a more familiar concept in North America. In the United States, the Morrill Act of 1862 provided land-grants that established public universities for students who could not afford to attend private universities. These students focused on the agricultural and mechanical arts and were often the first people in their families to receive a university education.

The majority of students attending public land-grant universities today have parents with college degrees. Thus, FG students are now in the minority at four-year universities. Further, FG students are less likely to attend college or to graduate from college (once enrolled) than students who have at least one college-educated parent. In the United States, the student body is more ethnically diverse than 25 years ago,[1] and the number of college-age students is expected to decline (Grawe 2018) through the 2020s. Thus, in addition to the social and moral imperatives related to equity and access, universities have a financial motivation to recruit and retain students. Mentoring programs are one intervention to achieve those goals.

This chapter describes two FG mentoring programs in the United States at the University of Arizona and Campbell University. The program directors provided information about their programs, which illustrate common elements of FG mentoring programs. The University of Arizona is a public, land-grant institution located in the American Southwest. About 35,000 of the 45,000 students are undergraduates.[2] Campbell University is a private university, located in the state of North Carolina. Undergraduate students make up about 3,700 of the nearly 6,000 enrolled students.[3]

DOI: 10.4324/9781003163862-13

Program goals

The First Cats mentoring program at the University of Arizona was established to support FG students as part of a financial need scholarship program in 2008. The program changed from a stand-alone financial aid initiative to become part of student success options in the Thrive Center. Michelle McKelvey is the director of the Thrive Center and Transfer Center. She reports that the program goal is to support students to "navigate through higher education and earn a college degree."

Michelle Pérez Ed.D, Associate Vice President, Student Success, oversees the 1st Generation Camels mentoring program at Campbell University. Pérez's arrival on campus occurred about the same time her boss read an article about a FG student mentoring program. There was an institutional desire to improve retention of undergraduates, and mentoring was seen as a way to support FG students. Thus, the program goal, supported by university leaders, was clear from the start – increase retention of FG students.

Program activities

McKelvey describes how the First Cats mentoring program will result in changes for FG students. She notes: "there are multiple peer mentoring opportunities focused on FG, cultural backgrounds, foster system, housing insecure students, etc. so that students have multiple points to enter into a mentoring relationship." FG students are invited to participate each year in a peer mentoring program. The peer mentoring program is designed to connect mentees to university resources such as tutoring, financial aid, and affinity groups to make sure they feel supported and welcomed on campus. Most students enter the program at the start of the school year, although students can join at any time if there are available spaces.

Students meet bi-weekly in their first year for 30–60 minutes. Peer mentors talk with students about academic, social, and financial topics. The program suggests topics for discussion that align with monthly workshops. The workshop topics align with the student life cycle – transition, study skills, getting involved, living on their own/at home, homesickness, making friends, and finding an apartment. Students enter the FG peer mentoring program at the start of the academic year.

In the second year students meet monthly and discuss topics related to their major and career choice. Conversations focus on career interests, finding internships and research opportunities, and preparing for graduate school. Sometimes, the "sophomore slump" may be a conversation topic for students who have a decrease in motivation or wonder why they are in college. Students in their third and fourth year of college can participate in a different peer mentoring program that is focused on the social mobility aspects of attending college.

At Campbell University, socialization to the university was viewed as critical to increasing retention. The program starts with an opening reception, where families could attend, and ends with a luncheon hosted by the university president. Participants are expected to meet regularly, at least three times a semester. The creation of peer mentoring support was also seen as a way to increase student socialization to campus. Thus, peer mentoring opportunities were created. For example, Pérez took on the teaching of a section of a one-credit course for first-year students when she saw that 22 of the first 50 students could enroll in that section. She arranged for the students to meet twice a semester as a group. After the first year, mentees created a 1st Generation Camels Club.

The 1st Generation Camels program started in the fall of 2018. There is a five-year vision for the program that supports the overall retention goals of the program while using the idea of small wins (see Chapter 8) to incrementally achieve the program goals.

- Year 1: New FG students will be invited to participate in the year-long 1st Generation Mentoring Program.
- Year 2: FG students will be invited to participate in the 1st Generation Camels Club to maintain a sense of belonging and develop new friends. The club might take on a greater role by hosting socials for new students during the year.
- Year 3: Launch Next Generation Mentoring program for FG juniors and seniors. A group mentoring experience would support these students to transition to life after graduation.
- Year 4: Offer peer mentoring to the first-year students. New FG students would have a faculty/staff mentor and a peer mentor.
- Year 5: Identify how to involve alumni in the Next Generation Mentoring program.

Participants

McKelvey reports that FG students are invited to participate in a formal mentor program every year. In 2020, there were about 300 students in the first- and second-year peer mentoring program. About 200 students participate in the mentor program for third- and fourth-year students, which focuses on preparing students for their careers.

The peer mentors develop their skills in a 46-hour training a week before the academic year begins. Most of the peer mentors were mentees in the program. A two-day retreat is followed by sessions to prepare them as paraprofessional mentors. A life management counselor provides about ten hours of the training. Topics covered are:

- self-awareness of identity and processes in college;
- trauma-informed care;
- when to refer students to other professionals; and
- self-care.

Students continue one hour of training each week during the program.

Role modeling is a central part of the 1st Gen Camels program. Thus, mentors are recruited from FG faculty and staff members. Between 40 and 50 students have participated each year in Campbell University's 1st Generation Camels Mentoring Program. Pérez notes that it was easy to recruit mentors: "faculty here engage more readily than any other campus that I have been in. They are willing to concede expertise and be part of it 'how can I help.' That was huge." A new academic advising office was created at the university in the second year, which made it easier to identify FG students to invite to participate. There is a one-hour orientation session for faculty and staff members who serve as mentors.

Program effectiveness

The goal of the First Cats mentor program is to support FG students to navigate through college. Thus, the data collected lets McKelvey know if the program helps students to stay in college. McKelvey says that they use propensity score matching to create a control group of similar students who did not participate in mentoring. She compares the persistence and retention rates of these two groups and finds that the mentor FG students are more likely to stay in school than the students in the control group. Mentees and mentors are surveyed about their satisfaction with the workshops and their overall program experience. McKelvey reports that they share the program success through newsletters, First Cats stories, and podcasts.

At Campbell University Pérez also examines grade point averages (GPA) and retention rates for evidence of the program's effectiveness. She finds that "The GPA of our cohort is higher than the other cohort students. Retention of the mentees is also higher than the first-year retention rate." Anecdotal feedback suggested some students felt "weird" talking to a mentor. Thus, this feedback led to the idea to include older students as peer mentors with a faculty/staff mentor as the program develops. Staff vacancies have presented challenges in collecting all the desired data and progressing into the planned incremental growth of the program.

Source: Interviews with Michelle McKelvey, Director, Thrive Center and Transfer Center, University of Arizona, and Michelle Pérez Ed.D, Associate Vice President, Student Success, Campbell University.

Resources

https://thrive.arizona.edu/first-cats
https://thrive.arizona.edu/
https://www.campbell.edu/students/student-success/first-year-experience/
camels-mentoring-program/

Notes

1 https://www.aacu.org/aacu-news/newsletter/2019/march/facts-figures
2 https://www.arizona.edu/about
3 https://www.campbell.edu/about/facts/

Reference

Grawe, N. D. 2018. *Demographics and the Demand for Higher Education.* Baltimore, MD: John Hopkins University Press.

Chapter 14

STEM mentoring programs

Introduction

Mentoring programs in science, technology, engineering, and mathematics (STEM) are a third area of interest and investment. Student-alumni/industry and first-generation mentoring programs are the other two areas of interest (see Chapters 12 and 13). STEM mentoring programs are designed to encourage people to go into areas of great market and societal need.

There continue to be disparities in who participates in STEM careers (National Science Foundation 2017), and mentoring programs are designed to reduce these disparities.

Mentoring programs in STEM are seen as one method to address projected shortages in critical workforce areas (Stelter et al. 2021). Medical fields are sometimes included and referred to as STEMM (Byars-Winston and Dahlberg 2019, 91). STEM mentoring programs are often one element of a programmatic intervention that can make it difficult to identify the unique effects of mentorship (Byars-Winston and Dahlberg 2019, 23).

Scholars believe that STEM mentoring programs work by helping individuals develop a scientific identity (Atkins et al. 2020) through engagement in a social community (Mondisa and McComb 2018) that confirms a person's STEM interests and aspirations. Affirmation of a science identity appears to be important for individuals who may encounter stereotypes counter to their interest in STEM fields. For example, STEM mentorship programs for women seek to counter the stereotype that women are bad at math (Byars-Winston and Dahlberg 2019, 58).

Approaches

The main types of mentoring programs for adults are through STEM-focused scholarships or fellowships at the undergraduate or graduate level; grant-funded programs; industry internships; and early career retention efforts. E-mentoring programs for young adults and early career professionals provide additional mentoring opportunities.

DOI: 10.4324/9781003163862-14

STEM mentoring efforts are provided at the college and graduate level, often in conjunction with scholarships or special stipends/internships for summer. STEM mentoring programs also seek to retain talented people in STEM careers, thus there are formal mentoring experiences for early career individuals such as the one experienced by Isaac Owolabi in Chapter 6 (see Case Study 6.1).

The Goodnight Scholarships Program at NC State University[1] is an example of a STEM-focused scholarship with considerable enrichment, including mentoring opportunities. The program has supported successful six-week peer mentoring for new scholars (Lunsford 2013). A focus on helping the scholars develop meaningful professional relationships with STEM faculty members and professionals is one of the program's aims. The Goldwater Scholarship program in the United States is a national example of a STEM-focused scholarship program that includes mentorship as a programmatic feature.[2]

In a similar vein, the national Graduate Education for Minorities consortium provides fellowships for minority students in STEM masters and doctoral degree programs in the United States. Like the programs just mentioned, mentorship is one aspect of the fellowship.

STEM mentoring also occurs through STEM internships in government or industry. For example, the National Aeronautics and Space Administration (NASA)[3] annually recruits thousands of undergraduate students for ten-week summer or 15-week semester-long internships. Site directors and STEM personnel provide mentoring to the interns, again with the hope of increasing their STEM interests in STEM careers (and possibly at NASA).

MentorNet is an example of an online STEM mentoring program in the United States that works with universities, corporations, and professional organizations. The nonprofit organization provides a short-term cycle of mentorship, with six facilitated interactions, that can be repeated.

An ambitious STEMM worldwide, e-mentoring program, *Global Talent Mentoring* (GTM), designed by Professor and Program Director Heidrun Stoeger at the University of Rengensburg, was launched in spring 2021. This program, funded and owned by the Hamdan Foundation, will provide ten years of support to exceptionally talented students in STEMM. As noted earlier, the role of social community is important in developing a STEM identity. GTM will provide community activities and engagements to increase mentees' sense of belonging to a group of like-minded individuals, which will help them develop an identity within their STEMM niche and STEMM more broadly (see Appendix A for a detailed interview with Dr. Stoeger about the program).

National funding agencies also devote considerable resources to STEM-oriented mentoring efforts. For example, the National Research Mentoring Network[4] has a well-developed website to provide resources for mentoring to diversify the biomedical workforce. The National Institutes of Health, in the United States, provided funding for the network. The National Academies published a detailed report *The Science of Effective Mentorship in STEMM,* which is another resource for program directors to consult (Byars-Winston and Dahlberg 2019).

Notes

1 https://goodnight.ncsu.edu/
2 https://goldwater.scholarsapply.org/our-mission/
3 https://intern.nasa.gov/
4 https://nrmnet.net/

References

Atkins, K., B. M. Dougan, M. S. Dromgold-Sermen, H. Potter, V. Sathy, and A. T. Panter. 2020. "'Looking at Myself in the Future': How Mentoring Shapes Scientific Identity for STEM Students from Underrepresented Groups." *International Journal of STEM Education* 7(1): 1–15.

Byars-Winston, A. and M. L. Dahlberg. 2019. "The Science of Effective Mentorship in STEMM. Consensus Study Report." Washington, DC: National Academies Press.

Lunsford, L. G. 2013. "Mentors as Friends." In M. Hojjat and A. Moyer. (Eds.). *The Psychology of Friendship,* 141–156.

Mondisa, J. L., and S. A. McComb. 2018. "The Role of Social Community and Individual Differences in Minority Mentoring Programs." *Mentoring & Tutoring: Partnership in Learning* 26(1): 91–113.

National Science Foundation. 2017. Women, Minorities, and Persons with Disabilities in Science and Engineering (NSF 17–310). Available online at www.nsf.gov/statistics/wmpd/ (accessed May 18 2021)

Stelter, Rebecca L., Kupersmidt, Janis B., and Kathryn N. Stump. 2020. "Establishing Effective STEM Mentoring Relationships through Mentor Training." *Annals of the New York Academy of Sciences,* 1483, 224–243 10.1111/nyas.14470.

Chapter 15

The future of mentoring

Introduction

Successful individuals often attribute part of their success to mentors. Some professions are designed such that mentoring relationships are at the core of how the profession perpetuates itself – for example, graduate education. You may be a mentoring champion who believes that mentoring programs will create an individual or organizational benefit. Perhaps mentoring is seen as part of your organization's people development strategy. Or you may have inherited a mentoring program and were told to run it.

Mentoring programs are structured experiences that are supported by the organization to achieve an organizational objective. These programs exist to connect protégés with individuals whom they may not otherwise encounter. Such programs take time and resources to administer well. The evidence is that mentoring programs are not equally effective, despite their proliferation.

As a mentoring practitioner or scholar, you will benefit from having a greater understanding of what we know about mentoring and the limits of mentoring. Knowledge about future trends in mentoring conclude the chapter.

What we do and don't know

We know more about mentoring relationships than we did ten or 20 years ago. Mentoring relationships are characterized by both friend-like and career or professional support (see Chapter 2). Many individuals have multiple mentor-like relationships. We know more about how these relationships unfold over time and what the critical tasks are at each stage (refer to Chapter 9). Chapter 3 highlighted findings from positive psychology that show how we engage with one another matters. Scholars have delineated the categories of outcomes that can be expected from a mentoring program (see Chapter 2).

Research suggests what elements are needed for effective mentoring programs. These elements include preparation and mentoring skill

DOI: 10.4324/9781003163862-15

development for participants and activities that support the goal of the mentoring program (see Chapter 6). Resources need to be devoted to the program, including a program manager who can support graceful exits from the program and provide skill development when needed. Intentional and targeted support is more likely to achieve participant and organizational goals. Chapter 2 discussed how effective mentorship works by giving protégés a sense of belonging and professional identity. Mentoring also seems to work best when individuals are at transition points and have needs that can be fulfilled through mentoring relationships.

The National Academies report (Byars-Winston and Dahlberg 2019) has advanced an evidence-based definition of mentoring (see Chapter 2). There is an opportunity for scholars and practitioners to converge on this definition to differentiate mentoring from coaching, tutoring, or other developmental relationships. Similarly, there are numerous types of mentoring relationships that have adjectives suggesting a precise meaning, for example "peer mentoring," or "reverse mentoring." Clarify what mentoring means in your program in terms of the people, processes, and behaviors (see Chapter 2).

There is plenty that we do not know about mentoring. Quantitative studies of mentoring and diversity suggest that demographic characteristics are not important (Eby et al. 2013), yet qualitative studies suggest that they are (Holmes et al. 2007; Barker 2011). Scholars are beginning to consider the role of relationship quality on mentoring outcomes (see Chapter 3).

Research suggests that mentoring relationships (formal or informal) do not produce a big difference in outcomes for those who participate in them (Baugh and Fagenson-Eland 2007). Further, it is unclear if mentoring is responsible for any outcomes for protégés – it might be that the more talented individuals are the ones who attract mentors to engage with them. Yet mentoring is prevalent across organizational contexts and ages. It appears to be a valued relationship, and a great deal of resources are invested in mentoring.

The limits of mentoring

Mentoring will not solve most, or even many, problems. Indeed, I remain unconvinced that everyone benefits or even desires to participate in mentoring relationships. However, mentoring can provide learning opportunities that benefit mentors and protégés. I admit to feeling a sense of pride and satisfaction when one of my protégés does well. A thoughtful conversation with one of my mentors leaves me energized to take on new challenges. Yet when we talk about mentoring programs, we often assume that great mentoring is always taking place – and usually it is not.

The information in this handbook will help you design a mentoring program and to promote a culture of mentoring in your organization that may increase the odds of powerful and transformative experiences for participants. Mentoring relationships may reveal our best selves at work, at school, or in our communities.

Future trends

It is likely that mentoring will continue to be part of community and organizational life, despite some scholars observing a recent decline in interest in mentoring (Stoeger et al. 2021). There are five trends that may influence the future work of mentoring program managers. First, there will be increasing expectations that program managers have a responsibility to start, support, and sustain the most effective mentoring programs possible. The professionalization of mentoring is likely to continue. Standards and best practice will become better established, and it is likely that more professional development and education will be expected for those who support mentoring relationships.

Second, there will be a greater emphasis on mentorship skill development. Scholarly work on positive organizations and positive psychology is influencing how we think about engaging in mentoring relationships. There will be a need for skill development on how to support learning and change through conversation and collaboration. In the future, program managers will be expected to support others in developing high-quality mentoring relationships, rather than oversee a mentoring program where it is unknown if mentoring relationships exist in name only.

Third, advances in technology will continue to influence how we interact. Mentoring has long been viewed as a face-to-face relationship. Yet web-assisted technologies have changing how we engage in mentoring relationships. Some mentoring programs are established already as virtual experiences. Improvements in telecommunication make it easier to simulate an in-person conversation, even when individuals are not co-located. Virtual assistants or 'bots' are already being developed to provide tips about mentoring. Software platforms are becoming common to manage mentoring programs with more than 50 dyads. Program managers will need to be versed in technology solutions that support mentoring programs, both in person and virtually.

Fourth, greater attention will be expected to ensure mentoring programs are inclusive and do not perpetuate organizational inequities. It is unclear exactly what skill development will be most effective. However, work on the development of cultural competency skills is one avenue that warrants exploration.

Fifth, networks will become more important as organizations become less hierarchal and individuals change jobs and even careers more frequently. Thus, mentoring programs will need to facilitate the development of mentoring networks and not just singular relationships between one mentor and one protégé.

Conclusion

A final reminder may be useful: Be a friendly skeptic of mentoring. Add to the field by investing in your professional development and increase your knowledge about mentoring. Find an organization, such as those listed in Chapter 1, to keep up with advances in our knowledge about mentoring relationships. Experiment to determine what mentoring activities best align with your organizational goals, seek out the exemplary relationships, and eliminate or reduce mentoring activities and practices that do not promote excellence. After all, we may learn a lot through our relationships with others.

References

Barker, M. J. 2011. "Racial Context, Currency and Connections: Black Doctoral Student and White Advisor Perspectives on Cross-Race Advising." *Innovations in Education and Teaching International* 48(4): 387–400.

Baugh, S. G., and E. A. Fagenson-Eland. 2007. "Formal Mentoring Programs." In *The Handbook of Mentoring at Work: Theory, Research, and Practice*, edited by B. R. Ragins and K. E. Kram, 249–271. Los Angeles, CA: Sage Publications.

Byars-Winston, A., and M. Dahlberg. 2019. *The Science of Effective Mentorship in STEMM*. Washington, DC: The National Academies Press. 10.17226/25568.

Eby, L. T., T. D. Allen, B. J. Hoffman, L. E. Baranik, J. B. Sauer, S. Baldwin, M. A. Morrison, K. M. Kinkade, C. P. Maher, and S. Curtis. 2013. "An Interdisciplinary Meta-Analysis of the Potential Antecedents, Correlates, and Consequences of Protégé Perceptions of Mentoring." *Psychological Bulletin* 139(2): 1–36.

Holmes, S. L., L. D. Land, and V. D. Hinton-Hudson. 2007. "Race Still Matters: Considerations for Mentoring Black Women in Academe." *Negro Educational Review* 58(1–2): 105–129.

Stoeger, H., D. P. Balestrini, and A. Ziegler. 2021. "Key Issues in Professionalizing Mentoring Practices." *Annals of the New York Academy of Sciences* 1483(1): 5–18.

A conversation with program designer and director Heidrun Stoeger about Global Talent Mentoring, a long-term online mentoring program for outstanding youths in STEMM

Introduction

Appendix A highlights the development and launch of Global Talent Mentoring, a worldwide online mentoring program. The program provides long-term, research-based support and guidance to outstanding students (around the age of 16) from all over the world who excel in one or more fields in science, technology, engineering, mathematics, and medical sciences (STEMM) and are committed to developing their specific STEMM interests. Services are provided to mentees for up to ten years for free. The mentoring program development is described here. The interview follows the internal structure of the chapters found in this book and was shortened for brevity.

Step 1: Identify the why

Global Talent Mentoring supports the talent-development needs of youths who are outstanding in a STEMM area and motivated to develop their specific STEMM talent. Such youths often lack the subject-specific guidance they require for making progress. With its global scope and virtual format, Global Talent Mentoring can match mentors and mentees who would not otherwise be able to work together. It provides an opportunity to connect experts with inquisitive, hardworking young academics.

Step 2: Map your theory of change

The goal of Global Talent Mentoring is to develop STEMM talent in youths in order to foster excellence and innovation in STEMM. Three program elements support that goal:

1. one-on-one mentoring,
2. goal-directed learning, and
3. networking.

First, eminent scientists often note that mentors played pivotal roles in their paths to eminence by providing instrumental support (e.g., teaching new knowledge and skills, providing feedback, and giving academic and career advice), psychosocial support (e.g., how to deal with setbacks, remain focused, and persevere), and role modeling. Global Talent Mentoring relies on mentoring as the primary mechanism to bring about changes by supporting the talent development of promising youths as they strive to become next-generation STEMM leaders.

Second, Global Talent Mentoring helps students to define and pursue their individual learning pathway to facilitate goal-directed learning. For both one-on-one mentoring and working with other program participants in group projects, the program encourages mentees to set short-term goals aligned with their long-term goal and their individual learning pathway. Global Talent Mentoring trains mentees on planning their learning pathways, setting appropriate goals, and defining tasks to achieve their goals. Program representatives continuously monitor mentees' progress and help them adjust when necessary.

Finally, Global Talent Mentoring fosters a sense of belonging and networking in a global community. Community activities and engagement will increase mentees' sense of belonging to a group of like-minded individuals, which will help them develop an identity within their STEMM niche and STEMM more broadly. An increased sense of belonging and competence will boost mentees' self-efficacy in becoming successful STEMM professionals.

Step 3: Recruiting and preparing the right participants

It was essential to the Global Talent Mentoring goal to include talent from a variety of cultures. Thus, Global Talent Mentoring built relationships with mentee-nominating institutions and mentor-nominating institutions. For the pilot round of mentoring that started in April of 2021, the program identified potential institutional partners in more than 80 countries.

Mentee-nominating institutions have local expertise in identifying and developing academic talent among youths (e.g., talent centers, ministries of education, leading STEM secondary institutions, universities). All mentee-nominating institutions assisted Global Talent Mentoring in expanding its pool of qualified STEMM experts as volunteers (e.g., university professors or other experts doing advanced work in a STEMM field). Mentor-nominating institutions include a variety of organizations (e.g., professional associations, universities, technology start-ups) that are investing in the STEMM talent-development pipeline.

As of this writing, 29 mentee-nominating organizations in 28 countries nominated 590 outstanding youths around the age of 16 according to the program's mentee description (see https://globaltalentmentoring.org/). Nominated youths were invited to complete an application on the Global Talent Mentoring platform. An extensive, holistic application system requested information in three areas: background information, motivation, and STEMM competence. As plausibility check for applicants' self-reported scholastic achievements and English competencies, applicants also completed a test of college-level mathematics and English usage. Of the 262 youths who completed the application, 122 youths were selected for participation in the program, starting with the pilot round. Participation in the Global Talent Mentoring is free.

To date, 301 STEMM experts have volunteered as mentors. Volunteers who fulfilled the basic mentor qualifications (see https://globaltalentmentoring.org/) were invited to a structured video interview with trained program staff. Mentors agreed to verify their identity and confirmed that they had no criminal records. Mentor volunteers for whom the internal review and the interview indicated program compatibility were matched with mentee participants according to the mentors' areas of expertise and the mentees' areas of interest. Qualified mentors for whom no mentee was found remain part of the mentor-volunteer pool for later matching. Mentors volunteer their time.

Each mentee receives a mentor, who is an expert from a STEMM field aligned with the mentee's interest area. The main methods of program support are one-on-one mentoring and community activities. Global Talent Mentoring combines mentoring with collaborative and inter-disciplinary discussion of and work on STEMM topics in projects and challenges.

Global Talent Mentoring creates and implements training for mentors and mentees. Before mentors and mentees meet, they have access to "kick-off" training units, which cover getting started on the platform, program orientation, ethics and safety issues, and how to prepare for the first mentor–mentee meeting. Thereafter, mentees and mentors receive ongoing training to help them cultivate good mentoring relationships, network, create individualized learning pathways, and work on talent development. Early training topics cover getting started on the online platform, program orientation, ethics and safety issues, and how to prepare for the first mentor–mentee meeting. Ongoing training helps participants to establish and maintain good mentoring relationships and to create individualized learning pathways and work on talent development. Training units also cover getting the most out of the program's mentoring and networking offerings (e.g., navigating and operating the platform, aligning expectations, setting goals, cross-cultural communication).

Global Talent Mentoring assigns a program representative to each dyad. Program representatives conduct check-in conversations and surveys with mentors and mentees about their relationships, platform-use experiences, and goal-directed learning. Feedback from the check-ins allows program staff to identify possible problems early and intervene as needed.

Step 4: Collect the right data

Global Talent Mentoring was conceptualized, created, and piloted by a team of researchers led by Heidrun Stoeger at the University of Regensburg. The four-year research project was funded by the UNESCO-recognized Hamdan Bin Rashid Al Maktoum Foundation for Distinguished Academic Performance (Dubai, UAE), which owns the program created during the research project.

The funding makes a comprehensive evaluation effort possible. Findings will provide valuable insights on a range of research topics – including STEMM talent development in gifted youths and online mentoring – and be used to make regular enhancements to the program.

Questionnaires (validated scales), interviews, and logfile data will be used to analyze the learning processes and talent development of the participants. In the long run, the developmental trajectories of the mentees will be compared with a waitlist control group of comparably STEMM-talented and STEMM-motivated students.

Data will be collected on successful mentoring processes and what characterizes them. Collection of process data and outcome data will allow the staff to monitor mentoring and program activities and determine their effectiveness. The mentoring activities will take place on the online platform. A database will automatically collect information about users' online activities (e.g., timestamps of participants' logins and logouts, creation and completion of goals, and utilization of training materials) and store the resulting process data systematically. The process data and regular face-to-face check-ins and online surveys will help program staff gauge whether the intended program activities are being carried out and whether these program activities promote the desired outcomes as hypothesized in the program's logic model.

Network and communication data (e.g., data about communication initiation, frequency, and methods as well as about the size and structure of resulting networks) will help the program staff monitor and support mentor–mentee interactions as well as mentees' network development on the platform.

Outcome data include STEMM-related outcomes, mentoring-relationship outcomes, and psychosocial outcomes. Mentees' STEMM progress and accomplishments will be assessed every six months by examining their completed goals, reported STEMM activities (e.g., finished projects, manuscripts) and engagement, and growth in STEMM knowledge and skills. One proximal STEMM outcome is, for example, participants' STEMM-focused communication on the platform. This will be measured by examining – with users' permission – the percentage of STEMM-focused communication in user-generated texts on the platform. Previous mentoring studies found that the amount and kind of STEM-focused communication (Hopp et al. 2020; Stoeger et al. 2017) predicted mentoring outcomes such as elective intentions in STEM (Stoeger et al. 2019; Stoeger et al. 2021).

The quality of mentoring relationships is being examined using quantitative and qualitative measures. Validated mentoring-relationship scales assess the appropriateness of matching criteria, types of support mentees perceive receiving from their mentor, and mentoring skills that were most valued in the dyads. Qualitative methods such as in-depth interviews and focus groups provide a deeper understanding of this unique type of mentoring (i.e., long-term online mentoring for outstanding students in STEMM in a global context) and the key ingredients of successful mentoring relationships. Finally, interviews and focus groups help program staff gather feedback from the participants about what they particularly appreciate and what they feel is missing.

Step 5: Success story

This program is just beginning. However, Stoeger and her team have envisioned the data needed to tell the success story about the program. It is expected that outstanding youths who participate in Global Talent Mentoring will profit from doing so and will become STEMM experts themselves. Each year, additional mentees and mentors will be selected to join the members-only community, allowing the overall size of the community to gradually grow and – thanks to network effects – increasing the depth and breadth of STEMM interactions and learning. The program allows mentees with specific STEMM interests to experience a richer ecosystem for their talent development than they will find locally and provides all participants with a unique opportunity to cultivate domain-specific interests in a community of like-minded individuals from numerous cultures. With the accompanying research, it should be possible to gain insights into (online) mentoring and talent development in STEMM that help improve Global Talent Mentoring and other STEMM mentoring initiatives.

Source: Written interview with Heidrun Stoeger. Dr. Stoeger is Professor of Educational Sciences and Chair, School Research, School Development, and Evaluation, at the University of Regensburg (Germany), and Director of Global Talent Mentoring. Dr. Stoeger's work on Global Talent Mentoring is funded by the Hamdan Bin Rashid Al Maktoum Foundation for Distinguished Academic Performance (Dubai, UAE).

References

Global Talent Mentoring. n.d. Available online at https://globaltalentmentoring.org/ (accessed April 29, 2021).

Hopp, M. D. S., H. Stoeger, and A. Ziegler. 2020. "The Supporting Role of Mentees' Peers in online mentoring:Online Mentoring: A Longitudinal Social Network Analysis of Peer Influence." *Frontiers in Psychology* 11. 10.3389/fpsyg.2020.01929

Stelter, R. L., J. B. Kupersmidt, and K. N. Stump. 2021. "Establishing Effective STEM Mentoring Relationships through Mentor Training." *Annals of the New York Academy of Sciences* 1483(1): 224–243.

Stoeger, H., T. Debatin, M. Heilemann, and A. Ziegler. 2019. "Online Mentoring for Talented Girls in STEM: The Role of Relationship Quality and Changes in Learning Environments in Explaining Mentoring Success." *New Directions for Child and Adolescent Development* 168: 75–99. 10.1002/cad.20320

Stoeger, H., M. Heilemann, T. Debatin, M. D. S. Hopp, S. Schirner, and A. Ziegler. 2021. "Nine Years of Online Mentoring for Secondary School Girls in STEM: An Empirical Comparison of Three Mentoring Formats." *Annals of the New York Academy of Sciences* 1483: 153–173. 10.1111/nyas.14476

Stoeger, H., M. Hopp, and A. Ziegler. 2017. "Online Mentoring as an Extracurricular Measure to Encourage Talented Girls in STEM (Science, Technology, Engineering, and Mathematics): An Empirical Study of One-on-One versus Group Mentoring." *Gifted Child Quarterly* 61: 239–249. 10.1177/001 6986217702215

Index

Printed in the United States
by Baker & Taylor Publisher Services